Opening Dialogue: Understanding the Dynamics of Language and Learning in the English Classroom
MARTIN NYSTRAND with ADAM GAMORAN, ROBERT KACHUR, and CATHERINE PRENDERGAST

Reading Across Cultures: Teaching Literature in a Diverse Society
THERESA ROGERS and ANNA O. SOTER, Editors

"You Gotta Be the Book": Teaching Engaged and Reflective Reading with Adolescents
JEFFREY D. WILHELM

Just Girls: Hidden Literacies and Life in Junior High
MARGARET J. FINDERS

The First R: Every Child's Right to Read
MICHAEL F. GRAVES, PAUL VAN DEN BROEK, and BARBARA M. TAYLOR, Editors

Exploring Blue Highways: Literacy Reform, School Change, and the Creation of Learning Communities
JOBETH ALLEN, MARILYNN CARY, and LISA DELGADO, Coordinators

Envisioning Literature: Literary Understanding and Literature Instruction
JUDITH A. LANGER

Teaching Writing as Reflective Practice
GEORGE HILLOCKS, JR.

Talking Their Way into Science: Hearing Children's Questions and Theories, Responding with Curricula
KAREN GALLAS

Whole Language Across the Curriculum: Grades 1, 2, 3
SHIRLEY C. RAINES, Editor

The Administration and Supervision of Reading Programs, SECOND EDITION
SHELLEY B. WEPNER, JOAN T. FEELEY, and DOROTHY S. STRICKLAND, Editors

No Quick Fix: Rethinking Literacy Programs in America's Elementary Schools
RICHARD L. ALLINGTON and SEAN A. WALMSLEY, Editors

Unequal Opportunity: Learning to Read in the U.S.A.
JILL SUNDAY BARTOLI

Nonfiction for the Classroom: Milton Meltzer on Writing, History, and Social Responsibility
Edited and with an Introduction by E. WENDY SAUL

When Children Write: Critical Re-Visions of the Writing Workshop
TIMOTHY LENSMIRE

Dramatizing Literature in Whole Language Classrooms, SECOND EDITION
JOHN WARREN STEWIG and CAROL BUEGE

The Languages of Learning: How Children Talk, Write, Dance, Draw, and Sing Their Understanding of the World
KAREN GALLAS

Partners in Learning: Teachers and Children in Reading Recovery
CAROL A. LYONS, GAY SU PINNELL, and DIANE E. DEFORD

Social Worlds of Children Learning to Write in an Urban Primary School
ANNE HAAS DYSON

(Continued)

# Jeffrey D. Wilhelm

*Foreword by Michael W. Smith*

# "You Gotta BE the Book"

*TEACHING ENGAGED and REFLECTIVE READING with ADOLESCENTS*

Teachers College
Columbia University
New York and London

Some data presented in Chapters 4 and 5 also appear in:

Jeffrey D. Wilhelm (1995). Reading Is Seeing: Using Visual Response to Improve the Literacy Reading of Reluctant Readers. *Journal of Reading Behavior (27)*4, 467–503.

Jeffrey D. Wilhelm (in press). The Drama of Engaged Reading. *Reading and Writing Quarterly.*

Published by Teachers College Press, 1234 Amsterdam Avenue, New York, NY 10027

*Library of Congress Cataloging-in-Publication Data*

Wilhelm, Jeffrey D., 1959–
    "You gotta be the book" : teaching engaged and reflective reading with adolescents / Jeffrey D. Wilhelm.
        p.    cm.—(Language and literacy series)
    Includes bibliographical references and index.
    ISBN 0-8077-3567-1 (alk. paper).—ISBN 0-8077-3566-3 (pbk. : alk. paper)
        1. Reading (Secondary)—United States.    2. Junior high school students—United States—Books and reading.    I. Title.    II. Series: Language and literacy series (New York, N.Y.)
    LB1632.W54    1997
    428.4′071′2—dc20                                        96-28696

ISBN 0-8077-3566-3 (paper)
ISBN 0-8077-3567-1 (cloth)

Printed on acid-free paper
Manufactured in the United States of America

04    03    02    01    00    99    98    97        8    7    6    5    4    3    2    1

I dedicate this work to all of my own teachers, especially:

James Blaser
William Strohm
Jack Wilhelm

# Contents

# Foreword

In David Lodge's *Small World* the hero brings the MLA convention to a halt by asking a panel of the world's most famous literary theorists what seems a very natural question: "What follows if everybody agrees with you?" The joke, of course, is that just asking theorists to think about the practical consequences of their theories could be so startling and cause such an uproar. The portrait of the literary theorist who debates arcane points that have little bearing on the "real world" has become a commonplace. Secondary school teachers of literature have done little to dispel this commonplace. As Applebee (1993) noted: "In our case studies of programs with reputations for excellence, we also asked teachers directly about their familiarity with recent developments in literary theory. Some 72 percent of these teachers reported little or no familiarity with contemporary literary theory. As one teacher put it, 'These are far removed from those of us who work the front lines!'" (pp. 121–122).

Until now. For in *"You Gotta Be the Book": Teaching Engaged and Reflective Reading with Adolescents,* Jeff Wilhelm does something that no other teacher or theorist or researcher of whom I am aware does: He builds a powerful theory of literary reading from the reading of students, and he uses that theory to build a powerful theory of the teaching of literature.

Wilhelm argues that literary reading depends on what he calls engagement: entering and becoming involved in a story world and using that involvement to interpret characters, setting, thematic possibilities, and so on. He grounds his theory on his study of three of the most engaged seventh-grade readers of the 123 that he taught the year he collected his data. From this study—and from each of the three studies Wilhelm reports here—we as readers get a multitude of riches. Wilhelm details a variety of innovative and exciting methodologies, most notably his use of visual protocols and symbolic story representation interviews. He situates his findings in a discussion of a wide variety of literary theory and reading research, notable for both how he uses theory and research to explain his findings and how his findings challenge, extend, and refine the theory and research he discusses. He provides a moving intellectual history by drawing on over 10 years of his teacher's journal. He gives us portraits of readers who will be in our heads long after we finish the book.

The energy and insight of Wilhelm's respondents is remarkable and moving, not the least in the effect they had on Wilhelm's other students. My particular favorite is an exchange that Ron, one of the three highly engaged readers who worked with Wilhelm on his study, had with his reading partner Jon, after Ron shared a symbolic story representation that revealed how he positioned himself as a reader:

> Jon: I can't believe you do all that stuff when you read! Holy crap, I'm not doing . . . like nothing . . . compared to you.
> Ron: I can't believe you don't do something. If you don't, you're not reading, man. . . . It's gotta be like wrestling or watching a movie or playing a video game . . . you've got to like . . . be there!

Wilhelm's research provides dramatic testimony that we too often undervalue the contributions students can make to our understanding of reading literature and to each other—in itself a significant accomplishment. This testimony, I believe, has the capacity to have the same kind of hortatory effect on teachers of literature that Nancie Atwell's *In the Middle* (1987) had for teachers of writing. But I also think that there's something more here. Whereas Atwell's book describes how she enacted the theories she learned from Murray and others, Wilhelm's book makes new theory.

And I think that it's a theory that will resonate with teachers of literature at all levels. I'm certain that many of us became English teachers because we love to read and talk about books, because we believe in the unique and powerful way of knowing literature provides, because we share with Gabriel Josipovici the belief that a book "can sink so deep that it alters our lives, and we know that its reverberations will never cease to be felt until the day of our death" (cited in Meek, 1983, p. 218). Wilhelm's theory of reading as engagement develops what often remains a tacit belief and explores the moves that readers make to experience the kind of engagement with literature that brought us to the field in the first place.

But as Wilhelm notes, many of our students do not share our enthusiasm. I think that there is a temptation to dismiss these students (or their generation) as different kinds of people or to look to the culture, especially television, to assess blame. What Wilhelm does instead is think hard about possible causes for students' hating or refusing to read. And he comes up with an idea that strikes me as utterly profound in its simplicity: students who hate to read can't see what they are reading.

Framing the problem in this way allowed Wilhelm to generate, in the second and third studies, a rich variety of instructional strategies that would help them see. Most notably, he discusses how using drama and drawing had a transformative effect on his most reluctant readers. Here again, his work is marked with a methodological and theoretical sophistication, and again it unfolds within a very real human drama, this time of kids struggling with and ultimately enjoying and succeeding with tasks that they had resisted.

In this portrait of six reluctant readers, Wilhelm challenges what has come to be an orthodoxy of at least some response-centered curricula. These students needed more than to be freed from top-down instructional approaches that didn't value what they could do; they needed to be taught. Wilhelm recognizes that he has expertise from which his students can benefit. The instruction he describes shows just how humane sharing that expertise can be. But he never casts himself as the only expert. Indeed, he finds that his emphasis on drama and especially art confounds hierarchies that existed in the class. All of a sudden, kids who had been punished throughout their schooling for drawing and doodling were experts in what became the common project of seeing literature and representing what one saw so that others could share in it.

Wilhelm's book is ultimately very political. It challenges the politics of traditional classrooms by casting students as experts and by expanding the notion of what counts as expertise. At its core is a profound belief in the importance of critical literacy in a democratic society. It exemplifies what can happen when teachers reimagine themselves as what Giroux (1985) would call transformative intellectuals. And it offers an articulate critique of the politics of literacy research and the place of teacher research in the field.

There's an irony here. Wilhelm writes as an assistant professor at the University of Maine. I know Jeff Wilhelm. I know how hard it has been for him to make the move to the university. I know that he misses the kind of energy that only exists in a middle school. I know that he still thinks of himself as a middle-school teacher and I suspect he always will. I'm saddened that such a wonderful teacher has left a place where he did so much good for so many kids. But I also know the costs he paid as he struggled to fit his writing into the life of a dedicated husband, father, and teacher. One of the most powerful critiques he makes of the system is that he had to leave it.

But leave it he did, so that he could write this book and continue his studies of learning and teaching and his advocacy of the importance of teachers and students working together to understand and develop a critical literacy. Only a remarkable book could balance the loss of the kind of teacher Jeff Wilhelm was. This is a remarkable book.

Michael W. Smith
Rutgers University

# REFERENCES

Applebee, A. (1993). *Literature in the secondary school: Studies of curriculum and instruction in the United States.* Urbana, IL: National Council of Teachers of English.

Atwell, N. (1987). *In the middle: Writing, reading and learning with adolescents.* Portsmouth, NH: Heinemann, Boynton/Cook.

Giroux, H. (1985). Teachers as transformative intellectuals. *Social Education, 49,* 376–379.

Meek, M. (1983). *Achieving literacy: Longitudinal studies of adolescents learning to read.* New York: Routledge & Kegan Paul.

# Acknowledgments

I wish to thank many people who were important to the thinking, conversing, and drafting that went into the completion of this book. The completion of such a project would have been impossible without the help and support of many people, to whom I am very grateful.

Above all, thank you to my wife, Peggy Jo, for her understanding support through the past several years. Her loving kindnesses and her constant belief that I would grow significantly through the long process of sustained study and writing—not to mention her constant belief that I would actually finish what I had set out to do—were of great and necessary importance to me.

My appreciation and thanks go to David Schaafsma and Stuart Greene for their generosity of time, energy, and thoughtful response to much of my work. Their encouragement and expertise have been much appreciated.

Thanks also to Wayne Otto and Deb Brandt for their reading of this manuscript and their very helpful suggestions.

A special thanks must go to Patricia Enciso for guidance, help, and selfless sharing of her own expertise and many insights. Michael Smith also offered constant encouragement and support. Brian Edmiston was a great help to me as I planned, implemented, and analyzed the drama activities.

I would like to thank my team teaching colleague Paul Friedemann for his support; my friend Brian Ambrosius for serving as a model reader and a model tennis partner; Leon Holley Jr. for his collegial support and friendship through the years; and Erv Barnes for many discussions on our companionable trips down to Madison, Wisconsin. Thanks to my colleagues Brenda Power, Jim Artesani, and Kelly Chandler at the University of Maine for their help during the final drafting.

Thanks to my father, mother, and my many dedicated teachers through the years, most notably James Blaser and William Strohm.

# Really Among Schoolchildren

As I read my early teaching journals and reflect, I look back through cloud banks of memory and am more than a little bit dubious of the confidence my younger self often expressed. I was certainly enthusiastic, totally in love with what I was experiencing with my students. There are days now when I would like to plug into that sort of positive energy. I wrote about *knowing* how to teach literature and *knowing* how to teach writing. For a young guy I was pretty smug. "I'm getting it down cold," I wrote one day over 10 years ago. "I'm cruising down the curricular highway, nailing lesson after lesson, skill after skill. I feel like a batter on a hitting streak" (March 1984).

My association with the National Writing Project supported and excited my thinking about the teaching of writing. The cornucopia of college and graduate literature courses I had enjoyed made me think I knew literature, and therefore how to teach it. I knew lots of stuff, for sure.

## THE READING STRUGGLE

Today I find this sort of highly competent feeling about my own teaching almost unimaginable. All my original beliefs about learning and instruction have undergone intense changes over the past few years. I now regard all of my current positions as categorically tentative. I converse daily with colleagues and with students, looking for a slightly better way to do things. Margaret Meek's (Meek et al., 1983) question about learning, "What if it is otherwise?," has become almost a mantra. I search daily for ways to help my individual students learn more fruitfully. There are practices, such as directly intervening in student literary interpretations, that I have rejected, embraced, and rejected again before coming to some sort of compromise position that I am sure will be compromised again.

My reflections these days have more to do with how often I may have missed opportunities while navigating my students from September to June through the course of a school year. Was I oblivious to tremendously important issues occurring in the minds and hearts of my student crew, sealed off from the view of my chart room? Did the evidence I garnered to support the idea of my earlier successes come only from my most enthusiastic students? Were there students whose needs I missed or dismissed? What might I be missing now? Did I know how to look into the secret hearts of my students' reading lives? What windows are now available to me into student attitudes and reading processes? What opportunities and students might be slipping away at this very moment?

These days, the complexity and responsibility of teaching 130 individual students often weighs upon me as a series of almost awesome possibilities.

What changed for me? For seven years I had taught high school English and speech with panache and assurance. Then I transferred to the middle school to teach language arts and three courses of "remedial reading."

It was the experience of teaching eighth grade "remedial reading" that really shook me up for the first time. In retrospect, those classes were the knocks in my mental engine that became thrown piston rods. After "remedial reading" I no longer possessed the confidence that my teaching theories and practices could help many of my students on their journeys to becoming independent readers and learners, nor sustain me on my own journey as a teacher.

You see, those kids knew what it meant to be labeled a "remedial reader." With every move and comment they made, they damned the very label, the class they were in, and their whole history of reading education in school. My confusion and frustration began on the first day I met my "remedial readers," and it never let up.

Over the first few days of school they strode into class and greeted me with hurled gauntlets such as, "I'm Jeff and I hate reading!"

"You can't make me read!"

"I'm a terrible reader. That's just the way it is. Sorry."

This message was repeated through a myriad of other explicitly and subtly insistent ways during that confusing first semester. Early in February, I made this journal entry:

> What a day! What a week of days! What a year of days! The eighth graders simply hate reading, or say that they do, and they refuse to even try to do it. Whether this is a defense-mechanism, a learned behavior or what, I don't know, but they won't be shaken from it. And another thing I don't know is how to help them change so they'll have a chance to become better readers. I have tried plan A, B, C, and D and I don't have a plan E! And if I don't find a parachute quickly I believe that I am going to crash and burn and take all of my little kiddies with me. And then I will be the biggest smoking black hole in family history. (February 1989)

This is how the year unfolded: After a first few dismally unsuccessful weeks, I put the basal readers and reading skills workbooks onto the shelf. Then I tried using newspapers, short stories, and journal writing, then free-choice reading and literary letter writing. Nothing worked. The students wouldn't bring any reading materials to class. They wouldn't choose books from our classroom library. Neither comic books nor magazines appealed to them. Trips to the library left them unmoved. They refused to write literary letters to each other, or would write the most cursory letters imaginable: "Hi Trudy. My books stupid. See you after school."

Finally I went exclusively with what I prayed would work: the reading of stories and trade books together as a class.

On this particular February day we were reading *Deathwatch* by Robb White, a story of a young man who guides a rich hunter into the desert. When the hunter "mistakenly" kills an old hermit and his guide insists that it must be reported, the hunter strips the boy and drives off without him, vowing to wait and watch until the boy dies of exposure. It's a disturbing yet powerful story, full of visceral injustice, action, and adventure. The students selected it themselves from several options.

We began the unit with a desert survival simulation that actually worked! The students imagined that we had been stranded by an airplane crash in the middle of the desert. Each class eagerly bought into this imaginary situation, which surprised and relieved me. As a group, the students had to rank the items available on the plane in order of importance to their survival. Finally, the class had to reach consensus about a plan for achieving their survival. All three of the classes were animated and fun. I wrote that "it was the first time all year I didn't feel it was a struggle to get through class" (February 1989).

The girls enjoyed the first few chapters as well as the boys, reacting mostly to the "unfairness" and injustice of the protagonist's situation, much as the boys engaged with his struggle for survival against an evil enemy and the forces of nature.

But after just three days of reading, things slowly fell apart. The students would listen when I read aloud, but many would not follow along. When I asked them to read in pairs or small groups, they resisted. So I asked them to read on their own. On one bleak Thursday afternoon, half the class closed their books and put their heads down. Three girls began chatting about their weekend plans. Two girls were actually reading, but none of the boys. I went to each student in turn, asking why? why? and WHY?

Perhaps because I was polite, the students were generally polite in return, but insistent. "I don't like to read," Jamie told me. "It's OK when you read out loud," Troy said, "but there's no way I'm going to read it by myself or with any idiot from this class."

In short, the class simply shut down. They would listen to me read, but there was "no way" they were going to try it on their own.

By now I was pretty thoroughly entangled in the strings of parachute D and I had nowhere to turn, except perhaps down—where I could see the hard cement of classroom reality rushing up to meet me.

## PERSONAL READINGS

During the same time frame, I was hugely enjoying several books on my own, books that I read in every free moment, books that I stayed up late into the night to read, books that haunted me, books that made me not want to speak for hours or made me call a friend to talk, books that stayed with me for days and were replayed in my dreams, books that insistently tapped on my memory and wove themselves into the tapestry of my life.

I read Flanagan's *The Year of the French* and imagined myself, each morning at breakfast, as an Irish peasant eating bacon for the first time in my life and enjoying it intensely. I savored the food all the more because I deeply suspected that the French would betray us and I would be hanged as a traitor. And I would never eat bacon—or anything else—ever again.

I read Ishiguro's *The Remains of the Day* in one sitting and was compelled to take a long silent walk in the woods. I sat down on a bench and silently cried for the main character and for my own foolish losses and decisions. As I thought about my experience with the book, I wrote my wife a series of intense letters that I left for her each morning at the breakfast table. I read Paton's *Too Late the Phalarope* and finished it when I should have been coaching. My assistant coach, a brother in the reading fraternity, had told me to "finish it, and then go home." He had read the book, too, and knew that I would be worthless for coaching after the experience of its conclusion. He would take the practice. It was a generous offer, and good advice, because I was so deeply inside the book that I could have been at the bottom of the sea. There was no way to quickly resurface without getting the bends.

I have had these experiences with books as far back as I can remember. My best friendships involve books; some friendships are because of books. There are authors and characters that I feel I know so well I regard them as friends, great-hearted people whom I get to know better each time I read. Seeing that they have written a new book or story is like receiving a dinner invitation: a chance to get to visit and know each other more.

When I finish a book, I have in some way finished a chapter in a relationship that I will continue to nurture. There are always two or three more books awaiting that I have already started, and another pile near my bed that have aroused my interest from their former place on a friend's bookshelf, the library, or a bookstore. I carry a book with me everywhere, just in case a train comes by or I'm stuck in a waiting room. I cannot imagine a day of my life without reading. This is why I studied literature in college. This is why I became a teacher: to share in grand conversations about books, to spread the joy, to initiate and welcome students into the fraternity, into what Frank Smith (1988) calls "the club of clubs," to travel with them into wondrously familiar or incredibly strange imaginative worlds.

As I considered the intense meaning of reading in my own life, I felt that there were significant numbers of students who were sleeping in their seats as I developed my own classroom literary flight plans. The plans and the journeys were my own, and seemed inaccessible to many of these eighth graders. What experiences did they lack that might help them to develop a love of reading like my own, or at least to glimpse the potential of stories? How might I change my teaching, adapt my chosen modes of curricular transportation, to make the students active planners and participants in their own sojourns?

## CHILDREN'S HOUR

At night, after struggling with my eighth graders, I often found myself happily reading to small children: my niece, the neighbor boy, and my own small daughter, Fiona. The experience was always the same. At the sight of me, the child would run to find a book, yell something like, "Let's read!," and jump into my lap, sometimes before I even had a chance to sit down. And one book was never enough. Oh no! These children consumed books as if they were Lay's potato chips. It didn't matter what book; no one could read just one. Fiona to this day opens her own negotiations with the question, "Two books or three?"

After reading, I would pronounce "The End" like a solemn "Amen," bringing closure to our shared reading experience. There would be a moment of thoughtful silence, perhaps a question, then the cathedral-like silence would shatter like a baseball thrown through stained glass, with "Read A-nudder One! Please, please, please, please, PLEASE!" (And how can one refuse a request like that?)

Reading with these children was a series of joyous surprises. Sometimes they would sit silently, soaking up the world of the book. But more often than not, they would interrupt me, pointing at pictures, telling stories about their own lives, laughing, asking questions, judging, elaborating, and even getting up to make faces and act out scenes from the book. I made several journal entries about our reading, commenting always on how reading, for them, was much more than "words." In fact, I was sometimes irritated with all the interruptions to what I regarded as "the story." For them, reading was an adventure that was unique each time. The books were suggestions, maps to be consulted, edited, deviated from. For these children, a book was a promise, and reading was an experiential fulfillment of the promise.

While reading a simple little story by Hans Wilhelm entitled *Waldo Goes to the Zoo*, my daughter interrupted on the very first page, telling a story about how "we went to the zoo and we saw the walrus and he spit at us, didn't he, Daddy?" She later pounced to the floor and roared like a lion, strutted like a giraffe, and then glided back to my side to continue reading, without commentary or explanation.

After *Waldo* it was *Madeline's Rescue* by Ludwig Bemelmans, which we must have read for the next 10 nights running. When I asked if we could read *Madeline* or *Madeline and the Bad Hat*, Fiona was most insistent; only *Madeline's Rescue* would do. "I want to read this one!" she insisted. (In my journal that night I ruminated about how I discouraged students from re-reading a book or even an author that they had already read.)

On the first page, Fiona chimed in to read the final rhyme of each couplet, cheering out the words and laughing. She pointed at the vines on the house and said, "Look, here's the vines!"

On page two, before a word could be uttered, Fiona yelled, "Oh no! Madeline shouldn't do that!" upon seeing that Madeline was walking on the railing of a bridge.

Without letting me read out the words, she turned the page and told me, "Don't worry, the dog will save her," as we studied the picture of Madeline sinking into the Seine. She pointed out various details: the blue house, the painter—"he's mad, isn't he, Daddy? Why were you mad at Jasmine [her baby sister] today?"—the policeman, and even Miss Clavell holding her head. "Don't worry, Miss Clavell!" she advised Madeline's teacher and caretaker. She even attempted to comfort Miss Clavell's picture, by patting the nun's back with her finger.

And on it went. Lord Cucuface was "mean. He's a bad man!" Miss Clavell was "nice," Madeline "naughty . . . sometimes, like me." A monologue followed explaining how she was mostly good but could still be "contrary" sometimes. Two stories were told about our neighbors' dogs, Cody and Monty, who had run away that past week.

At the end, when the puppies are born, Fiona laughed wildly, as she had each day for the past 10 days. "Look at all the doggies!" she gulped between giggles, proceeding to count the pups.

And before I could say "The End," Fiona turned to me and informed me, quite diplomatically, "I don't want to go to bed yet!" She shook her head sideways. "I'm not tired. Let's read another one!"

It was on this same night in February that the neighbor boy's mom came over in a distraught mood. At that night's parent–teacher conferences she had been told that her first grade son was doing poorly in reading, and that in fact he seemed to resist reading. The teacher had suggested testing and possibly enrollment in extra-help programs.

## COMPELLING QUESTIONS

Something was going on here, something as fishy and distasteful as cod liver oil. How could a boy who loved books, who loved sitting on a couch to read, who in fact continued to insist upon it in the comfort of his own home or my own, how could such a boy *not* like and succeed at reading in school?

There was clearly some sort of chasm for him between home reading and school reading, between what I came to consider engaged and unengaged experiences of reading.

And what about my daughter? As much as she loved reading now, could she become a nonreader who had lost the sense of reading's mystery, drama, magic, and camaraderie? Whatever had happened (or not happened) to my eighth grade students that they would not now give the act of reading another chance? As I thought about this, I began to formulate the questions that guided the subsequent years of classroom research and revised practice that I will report on in this book, primarily through the telling of three teacher-research stories.

Why do some kids love reading? What is rewarding and engaging about reading for these students? What do these engaged readers "do" as they read that makes the experience fun, satisfying, and engaging for them?

Why do other kids hate reading? What in their experience has contributed to their negative view?

I realized that year after year, I had encountered students who obviously resisted reading. But they seemed to be a minority, and eventually— I'm ashamed to say—I'd really just given up on them as far as becoming readers was concerned. It was when I encountered a whole class of them that I could not blame them instead of myself, the materials, or the method. Eighth grade remedial reading produced a crisis that required a new way of thinking about and teaching the act of reading. If I wished to pursue my job of developing readers, then resistance and lack of engagement were compelling issues that had to be deeply considered.

These considerations led to the central concern of this book and the theme of my most recent teaching: How might less engaged readers be helped to read in the way that engaged readers do, and maybe (just maybe!) become readers themselves?

## TENTATIVE ANSWERS

I considered these questions for several years, thinking about them, reading and writing about them, and testing out revised practices in my classroom. I kept track of what happened in class and interviewed students about their own attitudes, views, and experiences. I talked to my engaged readers and those who were unengaged and reluctant. I encouraged them to talk to each other.

As part of a graduate course, I used audiotaped protocols of students observing their own reading processes. The next year I used cued protocols, asking students to stop at various points in their reading and report their thoughts, feelings, imaginings. I kept questioning. I looked for any window that would make reading visible and offer me a glimpse of information about my driving questions. What has resulted is an evolving story about how my own student readers read and how they may be helped to read in more engaged and satisfying ways. The story I tell here is primarily the story of my students, how they revealed the moves they make as readers, what they made happen, and what happened for them when new classroom practices such as art and drama were put into play. But it is also my own story, and that of my own developing perspective on the teaching of reading and of the practice of literacy in classrooms.

For a problem such as this, I wanted advice, but I knew I had to find my own answer. No one else could know my students, or see what happened when we tried new things together. I took myself, as jazz musicians like to say, "out to the woodshed" for some heavy thinking. I tried to become aware of my implicit theories, think clearly about what I could do in the classroom and what ends I thought might be achieved through new practices. I became, for the first time, what I regard as a teacher-researcher: a teacher who is consciously questioning, observing, theorizing, testing, adapting, and learning something every day in the classroom. Teacher-research revitalized my passion for teaching, for reading literature with students, and it helped me to both read and teach in more aware and powerful ways. The story of what happened to the students involves what happened, and continues to happen, to me as the teacher. I see my experience as a teacher-researcher as one of reclaiming my classroom for myself and for my students, of taking control, together, of what and how we will do things together. This active control, and the awareness and willingness to use it, is what "empowerment" means to me.

The professional landscape of education has long been occupied by people who aren't teachers, and though I know these experts add valuable voices to the educational conversation, they can't be expected to have a teacher's perspective.

My experience as a teacher-researcher leads me to encourage teachers to become researchers who collaborate with students and share a community of multivoiced stories, providing a variety of classroom-based viewpoints from which to survey different parts of a highly complex topography of readers, literary experience, and learning. By combining our various voices, perhaps we can devise a map and a sense of the landscape that will help us all to become better and more independent readers of words and, as Freire encourages us, readers of the world.

## SETTING THE TASK

For the past four school years, my students started the year by anonymously completing attitude inventories. These inventories indicated that most of my own middle school students did not regard themselves as readers. Between 30 and 50 percent of the responses indicated that though the students generally regard themselves as "competent" readers, the activity of reading was something they saw solely as a necessary life skill and school activity. In their private lives, nearly half of my student population noted that they were "nonreaders," that they read "rarely," that they regarded reading as something required by "school," instead of something to do on your own, at "home," for "personal satisfaction," or with "friends" or "family." They wrote that they would not choose to read as a leisure-time activity, ranking it far below television, video games, sports, and, for some, even below "chores"! A variety of other responses also hinted that they generally held negative attitudes toward reading.

Each year, I am continually astonished by these results. I had always been aware of a few highly resistant and unengaged readers, some who were out of the closet and some who did their best to hide. But I had never dreamed that so many would anonymously express a total lack of interest in reading as a personally fulfilling pursuit. There were so many!

I began asking students to voice their opinions about everything that they read. I provided time during each class to log and write letters about what had been read the previous day: books, magazines, newspapers, cereal boxes, STOP signs, anything. And the results were consistent with the inventories. About half of the students just didn't read on their own. Half.

God, that there would be so many!

The inventories, logs, and subsequent interviews showed that students regarded reading as the finding of meaning in the text or as the passive reception of another's meaning. One student told me that reading is being able to answer the questions at the end of a story. This is an attitude, I think, that schools and textbooks actively endorse and reinforce, and that disenfranchises readers (see, for example, Durkin, 1979; Hillocks, 1987). Many other students maintained that reading was "answering questions" or "finding answers" and that this sort of "snipe hunting," as my case study student Joanne put it, was what "makes me hate reading for school." I began to suspect that it was this view, and their school experience of reading, that contributed to many students' lack of interest if not outright disdain.

If we take the theoretical stance that reading is, in fact, producing and creating meaning, then the way reading education is traditionally practiced in schools must be rethought. If reading is creating texts in response to texts, something new must start happening in our classrooms. This something must take response beyond boilerplate questions and "correct" answers.

The students who *do* know that reading is producing meaning have gone underground to harbor and nurture their secret. School has forced them to be secretive. Most forceful to me was the coy testimony of Joanne. "You're not really interested in how I read," she told me early in the school year. "No teacher would ever be interested in that." What teachers are interested in, she told me, was "my getting it right—or what you all think is right." Because of this, Joanne continued, "I do what I have to in school and then I take my own book home and do real reading."

If reading truly is the producing of meaning, then all the materials of the curriculum become pre-texts, by which I mean an excuse or a reason to pursue personal inquiry and create personal meanings. If we are interested in student learning and transformation, then textbooks and stories become the texts that catalyze the real text that is the reader's response and new understanding. The questions and the answers will become those of the student and may be most fruitfully embedded and expressed through creative, artistic, and student-centered response "texts."

The studies and the stories that follow will pursue two intertwining paths of inquiry suggested by these initial findings and impressions:

• What can we discover about how highly engaged adolescent readers produce meaning?

• What can be done in the classroom to help reluctant readers reconceive of reading as a creative and personally meaningful pursuit? Can this be done in a way that guides and scaffolds their use of meaning-making strategies so that they actually develop as readers? How, in short, can they be helped to become developing readers?

# CHAPTER ONE

# Moving Toward a Reader-Centered Classroom

This past year, on reading workshop days, my seventh grade students had to show me an "entrance ticket" to enter the class. That ticket was a free-reading book. Each student would show me the book and, in an enjoyable ritual (that could probably only happen with young adolescents), would give me a high five and call out "I am a reader!" as she or he entered the classroom. Every student would do this except Marvin, who would flash me his book, give me a high five, and yell out, "Reading is stupid!"

Marvin and many previous students much like him have literally changed my teaching, if not my life. It's because of him and classes such as eighth grade remedial reading that I came to rethink the reading act. Because of students like him, I've come to express this argument about the teaching of reading: In order to develop readers, we must encourage and foster the creative attitudes and activities of engaged readers. We must do this instead of teaching sets of skills or teaching texts—which was what was probably done for (or to!) us—and which was what I was certainly taught to do in my teacher education courses. It's also what traditional anthologies and workbooks and all other prepackaged programs require us to do. By instead focusing our instruction and support on the construction of meaning, the classroom can become a place where students not only produce and share meanings, but a place where they share ways of reading and being with text, becoming aware in the process of their own strategies and those of others. And then, with a little luck, reading won't seem so stupid to our students.

Creating this new kind of reading environment was a new and difficult direction to move in as a teacher. It was uncomfortable to leave the security of an anthology that blanketed the year with reading selections, suggested activities, and questions. And it required really recognizing my beliefs about reading so that they could be reworked in ways that would serve my students.

## THE BOTTOM-UP APPROACH

On the first day of this past academic year, I was walking to school. It's a small town, and I know the kids whom I'll be teaching. I was following two of them, Randy and his friend Chris. We had to walk through the neighborhood elementary school grounds to get to the middle school, and I continued along about 10 paces behind them. Near the front entry stood a child, probably a kindergartner who'd just been dropped off by his mom, and he was *wailing*. He was a sandy-haired little boy in new clothes clutching a green Ninja Turtle backpack. Big, gulping sobs were heaving out of his chest like giant burps, and he was struggling to catch his breath before the next sob racked his body. I was hurrying over to him as Randy and Chris passed by. Randy leaned toward the child and said, "Chill out, kid. It only gets worse."

At this point the playground aide hustled the weeping child away, and I was left thinking about Randy. I said to myself: *This is my challenge, isn't it? How can I help Randy so school doesn't get even worse for him this year?*

A couple of weeks later I was conferencing with Randy and asked him about the incident. He told me that "school is a bunch of crap that doesn't mean anything . . . you just do a bunch of crap for someone else so you can get through the year." This description of being a student is strikingly close to Plato's definition of a slave: a person who does someone else's work. Randy especially hated reading, and told me that reading was "like . . . pain."

Randy, Marvin, and most of their classmates learned to read using a phonics-based approach. This model of learning to read is also labeled the "bottom-up" or "parts to whole" approach. According to this approach, the foundation of learning to read is understanding letter-to-sound correspondences, better known as "phonics."

I understand that students have to know some phonics to read. But I also think that this approach to reading has encouraged students like Randy and Marvin to think of the meaning of reading as something outside themselves. My students who did not recall being read to at home often reported negative memories of elementary school reading instruction, because, I think, their experience with reading consisted of worksheets instead of stories and conversations about stories. My LD (learning disabled) students (and Marvin was one of these), who often had been given extra reading help through approaches such as DISTAR—an intense phonics and word recognition approach to reading—had very negative and resistant attitudes toward reading, summed up by Marvin's favorite little chant.

Libby told me that "All I remember [about learning to read] is sitting around all the time." Another student, wondering about my language arts class, asked me, "How can you do reading without worksheets and vocabulary lists?" (It's interesting that you don't read, you *do* reading.) When I asked if she thought doing worksheets helped her to be a better reader or to enjoy reading, she just said, "No. I hate reading, but that's what we've always done." Again, I think that these students have never been helped to pursue reading in any personally meaningful way. By the time they arrived in my classroom, an intense demythologization of the reading act was in order.

Leading experts call this "bottom-up" approach the longest and greatest influence on reading instruction, and the one that is usually reflected in basal readers and reading programs. This view regards reading as a data-driven process, and is rather mechanical in that it emphasizes mastery of specific subskills and skills, moving from small units such as letters to bigger units such as words, phrases, and sentences (e.g., DISTAR). The idea is that once students have understood and mastered the subskills of reading, they can apply these in context to decode letters and words; they are then well on their way to becoming readers. The emphasis is on breaking the code because meaning is seen as being *in* the text. Print is therefore in control of the reading process, which starts with letters and words. The page is greater than the reader.

The majority of my own students seemed thoroughly indoctrinated by this approach, and several students a year tell me that reading well is being able to recognize words or being able to answer the questions at the end of a story.

## WHY JOHNNY WON'T READ

Once students have learned how to read, and move through middle and secondary school, reading is still regarded as a passive act of receiving someone else's meanings. This is due in part to a literary theory known as New Criticism that implicitly informs much if not most of our nation's literature teaching. The New Critical orientation toward literary reading, in a way, is a natural kind of extension of the bottom-up approach to learning to read.

Basically, New Criticism is a highly systematic and formalistic approach to rigorous, analytic readings of literary texts. The New Critics paid tremendous attention to literary form, and the structures of the "whole text." They called for an end to a concern with matters outside the work itself—the author, his life, the historical situation, and the implications of the work for society or for the individual reader. In fact, they denied "the psychological effects of the poem" in an effort to make an objective science of interpretation. Textual details work together to express one thematic meaning.

Teachers influenced by this approach may emphasize knowing and recognizing literary devices, getting at the "internal logic" of a text's construction by studying various patterns and codes, and relating a work's central "organic" meaning to how this meaning was expressed. There may be an emphasis on "rightness" of literary interpretation. Interpretive questions about the text will be answered after reading; thesis essays assigned; and discussions mediated by the teacher, who acts as the authority on the text. The text is what is studied, and it is an artifact regarded with something rivaling reverence.

Throughout my own first years as a teacher, I suffered from what I might now call a sort of theoretical schizophrenia. I adopted the implicit New Critical conceptions that surrounded my own school education. Reading was finding meaning in text, and there were strict methodologies to be followed to get at that "correct" meaning. I certainly wasn't alone; studies by Durkin (1979) in elementary schools and Hillocks (1987) in high school settings demonstrate that most reading and literature instruction involves seatwork and recitation that focus on cracking codes instead of creating meanings.

Through my high school and college literature courses, a blend of classical and New Critical theory was the order of the day and informed classroom instruction, literary interpretation, and grading. My notes from college classes recorded the "intentional fallacy" and the "affective fallacy"—which warned me not to be moved or affected by my reading—as pitfalls to be avoided, and New Critical tenets pepper my notes as a way of directing "correct" interpretation. Thesis essays were written to show how well I had read and interpreted the text, with evidence provided in the form of formal analyses and textual quotations.

Creative, personal response was taboo. One college professor was severely stricken by my parody of Shakespeare's *Troilus and Cressida* starring Steve Martin as a comedic Ajax. "The play is a tragedy! What right do you have to violate the text of Shakespeare?!" he practically gagged. Holy smokes, I thought, I had engaged in illicit, practically blasphemous activities! I was sure to be put on some literary blacklist and called up by the Congressional Committee on Un-literary Activities!

The result of my own education was a tragicomedy of sorts: my situation as a teacher-theorist. You see, I didn't even know that New Criticism was a theory; I thought it was just the stance and strategies you used to read well. I had digested it, unaware that it was just one theory of reading among a constellation of theories.

I was certainly not alone in my ignorance (which is a place where you usually find a lot of company). The elder Roger Applebee's survey (Squires & Applebee, 1966) of literature instruction found that New Critical beliefs about literary interpretation dominated American secondary and undergraduate education in the 1960s. The younger Applebee's more recent national survey (1989) found that little has changed in the practice of literature instruction since that time.

Despite the best of my own intentions and a lot of very hard work, I've come to believe that my implicit theory and methods (shared as they are by much of the school establishment) were a large part of the reason for many of my students' discontent.

You see, New Criticism assumes the text to be an integrated and coherent whole, and it monolithically determines meaning, which can be gleaned through "close readings" of the text. As such, the reader's role is akin to dentistry (or Plato's slavery): to extract someone else's meaning. The role of the reader as an active meaning-maker, one who connects personally to what is read, who spends pleasurable and stirring time with stories, and who might judge or resist the text and its author, is essentially precluded from the reading act.

A study by Newell, MacAdams, and Spears-Burton (1987) of three secondary literature teachers found their situations to be entirely similar to my own. These teachers' literary theories and beliefs did implicitly inform their instruction, though not in particularly consistent or conscious ways, and did not lead to significant study, discussion, or changes in their practice.

Richard Rorty, cited by Jerome Bruner (1986) in *Actual Minds, Possible Worlds,* characterizes Anglo-American philosophy as the pursuit of the epistemological question "how to know truth," which is an empirical question, versus "how we come to endow experience with meaning," which is the epistemological question that preoccupies the poet and the storyteller (p. 12). And as I wrote in the margin, this latter question is the procedural one that should preoccupy the teacher. How do we endow experience, especially the experience of reading, with meaning? How can readers who do not endow the reading experience with meaning be helped to do so?

Many teachers influenced by New Criticism work against the purpose of this procedural question. They often communicate that literature is not about the students and their most vital concerns, but about whatever some superior intelligence tells them it is about. As Aidan Chambers (1985) asserts: "Nothing could be more dishonest and more productive of a cynical and disaffected community" (p. 126). Such an orientation can also serve to disaffect teachers. There came a point in my own career when I wrote:

> If literature does not speak to student lives, then what good is it? If
> students don't come to love reading now, when will they ever read

later? If teachers cannot help students to read better, with more purpose, better attitudes and greater power, than what good are we? I am
sick and tired of teaching the "classics" and blaming the kids who
can't answer my questions as "lazy" or "below grade level." If I am
really going to be worthy of the title "teacher" then I had better start
understanding what this act of reading is all about, and I'd better find
out how to let kids in on the secret. (April 1987)

I had always asked what content I should teach, what literary works
and terms and ideas were most important for students to know. I tried to
convince myself that by teaching *To Kill a Mockingbird* I was helping students
to internalize types of questions and ways of reading that would lead to
"correct" interpretations. The harder I looked at this assumption, the more
reductive and incomplete it seemed to be.

This is what I was asking students to do when they read literature:
someone else's work instead of their own. This is why Randy thinks of school
as a "bunch of crap to get through" and why Marvin can maintain that
"reading is stupid!" As I tried to make reading literature a kind of personal
work that my students would do for themselves, my implicit New Critical
views began to give way to a reader-response orientation that reading is the
enjoyable and affecting act of producing meaning.

## THERE IS AN ALTERNATIVE

Instead of looking at reading as receiving the meaning in texts, reader-
oriented theories regard reading as the creation, in concert with texts, of
personally significant experiences and meanings.

Proponents of the "top-down" psycholinguistic model of learning to
read regard too much phonics instruction as misguided because of the ultimate irrelevance of phonics to the competent reader, the complex nature of
the rules, and the time that such instruction takes from real reading and
writing activity. They also see phonics programs as symptomatic of the way
schools drain away the juicy joys of reading and set out obstacles between
children and becoming literate.

Proponents of this approach, such as Ken Goodman (1982) and Frank
Smith (1978), see reading less as an ability and more as a highly social,
purposeful, and meaning-driven activity. The Whole Language movement,
though this is an umbrella term for a wide variety of classroom practice, has
been largely informed by the thought of Goodman and Smith. The point
for these theorists is not the array of skills the reader can deploy, but how the
reader actually makes use of skills as she explores and experiences meaning.

Reading is seen as an intensely human pursuit with intensely human purposes that must be foregrounded. Reading, instead of a complex set of skills, becomes a social practice and a search for meaning.

Goodman argues that reading

> is the search for meaning which preoccupies the reader. . . . That is why aspects of the process and how it works cannot be isolated from the construction of meaning that is the ultimate goal. Learning to read involves getting the process together. That is harder if instruction takes it apart. (1985, p. 839)

Still, with such an approach, the teacher must ask when to intervene, especially with students such as my own who are often reluctant or resistant readers. How can their attitudes be changed, their repertoire of strategies developed? Are there no bottom-up skills that would be useful to them?

One answer to these concerns comes in the form of a compromise "interactive" model that has been proposed by David Rumelhart (1985) and that conceives of reading as both top-down and bottom-up. Yes, readers search for global meanings, but they sometimes use decoding skills on a local level to achieve this end. Both the text and the reader play a part in the meaning-making process, and the relationship is constantly changing. When reading lyric poetry, for example, the reader plays the more powerful and vital role by supplying memories and emotions. When reading a legal document, however, the text exerts more rigid controls over the meaning-making process. As the reader interacts and constructs meaning with text, she uses multiple sources of information. She is a pattern synthesizer who uses syntactic, semantic, and orthographic clues to arrive at a most probable interpretation that both considers the text and is satisfying to her own purposes and needs.

This model stresses the prior knowledge structures or "schema" of the individual reader. Reading becomes a meeting of the reader's prior knowledge *and* textual meanings that work together to create a greater sense of things.

Frank Smith (1978), in particular, stresses the importance of what the reader brings to the page, a body of knowledge he calls "nonvisual information."

> There is only one way to summarize everything that a child must learn in order to become a fluent reader, and that is to say that the child must learn to use nonvisual information efficiently when attending to print. Learning to read does not require the memorization of letter names or phonic rules, or large lists of words, all of which are in fact taken care of in the course of learning to read, and little of which will make sense to a child without experience of reading. Nor is learning to read a matter of application to all manner of exercises and

drills which can only distract and perhaps even discourage a child from the business of learning to read. (p. 179)

As I prepare the final draft of this manuscript, my now four-year-old daughter Fiona knows her letters and is beginning to recognize words. Yet we have never used flashcards or drills. We have magnetic letters on the refrigerator, which she will sometimes ask her mother and me to help her use to write out a message. She writes notes that are a mixture of real words and scribbles. After reading with us, she will make serial illustrations of scenes on computer paper. She makes character books in which she draws characters from books and real people engaged in typical pursuits. At other times she will write her own story by drawing pictures and asking us to write the text, but she is eager to write for herself the words she already knows. She knows many of her books so well that she can "read" to her sister Jasmine, age two, by flipping through the pages and reciting the story—nearly verbatim.

Last night she and little Jasmine asked me to be the Big Bad Wolf as they acted out a rendition of "The Three Little Pigs." They gathered pencils to signify sticks and blocks to signify bricks. After I slid down the back of the couch they had designated as the chimney and into the box that was their soup pot, they pulled me out and invited me to stay for dinner, an ending they liked better than the one in the book!

And then, before bed, flipping through a *Newsweek* article on airplane safety, Fiona asked me to point out the word "airplane" and then spelled it out for herself, then asked me to read "the story for this picture." She asked questions such as "What's a bomb?" and "Why don't they take more care of the airplanes so they won't have accidents?" Even as a child just learning to recognize her first words, reading is a search for meaning and understanding. She applies what she knows and asks adults to help her understand and learn what she does not know. Reading is something fun to do together with others to both explore the world and to express how we would change it. And responding to her reading through a variety of artistic and dramatic texts is quite natural for her.

The interactive model of reading allows readers like Fiona to pursue their own reading and construct their own meanings, yet asks adults to teach background knowledge, skills, and strategies helpful to the reader's purpose in the context of real, personally purposeful reading and writing.

This kind of interactive approach allows for everyone to have a place in learning and experiencing the reading act: the author, the text, the teacher, and especially the reader. This approach to learning to read is a natural complement to Louise Rosenblatt's transactional approach to experiential reading that can inform how we teach preadolescent and adolescent readers.

It was the transactional approach that provided the antidote to my own New Critical orientation, training, and teaching practice. This resulting reader-oriented approach led me to a changed classroom filled with both goal-oriented instruction and independent reading clubs of students who express their understandings through art, drama, hypermedia (a multimedia computer platform), and videotape. This new approach helped my students to become more positive and productive readers willing to explore and create for themselves the pleasures of text.

## GETTING STARTED

As I considered how to change my classroom practices, I turned to the work of Rosenblatt, who is widely recognized as the founder of reader-response theory.

In Rosenblatt's theory, reading is a "transaction" in which the reader and the text converse together in a particular situation to make meaning. The reader makes meaning *with* the text, instead of solely on his own, as top-down literary theorists such as David Bleich (1975) would have it. The reader's experience with the text is called the "poem," and it is unique to each reader and reading. The reader's situation, the text, and the interpretive conventions it puts into play guide the process of making the "poem," but not nearly to the degree asserted by Fish (1980), who argues that meaning is constrained entirely by the "interpretive communities" to which the reader belongs. For Rosenblatt, the reader's own individual purposes, mood, and background experiences with life and reading become primary influences on the meaning that is evoked. As she expressed in her first major work, *Literature as Exploration:*

> The special meanings, and, more particularly, the submerged associations that these words and images have for the individual reader will largely determine what the work communicates to him. The reader brings to the work personality traits, memories of past events, present needs and preoccupations, a particular mood of the moment, and a particular physical condition. These and many other elements in a never-to-be-duplicated combination determine his response to the peculiar contribution of the text. (1983, pp. 30–31)

Her later book *The Reader, the Text, the Poem* (1978) is more specifically useful to classroom teaching. In this work, Rosenblatt criticizes literary instruction (such as my own) that focused on correct answers. She cites an anthology question that asks: "What facts have we learned from this poem?" as a way of highlighting the shortsightedness of such an approach.

As part of her argument she makes an interesting move away from the view that "reading is reading" by drawing a distinction between "efferent" and "aesthetic" reading. Efferent reading is pursued when readers adopt a stance in which they are concerned with what information they can "take away" from the reading. The text is treated as consisting of information. The aesthetic stance, however, is maintained for the purpose of "living through" an experience that is enjoyed while reading. Texts themselves are not intrinsically literary or nonliterary; the stance taken toward a text is what makes the reading aesthetic or efferent.

Rosenblatt emphasizes that readers will operate, during the reading of a single text, on different points of a continuum between efferent and aesthetic reading. As she points out, most classroom reading, questions, and texts are designed to elicit efferent responses, and assume that there are correct answers to these questions. In fact, the way literature is generally taught, she argues, predisposes students to take the efferent stance, and in many subversive ways invalidates the taking of the aesthetic stance that makes literature an experience to be enjoyed.

Empirical research conducted by Alan Purves (1973) on the typical response modes in the classroom supports Rosenblatt's dreary view. By setting a correct interpretation to be reached by students in advance of the experience of reading, the students are led to particular interpretations and an efferent mode of reading. Purves asserts that "the penchant for experiential reading . . . is driven out of the heads of readers by instruction" (p. 72).

When Brad explains that the purpose of reading is "to find out stuff" and Kevin tells me that it is "to answer the questions at the end of the story," they are taking an efferent stance.

If students do not know how to take an aesthetic stance as they read, then they will be denied the opportunity to "live through" the experience of a literary transaction. In my journal, I almost exulted:

> This is what is happening. Suddenly it is clear! These students have not ever experienced the world of a story. They read for information. Every anthology selection, every quiz, every class they have ever taken has reinforced the efferent stance of reading at the expense of the aesthetic stance. Even their literary letters were just summaries, with an occasional judgment. My God, no wonder reading is uninteresting to them. No wonder they don't understand the wonder of it. (November 1989)

This also threw light on another phenomenon I had been observing in my classroom. Those students who were avid readers had all gone underground. They did not want it pointed out that they liked to read, and they only agreed to speak about their reading in private situations.

> Today the strangest thing happened. We were talking about our reading and Sarah was discussing *That Was Then, This Is Now* and I was approving of her and her effort in various ways when Clancy yelled out, "But she's reading at home!" to which everybody else started yelling, "Yes, yes! She's reading at home" like this was a crime or the ultimate stupidity or something. There was this attitude that it was OK to read in school, in class or even in a study hall, but—as Jeff put it, "if you have nothing better to do at home than read you'd better think about getting a real life!" Reading as only something you do at school, to finish assignments? Where in the hell did they get that idea? (February 1990)

I was often surprised during the school year when in journal writings or through observation I discovered that some students were quietly trading books and writing notes about their reading. When I asked why they would not share their reading more publicly, I was told, as in the case of Stacey, "Mr. Wilhelm, try not to embarrass us. We like to read but we don't want it to destroy our reputations or anything and seem like geeks or nerds or something. Try to understand! We'll do the reading and stuff but don't embarrass us about it." I hypothesized that

> these students have discovered the aesthetic experience of reading, and that is something that many of their peers cannot conceive of or understand, and in fact they deride the very notion of it. Perhaps if all could be introduced to the aesthetic stance and experience of literature, a great nationwide movement could be undertaken to make reading "COOL" and "POPULAR." Yes, perhaps teens across the nation would buy and trade books like they were baseball cards. Maybe book clubs could replace gangs . . . Maybe . . . If this mission could be undertaken a great sweeping change would occur across the nation! (March 1990)

Rosenblatt had unleashed my prophetic powers and a vision of an America of readers. She was making a move that had explanatory and suggestive power for the classroom teacher and researcher. As Robert Probst (1988) points out, her model suggests that "students must be free to deal with their own reactions to the text," which also means that teachers should "ask students what they see, feel, think and remember as they read, encouraging them to attend to their own experience of the text" (p. 31). This focusing on the process of reading, instead of solely on what was read, became a major thrust of my own classroom practice and research, which I will describe in the next chapters.

## BUILDING ON ROSENBLATT

When I was in graduate school I always found myself teaming up and working with other practicing teachers. The following joke struck a chord with us, and we told it over and over.

There's a famous education professor at a large midwestern university and he hasn't taught a night class in 20 years. He's prevailed upon to do so, though he knows what kind of clientele he'll get, and he'd really rather avoid them. Yes, he's going to get practicing teachers. Sure enough, that's exactly who flocks to his course, and some of them are a real headache. Two in particular keep bothering him to come visit their school. School! He hasn't been inside a school for over two decades. But teachers can be persistent, and he finally gives up and agrees.

When he comes to the school, the two teachers really roll out the red carpet, and they proudly show him around. There are students working in literature circles and other cooperative groups. Kids are creating their own hypermedia and video documentaries to teach other kids. Teachers are working in integrated teams. There are reading and writing workshops; students are publishing their own weekly newspaper and a monthly literary magazine.

At the end of the day, the teachers escort their professor out to his car and wait expectantly. He pauses and says, "Well, yes. It all looks very good in practice. But my question is: will it work *in theory*?"

As I pursued my research with students, I struggled to put reader-response theory into practice. I became convinced that for most of my student readers, engagement with literature through the aesthetic stance did not occur naturally or spontaneously. Rosenblatt, like many literary theorists, seems to assume an Ideal situation versus the Real situation of the classroom. Despite free reading and reading workshops, journals, literary letter exchanges, and a variety of response activities, many of my students did not seem to improve as readers, and many more continued to resist reading.

In fact, many of my better readers did not experience literature in a way that I considered to be complete. They did not recognize and make use of conventional invitations to make certain sorts of meaning (Culler, 1975; Rabinowitz, 1987). They missed irony, didn't understand unreliable narrators, didn't fill in textual gaps, didn't seem to converse with or critique characters, authors, or other readers. Their interpretations of a text's meaning often seemed very far off the mark.

My students, I came to believe, would not be able to "converse with texts fully unless they learn how to take particular stances, deploy strategies to engage with text, and to make use of literary conventions to truly make meaning with text" (June, 1991). I worried that their ability to learn and be transformed by literary transactions would be severely impaired unless Rosenblatt's theory could be made more specific and user-friendly in regard to what readers must do to elicit meaning from the text in order to converse with it. Of primary concern to me was that

> Rosenblatt rings so true to me, but she doesn't give an answer about what can be done to help my middle schoolers see themselves as readers. Sure, take the aesthetic stance, but what do readers do to achieve an aesthetic reading? What are the moves that constitute the aesthetic stance? (August 1991)

Certainly there are general processes of reading useful in any situation: determining importance, summarizing information, drawing inferences, generating questions, and monitoring comprehension (Dole, Duffy, Roehler, & Pearson, 1991). But literary reading was, I agreed, a highly particular sort of meaning-making that involved particular strategies and moves. What were they, though? Rosenblatt never identified them.

It became clear to me that the general strategies used by many students to read a textbook in the efferent stance were not sufficient to achieving an aesthetic reading with literature. What special knowledge and specific strategies did they lack for achieving literary experience and understanding? And what perspectives on their lives, what experiences did they possess that they could be helped to bring to their reading?

Rosenblatt made it clear that it was the reader's responsibility to attend to the author's careful crafting of literary signs, to the conventions of text that were exercised. But how do readers learn to do this? And what must readers do with particular genres, or when faced with sophisticated literary conventions? How do expert readers recognize and respond to these conventional markers and invitations? How could students be helped to develop problem-solving strategies for doing so?

Margaret Meek and colleagues (1983) remind us that we must make public "those secret things" that expert readers know and do. Rosenblatt is not specific in this regard. These issues were of primary importance to me as I used Rosenblatt's theory in my classroom, and eventually led to interesting questions about the actual moves readers make with narrative fiction, and my attempts to help resistant readers make use of and enjoy these stances and strategies.

Though there are reports and research that explore the use of reader response in the classroom, there is no body of work available that is highly detailed, specific, and broad in its look at the actual meaning-making processes of avid and highly engaged adolescent readers. We have lists of what adolescents read, and brief summaries from survey research of what they say they do. But I wanted something more: What could be found out from looking very closely, in great detail, at the particular moves of highly proficient readers? This is what I set out to do over the course of a whole school year.

In my journal I listed these questions, which eventually came to guide the research that I report on in the following chapters:

• What can be done in the classroom to develop reluctant readers and extend the abilities of all readers?

• What do "mature" readers *do* to engage in "rich and powerful" readings?

• How can less engaged readers be encouraged to do these things, and with what effects?

• How can my students be helped to experience literature, and to tell the story of their reading, helping them to discover for themselves the power and variety of the literary experience? (May 1990)

CHAPTER TWO

# Looking at Student Reading

As I pursued the answers to my questions, I became very close to many of my students, sharing stories about reading and life with them on an almost daily basis. Later in the year, when I told Joanne that I was interested in her "story as a reader," she told me, "No, you're interested in the story of my life." But after thinking for a moment, she said, "But for you that means almost the same thing." And maybe she's right, because though she will be one of a few thousand students I will eventually teach, I will always be her seventh grade English teacher, and I hope that will somehow make a qualitative difference in her life.

The stories I'm going to tell here come from a school year during which I taught 123 students. All of the students were involved in the activities that I will describe. I analyzed and report the data from only nine hand-picked students who represented a wide range of student interests, abilities, and difficulties, and it is their stories that I will tell in the following chapters.

I was part of an integrated middle school teaching team that served all of what I jokingly called the district's "severely labeled population." This meant that our team taught all of the students labeled LD (learning disabled) at the seventh grade level. During this year 13 LD students participated in 2 mainstreamed language arts classes with regular education students. Our team also served other labeled students such as ED (emotionally disturbed), ADHD (attention deficit/hyperactivity disorder), and ESL (English as a Second Language) in mainstreamed situations.

The students live in a unified school district in a medium-size midwestern town and a large surrounding farming area. Most parents from town work in light industries such as metallurgy, shoe, cheese, and food-processing factories, or in the professions.

## THE YEAR BEGINS

At the very beginning of the school year, as I began to systematically collect information about how all of my students were reading, I was imme diately struck by several central themes that corresponded to my main frustrations and questions as a teacher.

First, through the initial interviews and conferences, it seemed that the real reading lives of my students were led outside of school. They did not expect school reading to be fun, engaging, or personally satisfying. If they regarded themselves as readers, then the reading they valued was pursued in study halls, at home, with friends and family—usually anyplace but the classroom.

Ron expressed to me that his experience as a reader was not captured by school activities. "I've read things in school that were pretty good, but it's kind of just good luck. Usually if I'm learning something or really into something it's nothing to do with school." Later he explained that "you can read something good and the teacher ruins it by asking you questions that you already know, that don't matter, that you disagree with . . ."

Some of my students who loved reading most, students like Ron, Mandy, and Lisa, had achieved marginal grades in school and became "anti-students," as Mandy put it, as they "tr[ied] to ignore what's going on in class." These three students were often in "trouble" for reading in class, or even in study hall—when they "should be doing their homework," as the math teacher told me (just one example of how literary reading is marginalized in school).

Even engaged readers who were highly successful students, like Cora and Joanne, expressed that teachers and school activities did not share or abet what they valued most about their own reading. "I do what's asked [in assignments], but it often has . . . very little to do with what I'm thinking and feeling and caring about [as I read]," Cora said.

There was another type of student who read and seemed to enjoy stories, but had great difficulty answering typical anthology or worksheet questions. Their lack of success at these activities undermined these students' confidence. Libby, labeled LD, told me, "I like to read, but I'm not very good at it, I guess, or at least I can't remember what I read because I'm not good at answering the questions." Kae, an ESL student, told me that "I read and I sometimes like and I think I know it but then I do bad on quiz . . . I like reading by home better."

There were students like Marvin who simply refused to read, and made an issue out of it. "Can't make me," he told me when I encouraged him to read early in the year. Then there were students who played along and appeared to be reading, like Brad, Kevin, Tommy, and Walter, but who just didn't seem to comprehend or experience what they had read. They all sometimes resisted reading, and expressed that they were not good readers. "Let's face it," Brad told me, speaking for his LD-labeled cohorts, "We suck [at reading]. And who cares?"

For these resistant students, the factual or interpretive questions typically asked by teachers and commercially prepared materials appeared to be no help in revealing, developing, or extending their reading abilities. Even when I was able to navigate them through a reading, their responses seemed totally off the mark, unconnected in any way to what I had understood the story to be about.

## WHAT MAKES VALID READING?

What makes a reading "valid"? Is any response a good one? This has been a thorny issue for me. Given the readers with whom I work and their often negative and submissive attitudes toward reading, my primary concern has been to help them gain confidence as producers of meaning. I wish to help them gain control over their reading processes and to merge into textual worlds in which they will exert this control.

Rosenblatt (1978) addresses this issue when she asserts that a "valid" reading requires that "1) the interpretation is not contradicted by any element of the text, and 2) that nothing is projected for which there is no verbal basis" (p. 115).

Though I accept and even encourage divergent readings from many of my reluctant readers, because I believe growth is being demonstrated as they begin to create meanings, I do keep "valid" reading as an ultimate goal to work toward. I think it is critical to consider the author's intent and meaning, embodied in the "actual accomplishment" (Rosenblatt, 1978, p. 109) of the text. This authorial consciousness gives the reader access to insights, experiences, and perceptions otherwise beyond her reach, thus allowing a reformulation of the reader's consciousness. In other words, reading can lead to self-discovery and learning—but only if we understand what an author has to say! Still, personal meaning will differ from reader to reader and remain valid. Rosenblatt takes pains to argue for honoring the individual nature of the reading act when she states that teachers need "to help *specific human beings*—not some generalized fiction called the student—to discover the pleasures and satisfactions of literature" (1978, p. 34, my emphasis).

From the very start of my project to understand the activities of my student readers, this is what I wanted to find out: How could the students and I create a learning climate that would be meaningful for all of us, one that emphasized our current readerly activities and human concerns? How could we run a class that helped to encourage vital and enriching reading experiences by building on what individuals already knew and could do, and that extended and developed them as readers from whatever starting point they now inhabited?

I was especially troubled by the students who appeared to be reading but who did not find it meaningful, and who did not discuss or answer questions about what they read. In my journal, I asked myself: "How can they be brought into the fold? [How can they be] convinced that there is something worthwhile about this pursuit [of reading]? . . . What are they doing that the questions miss? that I miss?" (May 1992)

## STUDYING STUDENT RESPONSE

So I became a researcher. As a teacher, I teach individual students, individuals whom I invite to become part of a community of readers. Every individual is my project; I know that I really cannot afford to neglect one. Each year now, I try to get to know each student as a person and as a reader. The methods and projects I will describe in the following studies have helped me to do this. It is an arduous and complex job, this process of knowing and teaching students. And I have never felt when a year ended that I have dealt with each student in nearly the best possible way. This is part of teaching, and why teaching really is an act of faith. You do what you can and believe that it will suffice. As I wrote in my journal:

> I only ask to win three of every five. I can't win them all, and if I can win at least three of every five lessons, three of every five school days, three of every five encounters or conferences, then my students and I can go to the World Series. (September 1991)

As a teacher, I study every student who comes into my classroom. To do less would be to not take each student with the seriousness she or he deserves. I share with each student what I have noticed about what she does as a reader, and ask her to share with me what I may have missed. We identify and celebrate what they do, and set about pushing back the boundaries of what might be done. I ask my students to tell me what they are trying to do next, and to set goals that I will help them meet.

As a teacher, I am concerned with big pictures, with overall development, with the long term, with vistas of the future. Some of my past students (whom I still regard as my own, and in whom I am still intensely interested) are married and have children. Some are highly educated professionals or highly skilled laborers who might write up my will or fix my car. Many write me notes and letters, call on the phone, or stop by—often to discuss their reading, but always to discuss their lives.

I am concerned with the sort of lives they are leading and how what we experienced together in a language arts classroom contributes to that. I am concerned with helping the students now in my classroom to live enriched lives. These are the big pictures I concern myself with, learning from one student what can benefit the teaching of all future students.

I would like to make it clear that as a teacher I am interested in both the uniquely individual and in what is regular and patterned. I need to know about both to be able to teach (cf. Bissex, 1987; Chambers, 1985). What I describe in the next chapter is what three individual readers do as they read, but what is described seems generally true to me of what all my most engaged readers do and have done as readers over the past several years that I have carefully observed and written about them.

To gain a window into my students' reading activities, my students and I used a blend of interviews, conferences, literary letters, a variety of protocols (or think-alouds), and a technique that I call the symbolic story representation, in which students use cutouts or "found objects" to dramatize both what they are reading and how they are reading it. (I discuss these methods in more detail in Chapter Three.)

These first three individual readers are the figures against a ground made up of more than 1,000 students. The special knowledge of a teacher is made up of an accretion of thousands of daily events, discussions, observations, reflections. The special knowledge of the teacher-researcher is not the knowledge of the university researcher who may choose to study a very few students on chosen occasions. There are costs and benefits to each approach. When I speak of what I know, it is from the perspective of 13 years of carefully observing and thinking about what children do when they read. But this observation is in the context of 180 days of busy classroom interaction, clouded by problems, interruptions, conflicts, a continual lack of time, sometimes by tragedy, often with laughter.

Therefore, though I concentrate first on the stories of three engaged readers and later on the stories of six reluctant ones, I do so to achieve some clarity and focus. Their stories will have to do the work of the thousands of stories I would wish to tell.

## THREE HIGHLY ENGAGED READERS: CORA, JOANNE, AND RON

During the first 12 weeks of the school year, I chose 3 highly engaged readers to be case study students. I chose Cora, Joanne, and Ron because they 1) said they loved to read, 2) proved it by reading constantly, 3) exhibited high levels of engagement while reading, 4) exhibited wide varieties and highly divergent types of response to literature, 5) were highly articulate about what they did as they read, 6) expressed a willingness and interest in becoming co-researchers, and 7) exhibited proficient readings that seemed to embody the ways I had observed other engaged readers reading over the past several years. In other words, their readings were rich, valid, and displayed a conscious sense of the reader as a meaning-maker.

I chose to work with these excellent readers so that I could come to understand more clearly what they did to make their reading meaningful. I then planned to use what I found to help my less engaged readers begin to use these same strategies.

Cora, Joanne, and Ron were all delightful kids to teach. Cora seemed to be a private person in some ways, but she loved to contribute in class and was very articulate. She struck me as mature and philosophical, a loner by choice who could nonetheless blend in with various groups. She had dark brown hair and experimented with a few wildly varied hairstyles throughout the year. She had her own uniquely stylish way of dressing that she called "funky but chic," kind of what you'd expect from a female lawyer who was going a little bit out on a limb.

Joanne seemed very shy. She didn't talk much in large group discussions, but she had a soothing voice and worked well with other students as a peer tutor and in smaller groups. She was willowy and tall for her age, with blonde curly hair that flowed over her shoulders, and that she would whisk out of her face with a quick flicking gesture. She always dressed very neatly, often in a corduroy jumper over a turtleneck or blouse—which was rare among her peers. She had a simply tremendous smile that flashed when she was enjoying a story or classroom exchange.

Ron was a nut. He seemed to always be in some kind of minor trouble with other teachers, but I loved him. He described himself as "a wild and crazy seventh grade guy." He was big for his age, extremely gregarious, and was going out with an eighth grade girl who caused him occasional but very temporary heartache. He liked jeans and t-shirts with environmental slogans or flannel shirts. He had some good friends in class, especially Chris, and they would exchange high-fives and simultaneously chant "Glory BE!," hum the ESPN *SportsCenter* theme, or engage in some other humorous inanity whenever the spirit moved them—which was quite often.

Cora and Joanne were both students who excelled in the language arts, though both were described as "average" students by their math and science teachers. They earned mostly A's, with a few B's in math and science. Ron achieved average grades of B's, C's, and an occasional lower grade in math, though his teachers agreed that he was "bright" and "creative."

These students were all conscious of and articulate about what they did and felt as they read. As was true of many of their classmates, they immediately knew what I meant when I asked what they "did" as readers or where they found themselves in relationship to a story. They were generally eager to share these details with me. Cora especially spoke spontaneously and at great length about her role as a reader, about authorial technique, and about the relationship she naturally took up with the characters and authors of books that she was reading. Joanne was initially guarded about sharing how she read, revealing that, "It's not the sort of thing teachers are usually interested in knowing or hearing about." Joanne, as did other students, indicated that she had gone "underground" with her intense interest and experiences as a reader. "I talk to a few friends about it, but no one else. I imagine being considered weird or something if people knew about it." In fact, in light of data regarding my students' attitudes towards reading, this fear was not unfounded.

## Attitudes Toward Reading

Of the three case study students, Ron indicated that reading should be graded on "the amount of time people read and how deep they get into it"; Joanne by "what they learned, how it effected (sic) or changed them."

Cora explained that "I don't believe reading can or should be graded. Reading is really important and personal. It's more of a hobby than a job you have to do, which is what tests sort of tell you it is. It just seems foolish to me to try and grade reading unless you have a way to get inside people's minds . . . there are so many things that are important about what and how I read that I could never tell anyone . . . [and in response to a follow-up question] because it might be too private, or because I just couldn't put it in words. And a teacher would grade me down because I couldn't!"

All three case study students indicated that they read for both enjoyment and to learn, or as Joanne said, "to grow knowledge, [to] kind of water your head," and that they willingly attempted to enter any story they encountered. Cora told me that she would rather read than do anything else. "I love it. It offers you worlds and people to know and . . . well . . . there's nothing like it, it can offer you everything." She told me that she only watched TV "when I'm too sick to read and I don't want to think."

Early in the study, before we began to explicitly discuss and share our ideas of reading, I specifically asked these readers to discuss metaphors for their reading experience. Interestingly, their metaphors are all consistent with Rosenblatt's notion of a literary transaction. Both girls directly state a relationship with an author, and Ron implies one. All three express an active sense of agency as readers within the flexible parameters set by the text. All three clearly imply that reading is an experience.

Cora: "Reading is like a relay . . . it's more than a conversation. It's as if the author decides on the race and the terrain and the strategy and gets it all going, and you have to figure out the rules of the race and how it's run and then you get the baton and have to continue on your own. And you can make, then, the sort of race you want to run on the course the author has set out. Basically, once you're out on the course you can make what you want. You can stop if you want, or go exploring if you want."

Joanne: "[Reading is] like a safari and the book is your vehicle and the author is like the driver inside who takes you places and points out things, but what you notice—either with or without his help—and think is yours, that's the real story."

Ron: "It's sort of like map-reading, except the map—like in the Narnia books—will turn real if you start to believe in it and then *KA-ZAM*—there you are in the real world of the map doing stuff with the people there."

## Intensity of Engagement

The intensity of these students' responses to literature and the powerful reality of the secondary worlds these readers created were striking to me. Ron, reading a story about a boy whose dog was killed, told me that he felt so strongly that he was the boy in the story "that I couldn't stand how sad I felt about it." He reminded himself "that I was just reading, but it took a long time to convince myself . . . I was like totally upset." When he did convince himself, he reentered the story, not as the boy, but as "the kid's grandfather. . . . I thought the whole thing would be easier to take and I would be in a better position to help out if I could sort of be the grandfather. . . . it still hurt, but not as bad."

Joanne told me, "Sometimes I'm thinking something and I can't remember if it really happened or if I dreamed it or read it. Then I'll go back and . . . I found it. I'd read it. I couldn't believe it hadn't really happened to me because I thought that it had, you know, *really* happened to me."

This fuzziness of the border between actual and virtual worlds was echoed by Cora. She constantly referred to literary characters as "people I know": "I knew a girl who . . .," "I know about a person who. . . ." She revealed that "when the author is good at writing then I get to know the people in the book and I carry them and their ideas around with me just like we were best of friends. And in a sense, we are, we really know each other, better than you almost always know people in real life."

The experiences reported by these students echoes D. W. Harding's (1962) reports that participation in story worlds is far more complex than terms such as "vicarious experience" and "identification" can possibly suggest. These readers used a wide variety of moves (described in Chapter Three) to engage with stories, to become active participants in the story world, to then connect with that virtual world as real readers, and to reflect upon their experience as readers.

## So, What *Is* Literature?

These three students were constant readers. They read a lot, and they read a real variety of materials. Cora read *Spin* magazine; Joanne sometimes read *YM*. Cora read books ranging from the Nancy Drew and R. L. Stine series to Chris Crutcher (who usually appeals more to boys), the Scary Stories series, the young adult novels of Katherine Paterson, biographies of Marilyn Monroe and Eleanor Roosevelt, and decidedly adult books such as Gage's *Eleni* or heady documentaries such as Gitlin's *The Sixties*.

Joanne read books such as *Alice's Adventures in Wonderland, The Wind in the Willows, Watership Down,* and Anne Frank's *Diary of a Young Girl*. While preparing to create a video documentary, she read the works on female psychology of Carol Gilligan (1982) and Jean Baker Miller (1976), and a slew of nonfiction texts about women in the workplace.

The two of them shared both traditional and quite contemporary young adult novels ranging from *Little Women, The Secret Garden, A Gathering of Days,* and *Anne of Green Gables* to Voight's *Come a Stranger* and Cole's *Celine*.

Ron read through many Tom Clancy and John Grisham novels, hefty as they are, but interspersed them with young adult books such as *The High King, Deathwatch,* the Holocaust comic books *Maus* and *Maus II,* and contemporary comics such as *X-Men*.

What does this suggest about the kind of materials we might want our students to read? Given the reading habits and choices of these highly engaged readers and a transactional view of reading, how should we define the idea of literature?

The transactional view, focusing as it does on the experience of reading, does away with any traditional idea of a "literary canon." What constitutes a literary text is any text that provides a particular reader with a deeply engaging aesthetic experience. This depends largely upon the reader: her interests, abilities, preoccupations, experiences as they are brought to bear on the literary transaction in a particular moment of time.

This implies a new role for the teacher as one who will help familiarize students with all kinds of stories in various forms and with various content, and who will validate the reading of these materials. An important goal will be for students to learn to find and select the sorts of materials throughout their lives that will speak to their current needs, desires, and concerns.

We must remember that the ways in which we mediate literature with students will have a profound effect on the kinds of readers they will become. Cora told me that she resented people, including teachers, who "expect me to read only one kind of thing. That would be like eating only one kind of food all the time. I hate it when people say, 'I can't believe you're reading *that*,' like it's a book for children or something." Ron said he liked to know about a wide variety of books and always loved it "when someone introduces me to something new. That's so cool!" Joanne asserted that the best thing a teacher could do was "to recommend a good story to me, and give a chance to talk about it. . . . Most teachers must not read," she said, "or they'd know how to teach reading and not ruin it for us."

Part of encouraging adolescents to read is knowing a variety of materials and encouraging kids to read different genres and authors to learn the scope of what is available and the field of their own taste. Part of knowing how to teach good reading entails learning what techniques and what texts will work best with particular groups and particular individuals, and what books will be new, surprising, and challenging—helping the student to grow. This requires getting to know students, their current interests and abilities, and their own stories of what and how they read. The research techniques that I used with my students (described in Chapter Three) provided windows into my students' reading activity and helped to make what they did as readers visible to me. This story of the reader must be known before the story can be written about what sort of reading they might do and what sort of readers they might become. These stories are helped to unfold by providing the opportunity for students to choose their own reading materials and share what they are reading with each other.

There are vital genres of literature known as Children's and Young Adult literature that speak directly to the concerns of these age groups, attempting to connect directly with their "current state of being"(cf. Chambers, 1985). There are comic books, mysteries and horror stories, historical fiction, fantasies, stories of death and dying, and nonfiction that different students of mine love and read with great intensity. In middle school, I teach many students like Cora, Joanne, and Ron who engage with all of these age-directed genres, with children's books as well as with popular adult books. When I began to work with Tommy, Walter, and Kae, picture and comic books were highly intriguing and helpful to them. Marvin eventually read High Interest-Easy Reading books. This was not the sort of literature I had studied in college as I prepared to be a teacher, nor was it the sort of literature I had read either in or out of the classroom, on my own or with students, since that time. I now see the necessity of immersing myself in it so that I can suggest books to students and converse with them about them.

This is only to reassert that learning to read begins with the reader. After Marvin and Kevin were helped to find stories that spoke to their interests and were accessible to them, they began to take some steps toward selecting their own books. They showed me that readers will develop the interests, willingness, and abilities to dive and swim in more challenging literary currents if they have first learned the pleasures of the swim in waters that are meaningful, safe, and engaging for them. Readers need to have books that understand them as they are and help them to consider and perhaps outgrow their current points of view. Then they will have the desire to deepen and expand their experience.

Ron, Cora, and Joanne all independently indicated that reading was an important way to get to know yourself, who you are, what you believe, and what you should or might do in different situations. Beyond this, Cora felt that reading meant getting to "know other people, getting to live with them in other times and places to see what it was like or would be like for you." Joanne said that "reading is a way to get inside other people. . . . It's a way to learn stuff that's impossible to learn any other way because you learn from the inside." For Ron, reading gave him the opportunity to know people in his own life better. "The best thing about reading is it gives you something chewy to talk with other people about."

The reasons these students give for reading indicate something I have long believed about maturity. Maturity entails, first, the recognition that you have a unique perspective and a view of the world that has value, and second, the recognition that there are different perspectives in the world and that these have value and are worth knowing about, too. This is the issue of developing social imagination so central to literacy education and to democracy. Our adult relationships, with books and with others, entail a balancing of this paradox. When students are helped to outgrow their current selves, they will have the desire to deepen and expand their experience. Any text that serves these ends must be regarded as literature.

To this end, readers should be appropriately encouraged to read both literature written for them and literature written beyond them from traditional literary mainstreams and outside these mainstreams. Multicultural literature, in particular, helps students to enter other perspectives. When we pursued readings associated with a cultural journalism project late in the school year, all three of these students were excited. "I never thought about how different people live . . . about how different things are and look to different groups of people . . . until I read these [multicultural books]," Ron revealed.

Many teachers and parents are upset by their children's powerful passion for pap, those formulaic books of mystery, intrigue, or romance. In fact, all three of these engaged readers enjoyed these books. All readers who transact with such texts are engaging in powerful literary experiences. I have been continually impressed by the depth and intensity of student response to the horror tales of R. L. Stine, though his books elicited no response but disgust during my own painful reading of them. My students often compare themselves and their situations to those fantastic ones described in the story, and have often discussed how such books provide lessons, as Brent told me, "for surviving in a teenage world." Cora told me that such stories "certainly make you feel, and they can really make you think."

Besides that, research shows that:

1) Adolescent readers of formulaic fiction go through a stage of intense engagement with such books, such as the Hardy Boys or Nancy Drew mysteries, followed by a desire for something "more," for something more challenging and sophisticated, for something offering another way of seeing and interpreting the world (Carlsen, 1980). I have seen this often in my own teaching. R. L. Stine leads to Stephen King leads to Ray Bradbury or Ursula Le Guin. Or R. L. Stine leads to Stephen King and R. L. Stine. The point is that these formulaic books speak to the students and are helping them discover the power of reading, and that they often lead to the reading of other material.

2) Adult readers of formulaic fiction often have wide-ranging tastes. They read formula fiction for particular purposes, such as entertainment, but they know and enjoy other sorts of texts for other sorts of purposes. They are readers, and they know the various purposes reading can fulfill. My wife, a constant reader, is a perfect example of this, reading mysteries to "rest" between what she describes as "intense" literary experiences such as that offered her by Pilcher's *The Shell Seekers*.

3) Perhaps most importantly, studies such as Radway's (1984) *Reading the Romance* show that readers of what might be considered trash literature (like the romance) actually use it in highly creative or resistant ways that must be considered "literary transactions." The women studied by Radway revealed that romance reading gave them power over their lives. First, it staked out a time during which they were to be left alone, to their own pleasures, and not to be bothered by duties of serving spouse and family. Second, their actual readings of the texts helped them find a powerful way of being in the world, and a vision and potential for transforming the contexts of their own lives. Finally, reading the romances connected them to communities of women with similar concerns, thereby providing them with a powerful support group of readers and writers. Any texts that provide such experiences must be considered literature.

Aidan Chambers (1985) argues that the seminal quality of literature is that it is "transformational" or life-changing in some way—whether this is a change in our views, our relationships with the world, or the way we read and regard books. Joanne echoes him when she says: "Every good book I ever read has changed me, it's like adding another layer of more sensitive skin on my body . . . or maybe on my brain." Literature, if read transactionally and creatively, may have the effect of transforming us as readers and as people. Transformative reading begins where the reader currently is, and works from there.

Chambers cites Kafka, who wrote: "We have need of books which act upon us like a misfortune from which we would suffer terribly, like the death of someone we are fonder of than ourselves . . . a book must be the axe that smashes the frozen sea within us. That is what I think" (1985, p. 17).

One job of teachers, I have come to believe, is not to define a narrow and exclusive view of "literature" and to familiarize students with it, but to put children in touch with a wide variety of books and ideas that will help them develop into readers who can recognize the books that can be their personal axes, readers who can take them up and wield them mightily to smash the frozen seas within. Any story that can do so, for them at this particular moment, must be regarded as literature.

Because literature encourages the reader to enter the experience and perspectives of others, and to measure one's understanding in relationship to others' ideas, it is a doorway into the world of conversing with and understanding others. It offers choices and possibilities for the world and how we want to be in that world. As will be seen, Ron, Cora, and Joanne all articulated this "imaginative rehearsal for living" as part of their reading experience.

But there are hurdles to overcome. Applebee (1989) asserts that though readers best learn how to read and respond to literature by spending time reading, today's adolescents spend little of their leisure time pursuing reading. Other studies indicate that students spend very little time actually reading *in* school. Some experts estimate that the average child spends less than five minutes a day reading—including schoolwork (cited by Healy, 1990, p. 23). And students express repeatedly that they see little reason to do so. By putting books that speak to them and fit their abilities into their hands, we can give them many reasons to read.

## WHY READ LITERATURE?

So, what might we say to critics and reformers (such as Willard Dagget) who maintain that we should be teaching technical and textbook reading, and that literature is pleasure reading that serves no important purpose?

I put this question to my case study students. Ron had this to say: "Because school is supposed to help you live better, right?"

Joanne asserted that "a story helps you to think. It involves you totally in thinking about things you could never think about except in a story."

Cora maintained that reading was like "a microscope and a telescope . . . helps you see things that are invisible—because they're too small or too far away. . . . It makes you think so much more than a video or TV."

In a school where the sole purpose is to manufacture competent workers for the nation's technological-industrial complex, perhaps the need for literary instruction and reading would not be keenly felt (though this position can certainly be argued, cf. Brown, 1991). But if schools serve a greater function, to help create empowered and attentive citizens who can both pursue fulfilling and fruitful individual lives and who can contribute in transformative ways to the life of a democracy, then literature must take a central place in the curriculum.

If "functional literacy" is to be replaced with a "literacy of thoughtfulness" (Brown, 1991), if students are to develop critical and creative habits of mind, then literature must be a major player in this enterprise.

As Ron, Joanne, and Cora informed me, literary experience is on the one hand intensely personal and individual, helping the reader to understand his or her self and situation. On the other hand, literature can be a social experience in which we share meanings and ways of making meaning.

Narrative, as Hardy (1977) and Schank (1990) argue, is a primary way of knowing and organizing our personal knowledge of ourselves and the world. Storying defines humanity, makes us human, empowers us in being who we are, and makes it possible for us to conceive of being more than we are. As Bruner (1986) tells us, storytelling is a unique way of knowing that cannot be replicated by any other epistemological form. Literature, Aidan Chambers (1985) explains, offers us images with which to think, imagine, and communicate. It is in our nature as a "culture building species" to make sense of our surroundings and ourselves, and to communicate our understandings (p. 6).

Just as Cora suggests, Chambers argues that it is "with words, by words and through words" that we make sense of ourselves, and that this pursuit is the special province of the sense-making function of language in the form we call narrative. Literature is more profound, even at its simplest level, than any other form of words. What we can do with ourselves is limited or enabled by what we can do with language to tell and imagine stories (pp. 4, 5, 6).

Literature is transcendent: it offers us possibilities; it takes us beyond space, time, and self; it questions the way the world is and offers possibilities for the way it could be. It offers a variety of views, visions, and voices that are so vital to a democracy. It is unique in the way it provides us with maps for exploring the human condition, with insights and perceptions into life, and with offerings for ways to be human in the world. Literature helps us to define ourselves as we are, and to envision what it is we want ourselves and the world to be.

Joanne told me that "I feel like reading a good book makes me someone new." I think she's right. The literary transaction helps to shape us; it can help us to shape the world. Perhaps this is why literature flourishes in repressive political situations: it can not only critique and protest, it can reach out to others and toward something better.

As the world becomes a more complex and smaller place, it seems that self-understanding and the willingness and ability to understand others will become ever more important. That is one big reason why I think literature is important for adolescents.

Ron, Joanne, and Cora helped me to ask and answer the questions of why literary reading was important for all students, and how I could put all my students in touch with a variety of books that might speak to them.

Perhaps most importantly, these three students helped me see how I could teach all of my students—especially the many reluctant and resistant readers—how to more actively and expertly read and enjoy books. What follows in the next chapter is a highly detailed description of their reading response throughout the course of their seventh grade year. The descriptions take a very close and fine-grained look at examples of all the kinds of moves they made as readers. I look specifically at the whole wide range of their reading activity because, to date, we do not have a specific and comprehensive case study of what highly engaged adolescent readers do as they read. That is the story that comes next, and it has a lot to say for how we can better teach our more reluctant readers—as will be seen in Chapters Four and Five.

CHAPTER THREE

# The Dimensions of the Reader's Response

As I tried to find windows to my students' reading activity, I asked them to try and make visible what they were doing, thinking, and feeling as they read and responded to their reading. This was a project that I pursued with all of my students throughout the school year, but most intensively with Ron, Cora, and Joanne, as well as with my other six case study students.

## CLASSROOM RESEARCH METHODS

I developed three criteria for any classroom research method I used with my students:

1. that it offered a window into my students' reading processes.
2. that it fit naturally into the life and flow of the classroom, being accepted by students as something interesting and even fun to pursue.
3. that it was pedagogically useful, providing students and myself as the teacher with empowering ways of seeing, knowing, studying, and sharing ourselves as readers and learners.

These criteria inevitably led to undertaking research collaboratively with students, to sharing findings with them and with other teachers, and to asking them to share with each other. I continually asked students to display and perform what they were coming to know, and to talk about what and how they were learning. To these ends, I used the following methods.

### Teacher Journal

The bedrock of my teacher research was my teaching journal. I have kept a journal and notes about my teaching experiences for the past 13 years. I record observations about particular students, assess what seemed to work or not work for the kids, tell stories, posit theories, make plans, and revise lessons that I hope will be more successful in the future. During the year described here, I recorded as many observations and conversations as I could regarding the nine students I chose as case study students. I was sometimes able to write in my journal during classes, but I usually did so during lunch, after school, or during my free period.

## Literary Letters

On an average of two times a week, students exchanged literary letters (Atwell, 1987) about their reading, both with me and with other students. All letters and responses to them were kept in the students' journals. The letters concerned what students read in class and the reading they pursued on their own. I sometimes asked students to write about not only what they read, but about how they were reading: anything they noticed about what they saw, felt, did, and thought as they were reading.

## Think-Aloud Protocols

Throughout the year I made use of four types of protocols: a free-response protocol, a cued-response protocol, a two-column written protocol, and eventually, as we began to study the use of art as a response to our reading, what we called a visual protocol. I modeled my use and analysis of protocols on the work of Flower and Hayes with written composition (1981) and after Newell (1984, 1990), who adapted protocols for use with both writing and reading.

### Free-Response Protocols

Several years ago, I began making use of "free-response protocols." I would ask students to read something—sometimes a story I had chosen especially for them because I thought it would be challenging or offer them rich response possibilities. As they read, I would ask them to simply stop and talk into a tape recorder whenever they noticed something about how they were reading. I modeled a couple of protocol responses for the class, and began making use of them during workshop conferences.

### Cued-Response Protocols

The going with free-response protocols was tough. Some students provided very rich protocol information, but most students revealed very little. Since I wanted to get a sense of how each student was reading, I began to make use of "cued protocols." I would provide students with a text and insert a carat wherever I wanted them to stop and talk into the tape recorder about what was going on with them at that point in their reading. If students were reading from a book of their choice, I asked them to stop and respond at the middle and end of pages. This technique worked much better.

Onc of the best things about the protocols is that "they have focused the attention of the class on *how* we read, and made this the very subject matter of what we do together" (November 1991).

### Two-Column Written Protocols

Despite the success of protocols in yielding rich data and supporting student thinking about "their thinking and their reading," I was somewhat nonplussed about the amount of time it took to record protocols with each student, and then transcribe and analyze just segments of them. As a teacher, I was just too busy and tired to spend that kind of time translating data into usable forms. So I began using two strategies: asking students to tape protocols at home and transcribe segments on their own, and asking them to complete two-column written protocols. In this technique I would provide a story on one half of a sheet, leaving the other half clear for their comments, which provided a kind of gloss of their activity as they read the corresponding passages. Later, we simply recorded observations in our journals as we read.

This procedure meant that every student could complete a protocol during a single class period, and it saved me a tremendous amount of time, as the data were immediately available to me. The protocols were in a form that could easily be shared by the students with reading partners or friends. This they pursued with gusto, comparing responses to particular passages and beginning to evaluate and borrow particular strategies for making meaning. This was and continues to be tremendously exciting for everybody.

### Visual Protocols

During the visualization study explored in Chapter Five, Tommy and Walter suggested that instead of writing down what they were seeing and thinking at a particular point in a story, they draw pictures of what they envisioned as they read. This was an option I made available but did not require of all students, and most used some form of artistic response on all of the protocols that followed. (On one protocol, 72 of 121 students drew pictures, without or with only a few words. With so many students indicating a preference for visual notemaking, perhaps we could encourage and build on this more often in our classrooms.) Some students used a combination of writing and drawing, drawing themselves or characters with thought bubbles, or using pictures with captions. Some framed off a picture of themselves as readers engaged in their reading activity inside a larger picture depicting the world of the story; others included themselves as readers in a picture of the story world. Some just drew what they were seeing at that point in the story.

## Symbolic Story Representation

In Patricia Enciso's research (1990), which catalyzed my thinking about reading and response, she developed and made use of a technique she calls the "Symbolic Representation Interview," which I adapted and made use of in my own classroom and called the "Symbolic Story Representation" (hereafter referred to as SRI so it will not be confused with the SSR of sustained silent reading). In this technique, students create cutouts or find objects to dramatize what they have read and how they have read it.

During or after their reading, the students, using an adaptation of the SRI, created cutouts symbolizing characters, character qualities, groups, or forces from the book; objects, scenes or settings of importance; motifs, themes, or ideas that played a role in the story; and a cutout symbolizing oneself as a reader. Some readers chose to create cutouts of the author, or special props and backgrounds for particular scenes they wished to talk about, but this was something they did on their own initiative.

The cutouts could be of any shape or design the student wished. Some students used little squares, associating the size or color with the characters in question. Most students made highly stylized cutouts, sometimes realistic—being a face or including the special features and dress of a particular character; sometimes highly abstract—consisting of an object associated with the character, or symbolizing a quality of the character.

When the cutouts were complete, the reader met with the teacher, reading partner, or classroom reading club. The reader then identified the cutouts he had made, and explained why this character, quality, force, or idea was important, and how the cutout worked to suggest or symbolize that particular referent. Next, students would use the cutouts to both dramatize the story events for their audience and recount their readerly experience of these events—or in the case of a short story, to recount their experience of the story from beginning to end. I encouraged students to interview each other throughout the presentations about the nature of the cutouts, the story, and how the story was read and presented by the reader. Throughout the year the students developed and encouraged each other to meet high critical standards for the creation and presentation of an SRI.

Some readers began to use pictures from magazines as cutouts, while others began to use actual objects instead of cutouts: dice for the idea of risk-taking, a tortilla for the quality of egotism or being "all wrapped up in yourself," playing cards for the characters of a king and queen.

The reader moved the cutouts around to dramatize the story and to show the changing relationships of various characters or forces, and used the reader cutout to show where he was in relation to story events, explaining how and from what perspective he was experiencing the story.

I began by videotaping individual students using the SRI. The data were so rich and the students were so enthusiastic about the procedure that I was astounded. "I sort of knew I was doing this stuff [when I read], but this helps me bring it out, now—it's like WOW! I like totally know that this is *how* I read," one student told me excitedly.

Just as with the protocols, I brainstormed for a way to include all students on a more regular basis in the use of the SRI procedure. On four different occasions during the year, I asked all students to prepare their cutouts as homework and choose a scene or story to talk about. The next day, as part of a workshop, students would share their SRI response in triads, then discuss their various responses and reading strategies.

On the first occasion, students dramatized one of several assigned short stories for each other and were asked to make use of a reader cutout to demonstrate some of their moves as readers. Thereafter the SRIs were used with readings students chose on their own. On the second occasion, students were asked to layer in cutouts that demonstrated the importance of setting or scene to their understanding of the story. On the third occasion, students included cutouts of recurring motifs or ideas of importance to the story, including a central focus or main idea cutout that was brought into play whenever this particular thematic statement was reinforced by events in the story. In the final required SRI, students were asked to include a cutout symbolizing their idea of the story's author, and to use that cutout whenever they thought of the author during their reading and SRI performance.

Some students did not make use of these cutouts of more sophisticated story elements, but I used the SRI to make them aware of these elements and to encourage and guide their eventual attempts to use them. (For more extensive discussions of how to use symbolic story representations with students, descriptions and exhibits of student work, and findings about how SRI works for students, please see Wilhelm, 1996.)

The use of SRI as a classroom activity was incredibly beneficial to the students who were trying to become aware of their own reading strategies and to share these strategies with others. Though I had noticed this phenomenon before with the literary letters and protocols, it now became even more pronounced: Students were sharing moves and strategies, trying out the moves described by others, and supporting each other in the use of such moves. It was mind-boggling.

> In addition to accessing just huge mother lodes of data about how kids read and think about reading, something amazing has happened that I never planned or predicted: the kids are teaching each other how to read in ever more sophisticated, imaginative and creative ways! I've got a classroom of readers teaching each other all these new and powerful ways to see, to read, and, to be! (February 1993)

SRI is appealing because it captures and encourages the creative and dramatic elements of reading. It also allows students a way to objectify the very hidden processes of reading and get them out where they can talk about them, and try to understand and improve them. For classmates and for the teacher researcher it provides a magical window into the inner world of the reader. This, in fact, is what I noted in my journal:

> Using the SRI makes the magic of reading so obvious! This is something that nearly all traditional classroom activities regarding reading seem to completely obscure and kill off! But not this! The kids are having an absolute blast with it, and learning from it. They are making the magic of reading visible and creating more magic by sharing it! (March 1993)

In another entry I write about my excitement regarding the sharing:

> I have never really structured my classroom for this sort of sharing. Students are seeing how differently they read and understand the same words, scenes, or stories. When there are differences in "readings" or interpretation, we are asking each other "What about you, what about who you are or your background or experience is making that difference? What is it that is informing your reading?" The students, I truly believe, are seeing their lives and the lives of others as resources for learning—learning about the world, and about themselves. There is a sort of metacognitive self-awareness happening here that I've never seen before. Their reading is being used as an exploration and extrapolation of selves and their possibilities . . . as individuals and as members of a group. It's unbelievable to think that it was a book or me as the teacher that used to be the sole resources for learning. How incredibly limiting it must have been! If I could only go back and teach all those years again! (March 1993)

In addition to the data collection methods described here, I also continually conversed with students, interviewed them informally, and conferenced with them about the portfolios they put together throughout the year to document their reading activity and improvement.

## THE DIMENSIONS

Through the process of analyzing the variety of information I collected about student reading, I came to think about 10 different dimensions of response that my students seemed to use as they created, experienced, and responded to literary worlds. As I worked with them, it became clear that these 10 dimensions fell into three different categories of response, which I labeled evocative, connective, and reflective.

### Evocative Dimensions

1. *Entering the Story World*—On this dimension students prepared to read and started thinking about what the reading would be like. They activated prior knowledge that would help them read.
2. *Showing Interest in the Story*—Students comprehended the literal meaning of the plot and became interested in it as they read. They made predictions and formed expectations about story action.
3. *Relating to Characters*—Readers created characters and took up relationships with them. The reader often became a presence in the story and made judgments about characters.
4. *Seeing the Story World*—The readers noticed clues for creating mental images and envisioned characters, settings, and situations.

### Connective Dimensions

5. *Elaborating on the Story World*—The readers built up clues from throughout the story to create meaning. The readers played detective, fleshed out clues, and filled in story gaps, often creating meaning that went well beyond that suggested by the text.
6. *Connecting Literature to Life*—The readers made explicit connections between personal experiences and character experiences, often looking for ideas that could inform how they could solve problems or think about situations in their own life.

### Reflective Dimensions

7. *Considering Significance*—Students asked how the text worked to create meaning and considered the significance of various events and behavior and how this contributed to the meaning of a story.

8. *Recognizing Literary Conventions*—The readers noticed that the author made particular kinds of conventional moves that they had to respond to, and they used previous experiences with conventions from their reading, viewing, or conversing to figure out how to do so.

9. *Recognizing Reading as a Transaction*—The readers recognized an author and the choices of the author in telling the story. The author might be embraced or rejected as a person to converse and agree with. The reader recognized that they create meaning with the author and her text.

10. *Evaluating an Author, and the Self as Reader*—The readers considered the author's agenda, and their own. They thought about the author's effectiveness as a writer. They considered their own reading processes and how these related to their personal identity.

As I coded data and thought about the dimensions, I was helped very much in my thinking by Judith Langer's (1989, 1990) work on the various stances students take on in regard to created "envisionments" as they read, and especially by Jack Thomson's (1987) work on what he identified as six stages in a developmental model of response. Though I came to differ from Thomson's views in many ways, particularly with his developmental view of response, I did borrow some of his categories and I feel very indebted to his work.

I describe the 10 dimensions as a way of organizing the data, and because I believe the description of various dimensions to be pedagogically useful. I do not think that I have exhaustively described all that adolescent readers do, nor that this is the only way of organizing the information my readers provided. The data, as organized, do point out very specifically that there are many types of responses that we typically neglect when we plan classroom activities, ask questions, and discuss readings. The dimensions show that there are important readerly activities that we ignore and perhaps devalue in the typical classroom, and why responding in various media and forms is important to the development of response and literary understanding.

In the pages that follow I provide detailed examples of the kind of moves my case study readers made on each dimension. This is because if we ask what engaged readers do—and if we ask, as I do here, how less engaged readers can be helped to develop the same repertoire of reading strategies—then a detailed picture is necessary, and none is currently available. A summary of what the readers did within each dimension, as well as questions and activities that can be used to encourage and develop response on that dimension, are included in Appendix A at the back of this volume. I borrowed many of the questions listed in Appendix A from Aidan Chambers's "Tell Me . . ." framework (1985), and from Wolfgang Iser (1978), and came up with many others with the help of my students.

The response information from my readers suggests how engaged readers employ very different ways of reading in different situations. Often they have indicated that they are reading a particular text solely to be "entertained" or "enjoy" themselves. In these cases, the readers have reported making many moves to evoke and move around in story worlds, but few moves of a reflective nature. If readers indicated wishing to learn something about their "own life" or about "what to do" in parallel situations, then their readings concentrated on connections that can be made from literature to life, and from life to literature.

In this way, the dimensions point out that there are various purposes and ways of reading. When reading in different ways, readers operate on different dimensions—privileging the ones useful to them and responding less, if at all, on other dimensions. One particular way of reading may offer less rich response than another way and still fulfill the reader's purpose.

Also, some ways of reading can be seen as a way to richer and more complete readings. For example, relational readings—which Michael Smith (1992) calls "association-driven readings"—those in which the reading seems only to stimulate related memories and life details of the reader, can be seen as a necessary step in the direction of evoking complete story worlds in the reader's mind. Instead of discounting these sorts of moves on the part of less engaged readers as irrelevant or tangential, they can be seen as a starting point. Reading in richer ways, ways that involve other moves, satisfactions, possibilities, and considerations, depends upon first having built a story world that depends in large part on associating real-life experiences with textual cues. This indicates that what a teacher might at first regard as an impoverished reading is in fact a necessary building block to richer readings that may be achieved later.

All of these points are important considerations for a teacher who is encouraging, responding, and evaluating student response, and planning what to do next with individuals and groups of students in the language arts classes.

## SURPRISES

As I asked all of my students to describe their reading through interviews, literary letters, and the protocols, I was continually surprised.

Though many students, as I expected, offered very little as they described how they read, I was surprised by almost 40 of the students. They represented nearly a third of those I taught. There was a veritable explosion of articulate and often lengthy descriptions of the various moves these students made. The number of dimensions they responded upon and their response moves on these various dimensions were more sophisticated, deeper, and much more varied than I had ever expected. I was also immediately struck by how often and how far they went beyond what was explicitly suggested by the text. I was surprised by this important role of elaboration in their reading, and the data eventually led me to consider it as a separate dimension of response. I was surprised by how many readers considered the author's use of particular choices—and again decided to treat this sort of response as a separate dimension (elaboration). I was also surprised that several of my seventh grade readers would sometimes take up active relationships with an author, and reflected on the politics of a text and their own role as a reader in shaping what they had experienced.

Perhaps most surprising was how naturally many of the students described and discussed their reading experiences. I had expected data to be sparse, like collecting flora in the desert—but it was as abundant as if I were struggling through a rain forest, having to choose what to collect and make note of. Most students knew exactly what I was talking about when I asked them about their "experience" in the "world" of the book, and were adept at considering and then describing what they were "doing" as they read. Quite a few students were initially reticent, only to become positively loquacious when they became convinced of my interest. It was almost as if they were getting to share and celebrate all of what reading really was for them for the first time, and they could not believe their good luck.

Also surprising were nearly 20 students who could offer absolutely nothing about how they read or what they lived through as they did so. The students were surprised, too. After Ron shared an SRI with his reading partner, Jon, Jon said, "I can't believe you do all that stuff when you read! Holy crap, I'm not doing . . . like nothing . . . compared to you!"

Ron responded that "I can't believe you don't do something. If you don't, you're not reading, man. . . . It's gotta be like wrestling, or watching a movie or playing a video game. . . . You've got to . . . like . . . *be* there."

Pairing students as they read and shared their readings and then asking them to share with other pairs turned out to be a powerful teaching move. Students learned from each other about ways of reading. I was also impressed by the type of student dialogue I witnessed. After videotaping groups of three sharing their symbolic story representations (SRIs), I wrote:

> I expected the students to describe the basic plot and situation of the
> scene they had chosen and then to describe in some way how they
> read it. I couldn't believe how elaborate many of the cutouts were,
> how many forces or ideas students included as playing a part in their

reading—like Katie's bubbles for character thoughts, or Greg's cut-outs of forces and feelings that they considered as they read. The descriptions of how they read were incredibly involved. Greg was a "mist who can float inside of people"; Megan was a "giant eye, like the sun, that's up in the sky and can see everything and even come down and focus in like a microscope on stuff"; Tommy was "a mouse. I can hide and like be a Peeper Tom."

And best of all, students were interrupting each other to ask questions like "Where are you now?" "Are you still identifying with her? Why not with him? Because I'm identifying with him now because he's the one who's hurt." And so on. The students were having extended discussions in small groups like nothing I have ever seen before—and the discussions were about readers and the experience of reading—as well as the meaning of the reading. The SRI seems to make ways of reading into objects that can be seen and talked about, and to therefore scaffold presentation and discussion of the reading. (January 1993)

The final and most pleasant surprise was how well I was coming to know my students as individual people and readers through the project. After interviewing Theresa about her reading, I wrote:

I felt like there was this very human bond between us. Sharing as people, and as readers. Theresa is the sort of girl I couldn't even describe physically to you in years past. Now I've looked in her face and really seen her, how her eyes express her feelings as she reads. I know how she uses her own house and friends and experiences to create worlds as she reads. As a result, I know her house, her friends, her life . . . I know her! That means that the other students know her, too. And I think she feels better about herself, the class, and her reading than she would have if she had been my student in a previous year. . . . This is the best thing about what I am doing this year, that I feel I know the students and that they are getting to know each other and that everybody is involved . . . that I can teach them better because of it, and that they know me, not just as a teacher, but as another reader. The subject of the class has become not only our reading—but who we are as people—it's about us! (October 1992)

## EVOCATIVE DIMENSIONS

Readers operating on these dimensions indicated a willingness to read, even an excitement or interest in reading, and began to "think about" what the reading would be like by recalling appropriate experiences from real-life and previous reading.

As they started to read, students would "enter" or "get into" the story world by comprehending literal meanings, taking an interest in the story action, and deciding to continue with the reading. They would begin to make predictions and form expectations as they recognized the "the rules" and "the game" set up by the text. The reader entering the story world also began to create rudimentary mental images, often stereotypes from television or films. Some readers, at this point, could be confused or tentative. They might give up their willingness to read and their interest in the story action.

## Entering the Story World

Cora, Joanne, and Ron all anticipated pleasure before they began reading. They often chose a book for themselves based on recommendations of friends, or in Ron's case on the recommendation of his father. All three also searched randomly through the library, "foraging," as Cora put it, for "tasty"-looking books. The two girls in particular often went to the library without a specific idea of the book they would check out.

Library books were chosen on the basis of topics that were interesting as indicated by the cover and book jacket. Cora indicated that "it's the title that jumps out at me. An author who has an interesting title can probably write an interesting book." These readers all indicated that they were willing to read, and that they expected to help create an aesthetic experience in concert with the text. They also considered their previous experience with similar genres and topics in order to begin creating meanings.

During an SRI, Cora said, "The author writes about something meaningful to understand it himself. Then he shares it and it's up to you to make something meaningful of it for you, to understand it in your own way, make it beautiful or whatever it's going to be."

Ron revealed that:

*When I get ready to read I always think about what kind of story it is, you know, and what I'll have to do to get into it. I kind of imagine myself in the story, even before I start reading, and what it's going to be like in there and I might kind of review stuff from other stories or from my life that I might need to know as I read. . . . If it turns out to be a different sort of story I might not want to do the things that need done, or I might not want to feel the way it makes me feel, so I'll quit. . . . I hate it when the cover or the beginning of a book sort of fakes you out and you get confused about what you should be doing. . . . You know because you're excited and ready to do some certain things and then you find out you have to do something else. Bummer!*

Ron specifically points out something that was also true for the two girls: the created story world of the reader was always made up of both intratextual and extratextual references. In other words, the words of the text were used in such a way that the reader's knowledge and experience of the world was brought to bear in the creation of a "secondary world."

Ron was the sort of reader that Nell (1990) calls a "ludic reader": he entered a trancelike state as he experienced what was, for him, the intense reality of the story world. He indicated that once he entered a story world he was never able to stop. He reported reading deep into the night, through weekends, and in every spare moment once he had entered a story world. He recited to me a litany of tricks used to keep reading: flashlight in his bedroom, fake book covers, book inside a math book (though this was getting hard for him as he was reading very thick books), and even faking illness—in extreme cases—because "it was like I couldn't go on living until I had got through the story." When he was forced to stop reading, he continued to live in it. I witnessed this myself during our class reading of *The Incredible Journey*. Ron finished the book on his own, but continued to read with the class for about two weeks. Before class and in the hallway I would observe him playing the part of characters in the book or elaborating on the plot. Here is an entry from my journal:

> When Ron comes into reading class, it's like he's entering a strange admixture of the class itself and the world of the story . . . he is reading. When we were reading "The Horse Hunters" he comes in, and addresses me as Dodge and says, "We gonna rustle up some horses this class period, pardner?" While reading *The Incredible Journey*, he told me, "On my way to class I looked out the window and saw two dogs and a cat heading into the forest" [there is no forest in sight of the school]. "I told my boss but he laughed at me [and] asked if I'd seen any elves." (October 1992)

Joanne and Cora, on the other hand, were able and often chose to read several different books, and various kinds of books, at the same time. They indicated the ability to leave and reenter stories at any time, almost immediately reorienting themselves to the story at hand. Joanne reported that:

> *I might have to do something [to reenter a story] but I can't tell you what it is. The story stays inside me and it's like as soon as I start reading again I'm right back where I was. The story stays fresh in my memory, sometimes for a long time. I just pick up where I left off. It's easy.*

Cora indicated that she liked different books for different moods and needs.

*If I'm mad I sort of like to read a mystery, or something like* The Secret Garden *or the* Anne of Green Gables, *stories that soothe me. Anne is always, well . . . in control of her life and makes things work out and that helps me. On the other hand if I have energy and I'm interested in something I'll read nonfiction. So I'll just pick up one of the books I've been reading that seems to fit. . . . I never really have trouble deciding which one. It seems pretty obvious.*

In light of this information, it is interesting to consider that Cora and Joanne were both excellent students, earning straight A's in all subjects. Their teachers reported that they were both very conscientious, turning all work in. In contrast, Ron's grades were mediocre, and his teachers reported concerns with work habits, missing homework, and a "dreamy" or "inattentive" attitude. Cora told me that she would hate to leave off reading a book if she had homework, but she knew that she "had to, and that I could get right back to the book when I had time." Ron, on the other hand, told me that "I just can't shake a book when it's got a hold of me. It's hard to think of anything else." Ron admitted to me that his reading habits interfered with his school performance, but that he didn't "know what to do about it. . . . I don't really want to do anything about it—I mean the stuff you do in school is sort of a waste compared to a great book."

Ron and Joanne reported that they expected to be engaged in a book by the first few paragraphs. Ron said, "Maybe the first line, if it's good." Despite these expectations to be immediately engaged, they both gave a book two or three pages to engage them if necessary. Cora would give a book much longer. "I'll probably read 20 pages or more if I can't really lose myself. Maybe longer if I have reason to think it might get good . . . like a high recommendation from someone I respect."

Ron entered the story primarily through what Bruner (1986) calls the "landscape of action" and through visualization of the setting that goes along with it. "I want to know where we are and what we're doing there, then I can see the place and I know what's going on and then I'm off to the races." During an SRI, when he was retracing for me how and at what point he was fully immersed in the story, he made this comment:

*When an author explains scenes it makes it easy to see. That's what helped me get into the book. I have to see the scene—like here it's the totally cold and completely snow-covered city totally frozen and quiet and windy—I have to see it to get into the place or I can't get to know the characters. . . . I can't see the characters until I see where they are. . . . It's like walking up to a house, checking it out, figuring out what sort of people would live like this before you ring the doorbell.*

Ron indicated that details about plot and the place helped him to enter the story. Though he felt that he was with other characters, "I'm really tuning in to . . . you know, to my idea of what's happening."

The two girls, on the other hand, tended to enter and participate in the story primarily through what Bruner (1986) calls the "landscape of consciousness." Cora reported that:

*I want to get to know people . . . characters, or even the author. It's like I'm not really into the story until I recognize and get inside another person. . . . I want some details of the place, but especially about the people. Just a couple of details and I feel like I know them and the whole scene just unfolds in front of my eyes and I feel like I've known them forever and what they're feeling and want and everything.*

On a separate occasion, during an SRI, Cora gave this running commentary:

*I pick up this book and I want it to be very detailed at the beginning. I want to learn about the characters and where they are right away. . . . I want to learn from myself, by [comparing] my personal life to the story; I want to learn from the characters and from the author. . . . I can't learn unless the author lets me in on how he sees the world and what it looks like to him and to his characters. Otherwise you can't know them or relate to them.*

Cora was adamant that getting to know other consciousnesses was the seminal part of reading.

*I can make plots up on my own. Reading is relating my life to other people and to do that you have to really know them, not just see what they did. . . . I can observe people doing things on my own and guess what it does to them. A book is to get inside people and events. That's what a good author helps you do . . . to get inside characters and inside him, the author, I mean, revealing his innermost feelings and visions and things. You have to read to understand. You can't tell someone about what you learn about people from a book and expect them to understand. They have to read and go through it themselves.*

Joanne concurred. "A great book is a book with characters you really feel you know and who you have very strong feelings about."

Flynn (1987) and Bleich (1987) found that males tend to take a more detached, action-oriented stance toward stories, and that females tend to have a more intense sense of participation in the inner lives of characters, finding themselves, as Bleich says, "in the teller and the tale." This was certainly the case with these case study students.

Joanne said that she would give up reading a book that "lacked details" or that was about

*a topic I don't know much about and don't enjoy . . . like hunting. . . . A story about a hunting trip couldn't enthuse me. . . . I'm a vegetarian and I don't like meat and killing animals. I like woods and animals and would read a story in the wilderness, but killing for fun? I don't want to get involved in that. If I find out I don't want to know about a topic, I'll quit.*

And reminiscent of Stephen King's distinction between "Gotta Read" books and "Wanna Read" books, Joanne said:

*If you have to read something for school you try to make it fun and interesting. But if it's a book you're reading for yourself and it's about something that doesn't interest you, why waste your time? There are so many good books . . .*

In these cases, Joanne did not wish to activate the necessary schema for understanding, nor did she have the desire to develop them. She would move on to something more naturally interesting.

Once a story had been entered, and these three readers all expressed that it was such an intense involvement that there was no mistaking their utter engagement, the readers began to engage in other dimensions of response in order to fully evoke the world of the story. Ron described the experience poetically.

*When you're not into a book yet, it's really obvious [laughs]. It's like you're standing in line for the diving board on a windy day and you're freezing your nuts off. If you'll excuse the expression [laughs]. Where was I? Oh yeah. It's like you're in pain and you have your arms wrapped around you and the concrete is scratching your feet. The first part of the story is the line and the ladder and the board. When everything comes together and you jump it's like you're in this underwater world like INSTANTLY and then you just stay down there and never come up until someone makes you.*

The initial contact with a story depended upon these readers comprehending literal meaning and getting themselves into the story's sense of play and action. Expectations were formed and predictions made. Some rudimentary images were created, and the readers began to acquaint themselves in at least superficial ways with the introduced characters. These readers recognized what Rabinowitz (1987) calls "rules of notice" to get a sense of story and their roles in creating it. These readers then accepted the game devised by the author, and attempted to understand the basic conventions of it. By this point, the reader decided, if engaged, to continue with the reading—or, if the book did not meet current needs, to give it up.

### Showing Interest in the Story Action

Having entered the story and been engaged by it, these readers immediately began to anticipate action and make predictions.

During a protocol analysis of a first-time reading of O'Flaherty's "The Sniper," Joanne's comments existed almost entirely of predictions based on noticed details.

"The Sniper" is a story set during the Irish Civil War. Two snipers, after discovering each other on opposite rooftops, play a cat-and-mouse game. The first sniper is wounded, but then he fools and shoots the other sniper. He then goes into the street, turns over the body, and sees that he has shot his brother.

When the sniper takes out a cigarette, Joanne said, "He'll get shot. I wouldn't take my life in my hands for a cigarette." When an old lady crosses the road to talk to the driver of an armored car, she commented, "If she reports him . . . now he'll have to kill both of them. He'll have to."

Ron indicated that when he had entered a book:

*I'll have this constant urge to find out more. I totally feel the excitement and live the action. I want to see what's going on and know why they are doing it. That's the feeling I love when I get into a book. It's like your brain is a Pac-Man totally hungry with curiosity.*

Once such initial contact and subsequent immersion was made, these readers made particular moves to flesh out the story world. Though the girls showed a propensity for perspective-taking, and boys, such as Ron, for visualizing, all the readers I studied engaged with both dimensions of response.

Readers who successfully entered a story world began to make new moves to relate to characters and to see the story world. They noticed cues for creating and sustaining a "secondary world" in their minds as they read. They created characters and felt emotions in relation to character activities and problems. Quite often, the readers would become a presence in the story world, and begin to move around in that world or manipulate it in some way. In this way they would project themselves and their real-world knowledge into the story world. They would also mentally create visual pictures of settings, situations, characters, and their physical features and gestures. The readers on these dimensions evoked a complete story world, and at this point the virtual world of the story had intense and comprehensive reality for them.

## Relating to Characters

Having entered and become interested in the story, one of the two types of moves these readers made to fully evoke the story world was to establish contact with characters. The case study readers typically took on a variety of perspectives, often switching during the course of a single story. Nonetheless, they tended to have a favored perspective in any particular story. As reported by Enciso (1990), these readers often took on the perspective of a main character, sometimes becoming the character, merging with him or her for short or extended periods, or becoming a friend. Sometimes the readers established a more distanced relationship, observing characters from outside, either from close in or afar, sometimes part of the story, sometimes "above" or "outside" it, as a "spy" hiding somewhere using cameras or "see-through" devices (Ron) or as an object such as a wall, a piece of furniture, a ship (Cora), or, in one case, a "fish." When outside the story, sometimes these readers still felt that they had a friendly relationship with a character, despite their inability to communicate. Joanne was a reader who often expressed what Enciso (1990) calls a "parallel focus," referring to characters as friends, and to her friends as characters in a story! As such, she imagined scenarios that seemed parallel to story events. Joanne also often took on the role of "agent" (Enciso, 1990), expressing the desire to act on behalf of the character, or feeling that she was actually doing so.

Joanne tended, at some point, to "become" the main character in whatever book she was reading. She professed that she liked to read about "girls, about my age . . . it helps me to become them and understand them . . . though I can become characters really different from me—even a boy or an older woman—if I know where I am in the story and have some similarity with them." She indicated that though at times she "really was the character—it's like Joanne herself is totally lost," at other times she "merged" (Enciso, 1990) with a character: "It's like we're Siamese twins in one body, both Joanne and whoever the character is all at the same time." At other times, characters were just too different from her and she became their friend; or the protagonist was too unsavory, and she became a minor character, or made herself, as Joanne, a presence in the book, sometimes resisting the main character and his agenda.

When Cora completed a protocol during a reading of a poem called "The Wreck of the Hesperus"(Longfellow, 1952), she said:

*I took the place of the ship. I could mostly hear the waves and the wind and the captain and his daughter talking through it. . . . I really felt like I was there. I didn't relate to characters as much as I usually do, but I mostly watched and judged them.*

Later in her reading she revealed, "Now I'm sitting in a chair down [on] the deck, but I still sort of feel like I'm the ship. Every now and then I've felt like I was the daughter and felt really afraid. As the ship I'm like an unfeeling observer." During a separate interview she said, "I'd rather follow characters around and watch them than become them, but sometimes I become them anyway, for a short time like a scene or situation, or a longer time and it happens almost automatically."

In her first self-evaluation, she wrote:

*I learn about the way others live[d] by putting myself into their lives, by watching them or putting myself into their characters. When I read I put myself in that person's position and sometimes really become them and that's really what I do best when reading. I don't want to sound snooty but if you can't read in a way to be a character then I don't see that you're reading. A lot of people don't realize that about reading and it's really too bad.*

However, when reading *A Gathering of Days*, Cora revealed that "I'm more of an observer in this book. I feel what she feels, and it feels to me like the story is taking place now, even though it took place a long time ago." When pressed about why she was an observer in this book, Cora explained that:

*because it's told like a diary, it's like I'm always looking in, like over someone's shoulder. There's something about the way it's written that is always reminding me that I'm a reader. . . . I mean, I liked the book a lot and was really involved in it, and sometimes, for a situation or a scene, I sort of became the character, but only for a while and then I was just watching again.*

Ron usually found himself in the thick of a story, as an unmentioned confidante or sidekick. When reading through a sequence of Tom Clancy novels, he began by being a CIA colleague of Jack Ryan, but quickly took on the persona of Jack himself for the duration of the books. When reading De Marino's *The Odyssey Project* (1989), he became a friend of the main character, Ted Amundsen, "shadowing him around, looking around him or through him." This was one of Ron's typical positions, "almost like a bodyguard," but he occasionally found himself "above the story, like high in the sky looking down on it."

Joanne described her relationship with the character of Nancy Drew as

*understanding her completely, and following her every move, and it was like I was living [right next] to her, but we were separated by this wall of glass and I could see and hear everything from her world but she couldn't see or hear any-*

*thing of mine. And sometimes she would be in danger or ready to make a stu-
pid decision and I was just screaming at her—in my mind I mean—but she
couldn't hear me and I was so upset. It was like I really wanted to contact her
and save her and it was terrible that I couldn't. In my mind I would write letters of advice to her and send them off. . .*

Perspective-taking, as pointed out by Enciso (1990), is a highly complex social-cognitive process that entails considering what someone else
might be seeing, thinking, or feeling. It requires, in conjunction with this,
the recalling of the reader's own experiences and the relating of these to
another person, and considering the most likely experiences and interpretations the other might have in a situation.

In nearly everything that they read, these case study readers indicated,
they had a preferred perspective, but they also took on multiple perspectives, continually shifting, if only briefly, throughout a reading. Benton and
Fox (1985) argue that this experience of taking multiple perspectives and of
shifting viewpoints is critical to the development of more sensitive and powerful readings that lead to greater understanding of self and other.

All three readers also indicated at times the use of "mutual perspective
taking" (Selman & Byrne, 1974), in which they eschewed the switching of
perspectives, adopting instead a third-party view as an attempt to reconcile
two other perspectives. As Joanne reported about her reading of *Just as Long
as We're Together:*

> *I'm really most strongly relating to Stephanie. But there's this other girl who
> really likes the same guy and I sort of related to the other girl and how she must
> feel, and to Jeremy and how he would feel when he found out and what he
> would do and I sort of saw that everyone had the same sort of problem of work-
> ing things out in a situation, I guess, that involved other people in ways they re-
> ally cared about, you know? Like I said, it helps you to see that love is crazy—
> for everybody!*

The students' alignments with characters were very important to their
reading experience, contributing in important ways to their creation of the
experience, and in their location of the conflict and interpretations of
theme, as will be seen later. This, too, is consistent with research in the field
(Golden & Guthrie, 1986; Rogers, 1988; Tierney & Pearson, 1983). I think
that it is important for teachers to note that differing student understandings and interpretations might be the result of how they have matched up
with characters in the story.

The case study readers often felt intense emotions about characters and
their actions, and often evaluated characters and their activities and situa-

tions. They began to elaborate a character's personality and life history, implicitly connecting what they knew from the text to what they extrapolated from what they knew. As they related to and elaborated a character, they would often begin to critique the elaborated character.

Joanne described her relationship with Stephanie in *Just as Long as We're Together* as follows:

> *Stephanie is sort of like me—gets good grades—quiet—not the most popular. I feel like I'm her and I can feel what she's feeling. . . . Like when Jeremy Kravitz is in the same room, I'm totally surprised and delighted and I could feel my heart beating faster. I can imagine how she would try to dress and where she would try to be to catch his attention.*

Even when filling the role of his hero Jack Ryan, Ron would be critical of certain activities:

> *Jack likes to work out, and I felt proud about my power and strength and stuff when I was Jack. But Jack, like my dad, is really outspoken and doesn't hold anything back. It was like I could hear myself [as Jack] saying something that I shouldn't and I'm thinking, Uh-oh, man, I shouldn't have said that, but I just couldn't help it and now I'm gonna pay for it you stupid klutz.*

During Joanne's symbolic story representation of "The Sniper," she revealed that it took her about a paragraph to enter the story. "Now I'm in it and I'm on the rooftop. . . . I'm sort of an extra unmentioned detail of the story. I'm there and I've jumped into it. The author didn't know that it would be me or where I'd be, but I'm there and I can tell I'm there though I can't affect anything, only watch." She immediately began to elaborate and evaluate character. "Boy! I'm thinking, you sure are stupid!" Joanne reported after the sniper was shot while lighting a cigarette.

> *He should have used the lighter as a trick for an ambush or something. It was stupid of the other guy to miss too. You can't blow a chance like that. Not in a war. I'm thinking that the other guy is nervous, he's probably not a real soldier, he's probably been drafted or fighting against his will or something.*

When the armored car enters the scene, Joanne switches perspectives:

> *I felt I was down in the street then [instead of on the roof]. . . . I could hear the car putting and feel how big it was and could see it rumbling down the road and I felt fear and disappointment that the scene was interrupted and keeps him from solving the problem. . . . I thought the old lady was helping the snip-*

*er's side but then I realized she wasn't. I felt for an instant like I was the sniper, and I was angry, but then I was scared for everybody. When the tank driver looks up I thought, Stupid! don't stick your head out!*

Her feeling for the sniper is different when he dresses his own wound.

*Wow, I'm thinking, he was careless not to pay attention to the other sniper, but I'm impressed with him. I'm watching in wonder. He's bleeding [this detail is not stated in the story] and his shirt is soaked and I don't know what he'll do. I wouldn't have planned for this. But he did. And he did what he had to.*

Cora, too, evaluated the characters that she elaborated. In response to the scene in *Roll of Thunder, Hear My Cry* when Cassie unwisely tells the temperamental Uncle Hammer about being harassed by Mr. Simms, she wrote this spontaneous literary letter in the persona of Cassie:

*Dear Mama,*

> *It's just been one big learning experience this week. When Stacey and I saw that ole shiny silver Packard in the barn I thought for sure that ole Harlan Granger was here, and boy was I happy and surprised to see Uncle Hammer.*
> *Mama, I just had too much hurt inside to keep it in. I know it was wrong, but I just ain't never been treated that way. It got scary when he [Uncle Hammer] got so angry and his eyes started bulging and I knew I should stop and I just couldn't. I know it's all my fault. I should of listened to Big ma's gestures for me to shut up but I was so steamed up and all. I just hate myself for being such a blabbermouth!*
> *Now I'm thinking back to all the good times and how safe we all is all together and now here I am gettin us all in trouble, good and deep. I'm just scared. I feel like I'm even jeperdizing (sic) your life, Mama.*
> *Oh, please forgive me if something bad were to happen!*

> *Love,*
> *Cassie*

Here Cora becomes Cassie, infers and elaborates her character, and then critiques this elaborated character. She told me, in regard to this letter, that

*As much as I feel like a character sometimes, I guess I'm always aware of myself, too, and that I'm reading. I really related to Cassie in the scene in Straw-*

*berry and when she told Uncle Hammer about it but at the same time that I
felt her anger and frustration I also was watching what was happening [telling
her story to the volatile Uncle Hammer] and I knew it was stupid and wrong
[for her to do].*

In this letter, Cora continues to relate to character by making inferences about how Cassie must be feeling, and what she must be thinking
about. The letter and her discussion of it show an understanding of the
greater context of the story, and the situation that the Logan family will
eventually find itself in. During the same conversation, Cora told me,

*I read to understand myself and others. I associate very closely with Cassie. I
learned by being associated with her that it would be hard to live during that
time. I read to understand people, their atmosphere, their emotion, their place,
so I can feel like I am them or I am there with them.*

## Seeing the Story World

Once inside the story world, the other move the readers continued to
make to fully evoke and flesh out that world was to create mental images of
the story landscape.

These readers began by noticing cues for visualizing a "secondary
world." All three repeatedly told me that they consciously looked for such
visual clues as they first began to read a story. Once such cues were found
and interpreted, these readers created and sustained a secondary world in
their minds, creating visual pictures of characters, settings, and situations
and mental images of affect. As more clues were processed, these visualizations were revised and deepened, or completely new visualizations were created. The visualization was typically achieved through the reader scanning
a setting, sometimes from "on top of the world," as Ron put it, and relating
extratextual real-world information about settings to the details of the text.
On occasion, the readers immediately related to a particular character and
created the setting through the eyes of that character.

Very early in the reading of any particular text, it was already clear that
decoding words and making verbal sense of a text was only a fraction of the
larger picture of how readers transacted with text. These readers' visualizations were related in many ways to their own real-life experiences, and
sometimes built upon them. Cora speaks of the pictures she sees while
reading:

*When I read a book that takes place in a house, and it isn't really described in
great detail, then I always see the same house in my mind. The house is a mix-*

*ture of all of the houses I've been in. But if there are details that don't fit my idea of a house then I have to change the house. Once I do, it stays changed for the story. If too many things are different, I have to imagine a completely new house, but I'm sure that's based on what houses I've seen in my life, too.*

*It's kind of an odd thing because whenever I'm reading these pictures just pop into my mind, and it's almost as though I don't control it. It happens the minute I open a book and find a detail that helps me to see. When I'm reading a book with mountains in it I always see the exact same mountains, unless, like this book I read about this boy in the Andes, the mountains are specifically described and then I'll like reshape things in my mind and that's the way it will be . . .*

When I asked Cora about recalling what the original house or mountains were like, before she revised her idea of them, she said,

*I can't really, because once you change your picture of something you change it back all the way through the things you can remember from before. I might know that it looked different, but I can't see it that way anymore when I'm thinking about the book.*

Cora constantly confirmed her mental images against new information, and made necessary adjustments. In one book:

*I got the idea that the Barkers were black. . . . But then she [Celine] could see Mr. Barker's black hair on the skin of his white hand and all of a sudden I know he's white and it really confused me because then I had to rethink how his wife looked and his son and I started to think about how I got the idea of their color anyway and if it was important or even if I was being racist or something, do you know what I mean?*

One or two clues was all that was needed for Cora to create the rest of an object or scene in her mind.

*When I was reading* Come a Stranger *she was at ballet camp and the author mentioned that it was like an estate or something and immediately I imagined that it was Elvis's house—I think it's called Graceland, but I put it on a hill because it was on a hill in the book. When she went home, I'd already imagined the sort of neighborhood where a girl like this would live and then the author mentions the color of the house, I think, and suddenly I knew it and pictured it as my old neighbor's house. And that really worked for the whole story.*

Both Cora and Joanne compared reading a book to watching a movie. Cora was able, she said, to "use slow motion, or flashback" as well as being able to speed up certain sequences, "especially if it's really exciting and I want to know what happens." She described this sensation even when she felt like a character in the story. Joanne reported that she saw some books in black and white, if they were set in a far-off time or if the story was sad or told "in a cold way." Most of the time what she visualized was in color, "just like you were seeing it in real life."

Ron, during an SRI, told me that "The only time a book is hard to read is where there's no scenery, only action. I like to feel the book was made for me, and that the author has given a way to see it." When reading a section of *The Odyssey Project*, Ron said:

> *The story is in Wisconsin and it's like a new Ice Age. So I just imagine scenes from Madison or other places I've been totally covered in ice and snow, like it goes halfway up to roofs. I needed to know a couple of things but not much in order to imagine the rest of it. You get those first clues and the rest is automatic. . . . It [the book] says that Torrance is big and has a beard. That's all I needed to see him. I know it's winter and he's going to help Amundsen so I see him in a coat, but it's white camouflage clothing so no one can see them. If he's a friend of Amundsen he's smart and won't give himself away. My dad has a book about the Battle of the Bulge and I flip through it sometimes. The battle was in snow and the troops wore all white, even white pants and so that's what I see Amundsen wearing . . . his face is sort of fat and red from the cold. I feel like he's a good guy, and dependable, and smiles a lot. I got all that, I guess, from those two details.*

Both Joanne and Cora spoke at various times about the different experience of visualization when they reread a story. (Ron rarely read short stories, nor did he reread, a phenomenon tied, I think, to his style of reading and preoccupation with the landscape of action.) Cora reread the story "High Beams," about an assailant hiding in the back seat of a woman's car who is foiled by the flashing high beams of a following truck driver.

> *It was different when I re-read because I could see more details, like especially around the edges, and I noticed more clues . . . like I could see flitting shadows that could be the man . . . that I know are the man on one level because I already read the story, but I act like I haven't so it's just a shadow that could be a man. I have the feeling there's more color when I re-read.*

These descriptions from highly engaged readers suggest both the value of encouraging active imaging and the value of rereading as a separate reading experience from a first reading. It also suggests the necessity of providing time for reading, rereading, and response activities. I had the experience of asking Ron one day what he was doing as he sat staring into space. "I'm thinking!" he hissed, in an obvious reaction to the "teacher tone" in my voice and the implicit suggestion that he was doing nothing of value. He then told me that he was thinking about a story, what it looked like "in there. I can't quite get it. There's a building and passageways and I need to get it straight." A story world and the experience of it are clearly highly complex, dynamic, and developing. This requires the deployment of strategies many readers may not naturally use, and in any case, time and energy for the construction of characters, settings, and situations. It shows, I think, that teachers might provide not only guidance and support for visualizing activities, but also allow more support and time for this to occur.

During the first 12 weeks of the study, many of the less proficient readers and all of the LD readers failed to reveal a single move on the dimension of visualizing or seeing what they read. For these readers there were no indications that they made personal associations as they read. Many expressed incredulity when I asked questions about what they were "seeing" or when other students described what they saw while reading. They seemed to be entirely unable to visualize a secondary world without some sort of artistic aid such as photos or drawings—or the chance to draw, make a collage, or flip through a magazine to identify what a character or a place probably looked like. Once these students were given the support to create a concrete visualization of a story, then they often became excited about reading that particular piece, and became capable of empathizing, connecting, and reflecting upon the literary experience (see Chapter Five). It became clear, in repeated instances throughout the school year, that these students had great difficulty in spontaneously visualizing the story world. And if the visualization did not occur, they were unable to respond in any of the other response dimensions.

## CONNECTIVE DIMENSIONS

These next two dimensions, of elaborating and connecting, were a kind of transition between the moves students used to evoke and experience story worlds, and the moves used to step back and reflect on that experience. One set of moves was used to elaborate on and extend the story world beyond what was explicitly described in the text and to set up and explore alternatives to the written story. The second set of moves was used to explicitly connect personal experiences to those of characters, and to consider how the reading experience might inform choices and actions the reader might take in his or her own life.

## Elaborating on the Story World

In this dimension, the case study readers used their real-world knowledge by applying it to the virtual world of the reading, not in an automatic or naturally occurring way as in the previously discussed dimensions in which they entered and evoked a story world, but by actively and often quite consciously playing detective to go beyond and extend cues and fill textual gaps. Scenes, events, and characters were elaborated in ways not required by the story and that went beyond the story, but made the meaning more powerful and personal to these readers.

Reading on this dimension was extratextual, going beyond what was stated or even suggested by the book. The story world became, in effect, what could be called a "reader's world." Response on this dimension included the conscious use of intertextual links, in which the readers sometimes drew on previous story experiences to create or augment the meaning of the current reading and to sharpen their understanding of it.

These readers were guided by the text and its conventions, but incorporated and added significant personally elaborated details into the creation of a secondary world. The readers sometimes began to imagine extra events not mentioned in the text, alternate events or consequences for story events, or parallel events to the story world as they might occur in real life. They seem to ask and answer many "What If?" questions, playing with possibilities and suggested potentialities of character, motivation and consequence. (When these "What If?" questions were also posed in regard to real life, the students were connecting literature to life, which is the next dimension to be described.) Elaborations were sometimes subject to revision if later textual information made them unlikely or impossible to sustain.

These readers' elaborations infused extratextual life into the text, enlivening it with personal meaning, which the readers brought to the dimension of connecting as they expressed personal principles of living explored through the text, and more global ideas about human experience.

### Intertextual Elaborations

Here Cora not only elaborates on character and extends the text of a story, but combines knowledge of different texts together in an elaboration.

> Roll of Thunder *reminded me of some things I read about Spike Lee, and I began to imagine Cassie and Spike meeting, and what they would do together. Because if Cassie was 9 [years old] in 1933 than she would be . . . [calculates] . . . 69 in 1993. She would have lived through all the civil rights marches and things down south. She's smart and she becomes tough in the*

*book and I think she will probably become a lawyer or someone . . . someone
who is ready to go out in the world to fight. I know she liked Mr. Jamison, so
maybe that's why . . . a reason to become a lawyer. . . . Spike spent his sum-
mers in the sixties down South, so they would have that in common [civil
rights struggle] but Cassie would know a much bigger history of it. I imagined
them meeting at some awards banquet or meeting, because Cassie certainly
had become a strong supporter of civil rights and Spike would be interested in
her story and probably . . . he'd consider making a movie of it.*

Both Ron and Joanne often used their knowledge not only of other
books, but of movies and television shows to make intertextual links. While
reading "The Sniper," Joanne commented:

*In the beginning I thought it would be like an Arnold Schwarzenegger movie.
But then as I was comparing like* Terminator *movies to this I was thinking
how this ["The Sniper"] was so much more about real people and real consequences that you never really get to feel in a movie because it's [the movie] so
thin and . . . like glamorized or something.*

In comparison to Cora and Joanne, who disliked seeing movies about
books they had read ("They never compare," Joanne said), Ron looked for-
ward zealously to the release of movies such as *The Firm*. "I can't wait to see
what they make of it and how it compares to the book. It'll be great . . . it
will be something to talk about." Upon further questioning, Ron revealed
that "reading a book and seeing the movie are different experiences but they
sort of build on each other. I use the movie to rethink the book and the book
to understand the movie more."

### Filling Gaps

In *Roll of Thunder, Hear My Cry* (Taylor, 1976), which we read as a class,
there is an important scene between Uncle Hammer and Mr. Morrison that
is completely left out of the book. Uncle Hammer is enraged that Charlie
Simms, a white adult, has humiliated his niece Cassie, "a colored girl," by
twisting her arm, pushing her off the sidewalk, and making her apologize
for not kowtowing to his daughter Lillian Jean. Hammer, upon hearing the
story and over the protests and pleas of Big Ma (his mother) and Mary (his
sister-in-law and Cassie's mother), jumps into his car, ready to use his rifle
to wreak revenge. Mr. Morrison jumps into the car as well in an attempt to
stop him, knowing that certainly Hammer, and perhaps the whole family,
will be lynched if Hammer goes through with his plan. The next morning
the two men show up at the family breakfast table, tired and bleary-eyed.
One brief reference is later made to what had happened in the night.

I have documented elsewhere (Wilhelm, 1992) how very few of my students recognized or filled in this quite obvious textual gap. Highly engaged readers, however, such as the case study students, immediately did so. This excerpt shows how textual gaps can be filled in a way that makes them an organic part of the story. It also shows how story details or events, even those that are just suggested, are elaborated by readers. Joanne reported:

> As soon as Mr. Morrison jumps in the car and they roar away it was like I was inside the car with them, I could even hear the car [sic] slam. It's dark in the car, but I can see their faces in the light from the dashboard. I can see the dashboard because it was described earlier . . . walnut, and I'm in the back seat leaning into the front. The seats are plush red and comfortable. It's almost like I've stopped reading and I'm dreaming, I guess . . . [laughs] . . . but anyway Hammer says, "What you here for? If you ain't gonna help me just get out, right now!" and Mr. Morrison, real quiet like, says, "You're bad as them, you do this thing." And then they just keep on arguing like that and it's like I'm right there with them . . . then I'm reading again but when I find out what happened I'm right back in that scene and I know what happened to them.

During an SRI regarding his reading of *The Odyssey Project*, Ron began to fill gaps in a similar fashion, elaborating on both event and character. He was moving character cutouts around and discussing their relationships during a climactic scene when Amundsen and Torrance pick off four enemy soldiers.

> The author didn't really describe these guys [enemy soldiers] at all. That's why I made them stick figures [points to symbolic representation cutouts]. But I guess I get to know them. I'm sort of imagining they're like Nazis with the same sort of helmets and long gray coats and stuff. . . . Now I'm pretty excited. . . . I'm starting to think that it was a trap, that these soldiers [points to stick figures] wouldn't be so stupid to be standing around, that they must be like bait. So I'm feeling worried. And like for a minute I'm over there with them and [none of the following details are suggested by the text] they're just standing around talking and smoking cigarettes and one guy stamps on the ground and another one spits and they all laugh. Their faces are pink from the cold and one guy blows on his hands. I feel like a spy, I guess, and I'm feeling relieved because I'm convinced that it's not a trap, but I'm also thinking how these are regular guys and they're in the army and probably didn't volunteer. All of this is going through my mind, I think, both before the shooting and during it and after they are all shot. . . . Maybe it was afterwards but I think it

*was all happening as I was reading. They were still the enemy and I didn't feel too sorry when they got shot, but there was like this instant . . .*

### Extratextual, Imagined Events

All three readers explored the possibilities of extratextual events they imagined in their minds. Cora said that she often imagined what:

*Anne [of Green Gables] would do if things hadn't worked out, or if she was in our school right now, how would she dress and deal with things, what teachers would she like . . . sometimes I like to think that I'm her and I try to deal with difficulties like I think she would.*

After a rereading of "The Sniper," Joanne spoke at length about what would happen after the story's end, when:

*he [the sniper] has to go home. He'll have to tell his mother what happened. She'll be worried about his brother and he'll know what happened. . . . He could lie about it, say he just saw it happen. . . . No, he's going to have to tell the truth, and his mother will really weep but she'll forgive him. . . . Oh, it's just so horrible!*

At the end of *Roll of Thunder,* Ron reported:

*I'm like, wow, man, what if things hadn't turned out this way? What if Mr. Jamison hadn't got there in time? What if Papa hadn't started the fire? Would the night riders have really lynched Papa and Mr. Morrison? I just had this scene in my mind where they come up to the house and they try to get Papa and Mr. Morrison and they [the Logans] have guns and booby traps and they just kill them! And Mr. Jamison is there watching and he knows that the whites were just asking for it and that the Logans were just protecting themselves and so they don't get in trouble for it. I can see why the author wrote the ending the way she did, and maybe it's better . . . more believable, I know, but I like my ending. . . . It makes . . . it relieves me somehow, makes me feel better, like those night riders never get what they deserve and I really want them to.*

This study confirmed what Enciso (1992) has pointed out, that elaboration becomes a key indicator, and in fact a prerequisite, of the link between participating in a story world and moving along a continuum toward a more reflective exploration of those experiences as a spectator. Iser (1978), as well, has pointed out that elaboration is the key to personal understanding gained through reading. Bruner (1986) goes so far as to argue that the elaborations can be interpreted as the most vital element of the story world: "Literary experiences invite the reader to consider implicit meanings, multiple perspectives and the subjectification of reality." This operation of the "subjunctive mode" is what constitutes the power of literature, "the trafficking in human possibilities versus settled certainties" (p. 35). Elaboration is the exploration of possibilities, of extending what is known, of probing character thought and attitude.

## Connecting Literature to Life

As was seen in both the dimensions of relating to characters (stance/perspective taking) and seeing the story world (mental imaging), readers naturally brought their knowledge of the world to bear, adding it to textual clues to build a secondary world with characters and places they felt they knew. As could be seen in the case of Cora, this sort of connecting occurred as she visualized "houses" by bringing her personal knowledge of houses to the text. She was bringing her life to literature.

Highly engaged readers, such as the case study students, seemed to naturally use actual-world knowledge, in ways invited by textual cues, to build a virtual world. The less engaged readers in my classes did not automatically do this, and seemed at a loss unless such strategies were scaffolded for them.

The data suggested that *without the bringing of personally lived experience to literature, the reverse operation, bringing literature back to life, did not occur.* This, I think, is a key finding.

In this dimension of response, the readers went beyond drawing on their repertoires of personal knowledge as readers and people, and the bringing of their personal experience to bear on the understanding of literature. Here a reverse process occurred: the readers made conscious connections from the fictional world that helped them to gain heightened awareness of their personal identities and to formulate guidelines for personal ways of living. These readers did not just apply knowledge of life to the reading transaction, but consciously derived implications for living their own lives from the transaction. These readers activated personal comparisons the text seemed to invite for them. On occasion, these students mentally or physically role-played what they would do in a character's situation should it occur in their own lives. Literature was related to life and brought back to it.

This sort of conscious relating or connecting seemed to depend on the reader first bringing a great deal of his or her life to literature, not only to take a perspective and to visualize, but to elaborate on the story world to infuse some personal extratextual life into the reading experience. Once this was done, then the readers seemed enabled to draw comparisons from the literary experience to their own lives.

### Learning from Characters and Events

Ron spoke in general terms about making personal comparisons to characters that helped him consider issues in his own life.

> *I guess I'm comparing myself to Jack Ryan a lot when I read stories with him. When he's in a jam, I think, what would I do if I were him? Could I do it? And then when I'm in a jam, I think about the stories and think, "What would Jack Ryan do if he were me?" What if I were like the "young Jack Ryan," you know, like the "young Indiana Jones," what would I do then?*

Cora, discussing her reading of *Roll of Thunder* during an interview, had this to say:

> *After I read it anyway, I thought a lot about what Cassie had to teach me. I was especially impressed about how she handled Lillian Jean. She was in control even when it looked to everyone else that she wasn't. I learned that . . . it's hard to express . . . like if someone is using you, and you know they're using you, then they're not—because you have a choice about them using you then and where it's going to lead and what you will do about it. Knowing—knowing what's happening puts you in control and it's better to use that control and not get angry.*

After her reading of *Just as Long as We're Together*, Joanne explained that:

> *a book might not give you an answer of what to do in your own life, but it helps you think about it. This [book] made me think about what I would do if my friend and I both really liked the same boy. I mean, is friendship or love more important? What's more lasting? Would I want to risk what I already have for something I might not get? I don't know . . .*

During her SRI with "The Sniper," notice how Joanne initially brings life to literature by making a personal comparison, and then makes a connection, bringing literature back to life as she formulates an idea about living.

> *[When the sniper was wounded] I felt the pain of the iodine. I even clenched my teeth and shook. I had something like that happen to me—[laughs]—it*

*didn't feel good. I could remember that so well. . . . When the other sniper he
shot fell over the side of the building, that really affected me. I pushed my sister
down once and she started crying so pitifully. I felt so terrible. It was the crying
that got to me, just like the guy falling and his bones being smashed when he
hit the street [last detail was elaborated]. You know, I'm thinking that it's
when you see the . . . consequences of what you do, that's when it gets you. It
makes me think that we should always imagine the unseen consequences of
what we do . . . that we should think, like what is it? The golden rule . . . that
we should imagine what it would be like from the receiving end before we do
anything.*

When the sniper kills his enemy, he is repulsed and throws down his
revolver, which then discharges. Joanne elaborates on the scene and indicates heightened personal awareness, which in turn leads to the formulation
of a personal guideline.

*He almost killed himself! It's ridiculous! [Laughs] I felt like he almost killed
himself for no reason. All of a sudden I feel like I'm there with him again and
it's cold and damp up on the roof like just before the sun rises and I'm shiv-
ering and the gun goes off and about blows out my eardrums and the bullet
whizzes by me . . . and it makes me think how you have to be careful . . . especially when you're angry about something or upset, not to do something stupid. It's like when I'm really upset I'll do something wild—oh, I'm seeing myself so well right now and how I could do the exact same stupid thing, out of
control, and it could really ruin things and that shocks you back to reality, and
I'm thinking the being upset has to be enough to shock you back so you don't
screw things up even more. You have to know yourself well enough that you
know you might do something like that and that is what has to stop you.*

### Role-Playing

Both Joanne and Cora reported mental "role-plays" in which they
would be the character in the story world acting out a scene as it was played
out, might be played out, or could have been alternately played out. Apro-
pos to the dimension of connecting and relating literature to life, they
reported that they would also role-play scenes in which they might find
themselves, in the context of their own lives, in a similar situation to the
characters. They would then role-play the scene, often revising the role-
play, and rehearsing over and over a particular enactment that pleased them,
or, as Joanne put it, "You might find really happening to you and you want
to make sure you get it right. So you can automatically do and say the things
you want right away instead of saying later, ohmygod I missed my chance."

Ron was the only one of the three given to overt, physical role-plays. He would sometimes enact a scene by himself as a single character, and sometimes play multiple roles. At other times he would begin a role-play hoping that others would play along, or he would actively enlist friends to try out a particular scene. His success in such schemes was erratic, especially when he had to explain a scene from a book others had not read and they quickly became uninterested. He was more successful role-playing scenes from texts the class had read as a group.

This highlights the importance of balancing shared and individualized readings. When students read individually, they can exercise their individual taste and response, and they can encourage others to read the books they have enjoyed. When readings are shared, students have the opportunity to create response together, to compare response and ways of reading, and to learn from each other about these ways of reading.

Ron's overt role-playing is not common, but neither is it unique. I have written several journal entries over the years about students spontaneously role-playing scenes or elaborations from their reading, and once I observed several remedial reading students enacting the tiger hunt we had read about that day (from Jim Corbett's *Man-Eaters of Kumaon*) on their way home from school.

Drama is a natural way of making meaning for children, yet it is a terribly underused part of American teachers' repertoires. Students, I think, lose their propensity for learning and exploring through drama partly because of school. But this propensity can be recovered and can work to support better reading, as we will see in the next chapter.

### Telling Others

Students who analogized principles or ideas from literature seemed to have a special urge to share their understandings with others. Cora indicated to me that she and Joanne were "reading friends," and that they enjoyed "sharing what we get out of books, what they mean to us," although they were not friendly in any other social sense. "Some books I don't need to talk about, only if, you know, there were things I learned from it about myself." Joanne said:

> *I share and trade books with a lot of girls, mostly Christie and Cora. We have the same taste. You have to find people with your own reading style, who know what you like to see and feel when you read. . . . One of the really nice things about reading a book someone gives you is that you can see what they learned from it and how it, well, not just what they thought about it but how it will change how they act. It's so much fun to talk about when and how we*

*might have the chance to act like the characters, or what we would do differ-*
*ently in their situation because of what happened to them.*

Ron expressed on several occasions that he loved to talk with his father about what he read, and that he actively enlisted friends to read certain books so "we can talk about them." He loved it "when people borrow me books [sic—this is a Wisconsinism]. Then I know if I read it we can talk about it."

## REFLECTIVE DIMENSIONS

In this last set of response dimensions, the case study students seemed to have separated themselves from their participation in the story and were looking at that experience in a more detached and objective manner. They seemed to be spectating on the reading experience and reflecting on it. Often this reflection would occur while they read, and it seemed to almost always occur after a reading. In fact, this reflecting on the textual experience seemed to be an organic and highly enjoyable part of the reading act for these students.

### Considering Significance

In this dimension, the readers asked various forms of Galda's (1982) analytic evaluation question: "How did/does the text work?" and "How does this particular detail or rhetorical move contribute to its working?"

Operating on this dimension, these readers vigorously interrogated the text, continuing to fill in gaps but consciously recognizing not only details but the openness of the text—of what is not told, of what is left for the reader—and considering the significance of such openness.

These readers became consciously concerned with what could be termed "a narrative world," or the way the story is told. Narrative conventions for interpreting text (cf. Rabinowitz's rules of signification, 1987) were applied, and the significance of certain details was considered. The implications of character behavior were considered and evaluated. These readers continued to reflect and elaborate on possible meanings that such details might convey. Story events were considered in relationship to possible themes and complex authorial generalizations that readers recognized the literature was attempting to make.

These readers formulated puzzles and enigmas and consciously welcomed, accepted, or rejected what Iser (1978) calls "hermeneutic challenges" to their interpretive, meaning-making abilities. In other words, the readers would set up detective games for themselves, posing sophisticated mysteries for themselves and then trying to solve them.

Details were considered in relation to previous details; these readers read along what Barthes (1986) calls "textual indices," building up meaning by adding together an accumulation of various details considered to be significant that were presented at different places in the text. These readers actively looked for patterns that evolved through a reading and considered matters of coherence and how separate elements fit together to indicate meanings. In contrast to extracting personal principles and guidelines from isolated events and details, as in the dimension of connecting, when operating on reflective dimensions the readers knew that the author was making a complex statement about life that could be understood only by considering the experience of the literary work as an organic whole.

As Ron commented: "Sometimes I'll be reading and something will just knock my socks off and I'll say, 'Whoa! How'd he [the author] do that to me?' I mean, how did he shock me like that or make me feel that way?"

### Interrogating the Text

Throughout the reading of "The Sniper," Joanne interrogated the text. When the sniper puts his hat on top of his rifle to fool the other sniper into shooting it, Joanne asked:

> *Could he really trick the other sniper that way? It seems so obvious. . . . I guess it was dark, but it wouldn't fool me . . . and why drop your rifle? It has his fingerprints on it and he just killed the driver and the old lady! Does he really have to do it to make the trick work? Now he doesn't have a rifle! He's laying everything on escaping and on his side winning. . . . I'm asking why are they all doing this? It makes me shiver. How can war be pushing them to do this when you see that they hate it [the killing]? I'm asking what it is they are fighting for that can be this important, especially when none of them really seem like soldiers who really know about fighting.*

At the end of the story, Joanne recognizes and considers the openness of the text.

> *I felt total awe at the ending. . . . The author doesn't tell what he felt so I could fill it in and feel it myself. That was a good thing to leave to me. I would have gone nuts, blown my cover totally, it's so terrible! So now I sort of take over the story and I'm asking "How could you have done this?" and "What will your life be like now?" and I'm thinking. . . . Now he doesn't know why he did it himself or why he's fighting and how he ever could have done such a thing.*

Interestingly, Joanne first thought that the story took place in Central America, "between the contras and the other people," but later thought, "It must be in Europe, I think because of the city rooftops and chimneys and stuff." At the end of the story, she said, "It doesn't really matter where, maybe the author doesn't want you to know where because it [the theme] applies anywhere people fight each other."

Cora considers how endings contribute to a story's workings and meanings at the same time that she shows that she has added together various pieces of information from throughout the story.

> *Like at the end of "High Beams" there's that twist, that it's not the truck driver who's the . . . danger. He's the hero who saved the girl [from the guy trying to kill her from the back seat of her car] by flashing the high beams whenever he saw the guy getting ready to hurt her. I was really surprised by the ending and . . . I think, "What did the author do to make me expect another ending?" and then I'll ask if there was a point to the twist or if it's just to surprise me.*

Later during the same discussion, Cora considers not only how details work, but also shows pleasure in the challenges she and the text set for her as the reader.

> *Then at the end I imagine what happens after the ending . . . I see the police grabbing the guy and dragging him away and he has this evil smile on his face. And I think, "What did he want?" "Why did he do this?" He must have had something, some relationship with the girl, or she must remind him of someone. I keep imagining—it's part of the fun of the way the story was written—but I never really want to come up with a final answer like some people do.*

Cora then considers the text as a whole as she considers its meaning.

> *When you consider all the clues you see there's a message, like . . . things aren't always what they seem. Yes . . . because it seemed like she was safe in the car . . . and that the truck driver was evil instead of good.*

### Revising Interpretations

All of these readers often expressed confusion when operating on this dimension. Often they were troubled about the meaning of a detail, or their particular interpretation of it. Nonetheless, these readers were quite adept at acknowledging a lack of clarity, or realizing that they lacked essential information: either background information, or essential information that, as Ron put it, "I must have missed. I had to have missed something. Damn!"

Sometimes they acknowledged that previous responses were too narrow or incorrect and needed revision. Cora, responding to the end of "Lob's Girl," said:

> *You see I thought the dog was still alive [when he came to the hospital to wake his owner, Sandy, from her coma], but when I found out he was dead then I went back and I saw lots of clues that showed he was dead. And I had to, well, rethink the story from that point [where Lob died] . . . and I was thinking how much he loved her, but then I thought how she came out of the coma because she thought he was there and I thought about how much she loved him and how she really had come back from the dead too! It's more than about the power of love and how it goes beyond the grave . . . I think it has something to do with memory.*

This is exactly the sort of attention to detail and consequent revising activity that most of my student readers rarely engaged in. I think that this building and revising of understanding based on accumulating and adding together details from throughout a text should be a reading activity that is modeled and encouraged. Another lesson for me as a teacher is to tolerate, or perhaps even contribute to, student confusion by pointing out details they might not have considered. Then time needs to be given to consider and work through the confusion. A further implication is for assessment and evaluation of student reading: confusion and the inability to answer certain questions may indicate growth, that is, that the student has taken on a new challenge that she is still struggling to meet. This kind of move needs to be applauded and encouraged. Error and failure may be a great indication of growth.

## Recognizing Literary Conventions

On this dimension, the case study readers exhibited an awareness that the literary event is a highly conventionalized and socially constructed experience. As such, the readers recognized highly sophisticated rules of signification that often undercut literal or usual expression. On occasion, I noticed that they considered irony, story inversions, narrator and author reliability, and symbolism. To interpret and construct the meaning such conventions implied, they drew on their previous experiences as readers and people, and upon the literary and cultural repertoires these experiences had developed.

We have already seen how these readers considered the constructedness of a text, the meanings of its revealed and withheld details. In this excerpt from a discussion of *Just as Long as We're Together*, Joanne considers the issues of withheld information and a narrator's reliability: "I know she's [the author] withholding information about Jeremy and I wonder why. I wonder if I can believe her, if there's a story behind the story. And whether, you know, I'm actually supposed to guess at that story behind the story."

Ron spoke in general terms about irony.

> *Sometimes I know I've read a story and you know you've understood all the words but the story just . . . doesn't make any sense. You just know you've missed something. And I'm racking my brain and all of a sudden I'll get it! Like, you know, maybe people weren't saying what they meant, but the opposite of it . . . like you weren't supposed to believe something or take it seriously . . . you know, like real people do all the time . . . and presto! The story makes sense.*

I took this opportunity to explain and illustrate verbal, situational, and dramatic irony to Ron. It was a lesson he was ready for, and he identified several instances of each kind of irony from his recent reading. Recognizing irony was becoming part of his repertoire; being able to name it helped him recognize and understand it more powerfully.

Ron showed the importance of activating a cultural and literary repertoire as he discussed his reading of spy novels.

> *You know, you're always looking for the mole. You know there's somebody you can't trust and you try to figure out who. [In response to a teacher's question, he added] You just know, because you've read a lot of books and a lot of movies and it always happens and usually there's been some clues of some sort . . . so you're on the lookout.*

Though these students showed some awareness of sophisticated literary conventions, like most other readers in their seventh grade classes they continued to have difficulty with such conventions and would sometimes completely misread a story despite many clues contrary to their reading. The most engaged readers, such as the three profiled here, did tend to recognize a misreading more readily than their peers, even if they had difficulty revising that reading.

I found Michael Smith's (1989, 1991) work on teaching such sophisticated conventions through sequences of textual experiences very useful for helping my own students. Smith suggests providing students with repeated exposure to particular conventions like irony, starting with simple texts such as cartoons and moving through shorter and simpler examples to longer and more subtle forms. The students build up the experience necessary to formulate heuristics, or problem-solving strategies, for reading and inter-preting such conventions. I think that such direct instruction is probably necessary for students to understand texts that make use of complex con-ventions, since even the case study students struggled to recognize and make use of these.

## Recognizing Reading as a Transaction

On the reflective dimensions, the readers consciously recognized that the text was constructed by a human and fallible author. Moreover, they expressed recognition that the author, through the textual construction, and they themselves as readers had to work together to create meanings. The author of the work was considered as an individual who created the work through artifice and the weaving of patterns to communicate a feeling or interpretation of some aspects of the human condition. In addition, the stu-dents recognized that they had a role in responding to the details and pat-terns.

The readers sometimes recognized an implied author and interrogated that author, evaluating the techniques used by that author to construct the story. An attempt was made by them to understand the story's expressed vision in terms of the constructed nature of the text. The author's represen-tation of the world was matched with their own, and that representation might be accepted, rejected, resisted, or revised.

The readers sometimes recognized and reflected on their own contri-butions to the literary event, and began to consider if the role they played matched the expectation of the author and the text.

Much of the data reported previously show how these readers consid-ered these issues, demonstrating that the dimensions discussed here are not really separable in practice. Nonetheless, I will cite some examples that do seem to highlight how readers considered their role vis-à-vis that of the text and the author behind the text.

Cora was one reader who almost always considered herself in conversa-tion or communion with an author. After reading *The Incredible Journey*, she noted, "This author must really love and understand animals." And in re-gard to several Katherine Paterson novels: "When I read her books I feel like I'm getting to know a very kind and sensitive person who has a powerful heart and . . . an ability to understand people."

As Thomson (1987) noted in his study, readers who read several works of a particular type, or especially by a particular author, are much more likely to consciously consider the notion of an author with an individual agenda, and individual interests, styles, and techniques for constructing a literary work of art. Students choosing their own reading frequently read several or all of the works by a particular author they have come to like. Yet this opportunity to know an author through multiple works is very rare in classes that are directed by a teacher or a planned curriculum. And then these kinds of moves will be much more difficult for students to make.

As Cora continued this train of thought, she said of Paterson:

> *Sometimes she lets me down and I'm a little disappointed . . . not in her so much I guess as the way she wrote something because I still think a lot of her. I was disappointed by the end of* Gilly Hopkins *and by the whole book* Park's Quest. *It just wasn't up to her standards. But then* Liddy *(sic) restored my confidence and put things back on an even keel.*

Ron, who would plow through several books by the same author on great binges, had similar reactions. "*The Firm* [by John Grisham] was great and I was thinking what a great author he is. Then *The Pelican Brief* was good too, but not as good."

These readers would sometimes compare the representation of the author with their own views of the world. Ron said,

> *I like Clancy a lot, but he has a really negative view of the world. When I read a couple of his books it wears me out. I need to read a fantasy as a relief from being dragged down by all the problems he sees in the world. I guess I just don't see the world as being that bad. Some authors just concentrate on the bad stuff and they don't give a complete picture and that can really get you down.*

Joanne recognizes and evaluates the constructedness of "The Sniper" at the same time she mildly interrogates the author:

> *I knew as soon as the author tells me he's going to check the body that he would know the guy. Why else would the author have him look? When he did that I thought, the author has to have a good ending. The guy who was shot . . . family member, definitely. It was still a shock to find out it was his brother. . . . I don't know if it's good, maybe the same point could have been made in a more believable way. But maybe it has to be the brother to have that force.*

Joanne also recognizes and reflects on her own contribution to the story:

> *Sometimes I'll read something and I'll think, "I just didn't get enough out of that. I wasn't up to it. I know there's more there." What's nice about this story is that I think I really . . . you know, thought and felt along with it. I think I did a good job. At the end I feel like I really related to the story.*

Toward the end of *The Great Gilly Hopkins,* Cora considers the role of a particular character. She related:

> *I'm thinking about her [Gilly's] grandma and why she's even been put into the story. I thought about it a lot and I guess it's for the plot, so Gilly will have a place she'll have to stay . . . but much more important than that is that the grandmother is suffering too and it's the first time Gilly has the opportunity to really understand someone else and help them from the very start.*

All three readers indicated that when they were confused about something they just simply read on, trusting that the author would eventually reveal enough for them to resolve the confusion. Often, as Ron said, "You just have to like get the problem straight in your head, so you can solve it when the chance comes. . . . You have to trust that the guy writing it knew what he was doing." This is reminiscent of Iser's view of the reader's setting up and solving "hermeneutic puzzles" (1978), and of Meek's (Meek et al., 1983) view that the practiced reader can tolerate uncertainty because she knows that if she continues to read, "the puzzles and suspense built by the author will be resolved."

However, this kind of ambiguity was difficult for my less engaged readers to tolerate and often caused them to give up their reading. Interesting, too, in this regard was the universal desire of the three case study students for "surprise." This desire was not shared by lower-level students, who were disconcerted by surprise, and who felt, as Walter told me, "screwed over" in their attempts to figure out the text.

Not only did the case study readers desire surprise, they desired different types: not only of event, but of style and metaphor. And they relished the opportunity to realign their readings with new revelations about the story world.

I interpreted this desire for surprise as a desire for new challenges as they outgrew the demands of formulaic fiction. Joanne, who read more formulaic fiction than the other two case study students, had this to say.

> *Like a Nancy Drew book is sort of comforting and relaxing. Every book is like an old friend, you can almost tell what's going to happen and when. It's predictable and easy. But it gets boring too and it's like having ate too much candy. You just get sick of it and you want a book that will really throw you for a loop.*

## Evaluating an Author, and the Self as Reader

The case study readers would occasionally seem to recognize the reader implied by the text (the reader imagined by the author as she wrote), and

Cora, especially, might even critique the role of the implied reader, or her own performance of the implied role. She would comment on the acceptance/resistance/rejection of the assigned role as implied reader, or the interpretive moves she made because it was expected of her, perhaps because she was a member of what Fish (1980) regards as a particular reading community.

These readers, when operating on this dimension, exercised reflexiveness, considering what the processes of reading and making interpretations revealed about their personal identities. A personal interpretation was sometimes compared to another reader's interpretation in a way that revealed a personally characteristic way of being in and making sense of the world.

Finally, these readers very occasionally seemed to consider the ideology or political agenda of the author and text, and the implications of such an ideology.

I gathered data about this dimension when these readers were sharing interpretations, comparing these to reveal their personal characteristics as readers and as people.

Ron would often enlist friends to read the books he was reading.

> *I like sharing. If you agree [about a book's meaning], then you share this excitement about thinking the same way, like being fans of the same winning team. If you disagree you get to see it in a new way and that's interesting. I think there's lots of ways to see a book and how you see it tells a lot about you.*

Ron believed that he learned about himself by comparing his literary interpretations to those of others.

For a period of time during the school year, Ron enlisted his friend Chris to read some Tom Clancy novels along with him. They would sometimes read aloud together, and did several cooperative projects together: a radio show, a story drama, a video newscast.

> *You know, Chris really likes sports and humor and action and stuff like that. When he read these books he was into the big climactic scenes. He always wanted to reenact these assassinations and big explosions and things. . . . Me, I was more interested in like the good and evil part of it, and could Jack Ryan save his family or friends. I guess how we read the books just showed what we care and think about.*

Joanne told me that she and Cora often shared books "to compare how we feel about them. We like talking about that. Sometimes I'll read a book and I'll want to know what she will think about it. Sometimes we think alike but there's always something different too. It's fun to think about what that shows about us."

Joanne often indicated that she had stepped back and was evaluating the author, the text, herself, and her own reading. When researching for her learning group's production of a video documentary on women in the workplace, Joanne wrote in her journal:

*The author of this really thinks women are always mistreated. But some females I know actually say that they aren't being treated unfairly. Is the author wrong? Has she really considered everyone's point of view, which she should if she's an author, or only her own? I think we should take a poll, because this is very weird, because I see both points of view. What I think is that females are just as prejudice to males as they are to us! Like maybe many of us prejudge them and lump them all together. Neat but disturbing thought!*

When Cora completed her reading of Katherine Paterson's *The Great Gilly Hopkins,* she was irate with the ideology of the text and the text's implied reader role. Here, as on other occasions, she perceives a shift in her reading experience. Often these changes are in character, plot direction, style, or tone. Here it is in regard to the role she feels the text wishes her to perform. After referring to Paterson's Christian orientation, Cora irately reported that

*The end of the book CLEARLY wants me to read it a certain way, and I don't want to read it that way. I mean, at the end, it's different than the rest of the book! It's like we get to like Gilly and get excited about how she's growing and then . . . at the end of the book, she [the author] wants me to be sad, and I am, but I don't want to be, but then I'm mostly angry. She also wants me to buy into what happens, that it's the way it has to be. . . . I feel manipulated by that. She wants me to think that Gilly should bear her cross, that this is what she asked for and now that she has it she has to . . . well, endure it, I guess. . . . I resent that sort of ending. . . . I mean, why can't Gilly go back to her foster home? What would be wrong with that? Why couldn't we have an ending like that? They're [the foster family] her family, not this mother and grandmother. Doesn't Gilly have any rights? Is it Christian to believe that she has to be unhappy because she's made mistakes and she has to live with those mistakes? What about Gilly being forgiven and having learned from her mistakes? Why can't she just admit she made a mistake and say she wants to go where she found love? Where's the Christianity in beating up on a kid? . . . I liked the book a lot until the end. I just . . . I just can't live with that ending and what the author is trying to feed me with it.*

Joanne, responding to the end of *Roll of Thunder, Hear My Cry,* had this to say.

> *One reason I really liked this book is that the author obviously had a lot of re-*
> *spect for me. I mean, I've read books like this that beat you over the head kind*
> *of [laughs] . . . like a fable with a big moral written all over it. In this [book]*
> *there's a moral too, like that blacks were really mistreated, and everybody . . .*
> *well lots of people accepted it. And that's bad because people like Mr. Jamison*
> *and Papa showed that you do have the power to change things and make them*
> *better. The story, I guess, is about people being treated equally . . . deserving*
> *to be treated equally . . . but the author, she doesn't beat you over the head*
> *with it, she lets you in on their life so you can feel their problems . . . see for*
> *yourself, well . . . their dignity, and you believe it and really feel it because you*
> *were allowed to come to it yourself. You know, I really believe people will only*
> *change if they are helped to see things for themselves. They won't change by*
> *someone telling them what to see. . . . Another thing I liked was how not all*
> *the whites were evil. Mr. Jamison helped them, even the Simmses [during the*
> *cotton fire] . . . Jeremy was nice, and Lillian Jean was . . . well, she changed.*
> *And they [the Logans] fought back. I read another book [about discrimina-*
> *tion] and the people just took everything and I couldn't believe that, or that the*
> *author would want them to do that . . .*

## EPILOGUE: WHAT WE LEARNED TOGETHER ABOUT READING

I pursued this study not only with Cora, Joanne, and Ron but also (to a much less formal degree) with all of my students for the whole of the school year. It became what we did together: sharing how we read, discussing it, trying new things. It was a giant reading experiment.

Studying how my students read helped me as a teacher, helping me to see that I had previously neglected how readers evoke and experience their reading, and how they connect and relate personally to that experience. I saw how I had privileged particular kinds of interpretive and reflective response through my past teaching and saw ways to take a new tack.

The process allowed me to see what my most engaged readers were doing, and to begin considering how I might help less engaged readers to begin making the same sorts of moves.

Our focus on the process of reading helped my students as they learned new moves from each other, trying on other readers' strategies and perspectives. Their personal experience of reading, whether relatively impoverished or highly engaged, was validated and expanded. Because of the way we ran the class, they were not told that they were "wrong," but that they were readers doing what readers did, and that they could be better readers by doing new and different things.

The students noticed and spoke often about how differently they would experience and understand the same text—discussing why this was so and if a particular reading was richer than another. They came to value different readings and different ways of reading.

Many students reconceived the reading act in a way that empowered them because it gave them a sense of their own agency as meaning-makers. They came to see reading as something they did, that they controlled, that they could talk about, think about, manipulate, and change.

Throughout the process, students were given a metacognitive vocabulary, frame, and voice. This is important because readers must become aware of and alert to their behaviors to be in control of them. Becoming aware of reading processes creates the possibility of changing and improving one's use of these strategic processes. As a result, I believe that students began to set about the business of learning how to learn and learning how to read in creative and productive ways.

What I learned from my students helped me to explore classroom activities and questions that would help elicit and develop evocative and connective response moves, helping many students to develop powerful and necessary response strategies that they previously knew little if anything about.

As I saw the intense visual experience of my engaged readers, and how vitally they related to or became characters during their reading, I was led to develop response activities including drama and art. Drama and art, I believed, could help to develop response and awareness of readerly activity in my many less engaged readers. It was a way of bringing the invisible secrets of engaged readers out into the open, where they could be observed and shared and tried on by other readers. Drama and art naturally engender involvement and a sense of ownership, which I wished to develop in my less engaged readers.

At the same time, I developed a new attitude toward how my less engaged readers were reading. I became aware that many readings that I had considered invalid or impoverished often served student purposes, and at other times provided a springboard to richer readings. This made me more accepting and less goal-driven, monolithic, and judgmental of variant readings. My new attitude helped me become a listener instead of a teller.

Through my research, I was helped to see that I needed to be more open and student-centered as a teacher, getting to know each student and what they could do so that I could teach them "where they were," responding to them personally and offering more opportunities for descriptive and artistic response, for free reading and sharing. The research methods themselves helped me to get to know my students as readers.

I expanded my notions of the types of moves and activities readers engage in. I developed a vocabulary to describe reading and discuss it with readers. My teaching became more informed, and new directions I could take as a teacher to develop and extend my student readers became clearer. I have become more forward-looking—toward the ultimate goals of the individual reader. My classroom, in a way, became "de-schooled," more personal and individual, more like a studio.

What I found helped me as a teacher because I asked and found answers to the question, How can I change my teaching to account for this or encourage that? How, as a teacher, can I build on what this student is doing so that she will start doing these other things as well?

In the following two chapters, I will describe two studies that made use of the response dimensions gleaned from the practices of these readers as a benchmark for rich and engaged reading. This rubric of response dimensions became the basis for shaping instruction that would help other, less engaged readers develop the strategies, stances, and attitudes exhibited by Cora, Joanne, and Ron. It also served as a benchmark to measure the growth of these less engaged readers in experiencing stories throughout the school year.

Perhaps my biggest surprise while studying the engaged readers was how much more sophisticated their involvement was than I had ever imagined. It made me ask how many students I had sold short over the years, not imagining they were "ready" for particular books or "capable" of participating in particular activities or discussions.

Seeing over and over again just how many different dimensions of response the students operated on, and how many moves they made on these dimensions, and how deeply they engaged with literature and with others whom they considered reading partners, I was left with a challenge: How could I help my many less engaged readers to have these same sorts of rich experiences with literature? This was a mission I had failed to complete with many students through my years of teaching.

A third of the way through the school year, I began to use drama as a vehicle for letting less engaged readers into the secrets of engaged reading. When this approach showed promise for some and not as much for others, I pursued a second project—encouraging students to use visual art as a response to literature.

# CHAPTER FOUR

# Using Drama to Extend the Reader

Reader response theorists have often focused on ideal reading, on the general stance and processes of proficient and engaged readers like Cora, Joanne, and Ron. Though I too worked hard to help my proficient readers outgrow themselves, I was especially concerned with those many other students who struggled with or resisted the reading act. I have always regarded reading of any kind, but especially of literature, as a unique and powerful way of knowing about self, others, and the world. Seeing students who went to great lengths to avoid reading made me ask what was different about their history, experience, and attitudes as readers from that of more engaged readers. I felt as if these reluctant readers had been sitting on the bench during the big game, completely bored, without even realizing they hadn't participated in the action. I asked myself how I could help them get into the game of reading and experience in some way its potential thrills and excitement.

I decided to use techniques of story theater (using the text as a script) to help students experience the world of a text, and techniques of story drama (using the text as a starting point) to help them explore the implications and possibilities at the edge of texts. The story I will tell in this chapter is about three reluctant readers who were helped by these dramatic interventions. Marvin, Kevin, and Libby were helped by drama to experience and take on for themselves some of the moves and strategies of more engaged readers. They also began, through the dramas, to rethink the nature and possibilities of reading.

Rosenblatt (1978) asserts that "the benefits of literature can emerge only from creative activity on the part of the reader himself" (p. 276). She argues that the reader must evoke and exert control over the ideas, sensations, feelings, and images that are experienced while reading. The text acts both as a stimulus that activates a reader's past experience and as a guide or blueprint for selecting, rejecting, and ordering that experience. Rosenblatt even makes a specific comparison between reading and acting in a drama: "We accept the fact that the actor infuses his own voice, his own body, his own gestures—in short, his own interpretation—into the words of the text. Is he not simply carrying to its ultimate manifestation what each of us as readers of the text must do?" (1978, p. 13). In this view, literary reading requires that readers both evoke and participate in imaginary worlds whose creation is stimulated and guided by the text. Reading literature is not the reception of meaning, but the reader's participation in a "transaction" with text that produces meaning. Yet this was a conception of reading that my less engaged readers failed to understand or enact, and that left some of them scoffing.

Iser (1978) argues similarly that "Apprehension of a literary work comes about through the interaction between the reader's presence in the text and his habitual experiences, which are now a past orientation. As such it is not a passive process of acceptance, but a productive response" (p. 113). For Iser, most stories cannot be fruitfully enjoyed and understood solely through explicitly articulated action because the text is filled with gaps that the reader must fill and elaborate upon to create a "virtual world."

Though Ron, Joanne, and Cora engaged in many elaborative reading activities, most of my other students did not. Eco (1978) calls such elaborative activities "taking inferential walks" and writes:

> Texts are lazy machineries that ask someone [the reader] to do part of their job. . . . Frequently . . . a text tells the reader about the event A and, after a while, about the event E, taking for granted that the reader has already anticipated the dependent events B, C, D. (pp. 214, 215)

I believe that at least for less engaged readers, the dimensions of response are order-dependent; I found that the less engaged readers I studied did not respond in connective or reflective ways to their reading unless they first overtly responded on all of the evocative dimensions. I would like to make the claim that this is the case with all readers, but the data are too murky. Engaged readers seem to respond simultaneously on many if not all of these dimensions, sometimes privileging a highly reflective dimension without really discussing their response on an evocative one.

The findings about the less engaged readers strike me as very important. The collected information reveals that we often ask less engaged readers to reflect on something that they have not experienced. This suggests that if we would help them to develop evocative, experiential response to literature, response on other dimensions would be possible for them— and the door to engaging literary worlds would finally be opened. Defining the dimensions of evocative response and thinking about questions and activities to encourage this sort of response seem to me to be important steps for teachers to take toward helping less engaged readers into the experience of reading.

My question at the point when I began to use drama, some 12 weeks into the school year, was, How could I help the rest of my student readers to think of reading as something that required the creation of meanings that were not completely printed on the page? How could I help them use words to create characters and pictures that went beyond the words? It was then that I began to think of *story theater,* or enacting *story events,* and story drama, or enacting story suggestions and possibilities, as a way to help these readers.

## WHY DRAMA?

Benton (1983) describes the act of reading as the creation of "secondary worlds" (a term he borrows from Tolkien, 1964) and the involvement and enactment of dramatic activity within those worlds. Harding (1937, 1962) and Britton (1984) support this view when they describe what they call "the participant stance" of the reader as an important dimension of reading. This stance puts the reader inside the secondary world of a story, experiencing and elaborating upon it from within. The reader taking this stance, as seen with Cora and the other engaged readers, makes moves to enter the story world and to move about inside it. These theorists also describe the "spectator role" (also exemplified in great detail by Ron, Joanne, and Cora), in which a reader sees the text as an object, reflecting and commenting upon it. Rosenblatt (1978) and others have pointed out that most teaching and research have focused on the spectator stance and how a reader interprets, evaluates, and reflects on the evoked world of the text. Little emphasis has been placed on what readers actually do to go beyond simple comprehension of story action to evoke the text and elaborate upon it as a "story participant." Students are thus often asked to interpret a story by gazing and reflecting upon what they have never learned to experience.

Theory and research agree that what highly engaged readers do as they read is dramatic in nature. In just this vein, Enciso (1992) describes engagement in reading as

> our entry into the world of the story and the intense involvement we feel as we imagine and interpret the characters, setting, events, and thematic possibilities of literary texts. It includes a complex interplay of imaginative and intellectual processes that are typically private and elusive, yet critical to comprehension and pleasure in reading. (p. 1)

Enciso (1990) describes engaged readers taking on and enacting various roles and intensely visualizing particular settings and scenes. These same activities were apparent in the responses of Ron, Cora, and Joanne, but I had little evidence that any of my other readers engaged with texts in this way.

Other research indicates that readers must first take interest in the action and setting of the story and begin to participate in a "story world" before response can occur on other dimensions such as connecting the story to their lives or reflecting upon the story, its construction, or its authorship (Thomson, 1987). The reader, after taking unreflective interest in the story, may then evoke and enter what Bruner (1986) describes as a "landscape of action" that is directly stimulated by the facts of the story. Such interest and participation are a prerequisite to engagement on "the landscape of consciousness," in which the reader is pulled by the possibilities and potentialities of the story facts into "what those involved in the action know, think or feel, or do not know, think or feel" (p. 14).

Many other average or less engaged readers tend to take only an unreflective interest in action, or may proceed to read in a more engaged fashion, but still only on "the landscape of action." These readers do not go beyond the text, they do not actively create meaning as they elaborate upon the story experience (Thomson, 1987; Wilhelm, 1992). Enciso (1992) points out that as Barthes (1986) suggests, these readers are often bored by reading, because without engagement on both of these landscapes the reader is unable to "produce the text, play it, release it, make it go" (p. 63).

## Pulling in Reluctant Readers

But what about my many less engaged readers? In spite of these views on productive reading, a body of research on remedial reading supports the view that many less proficient readers do not naturally and spontaneously experience literature as participants. This lack of involvement suggests why they are reluctant to read and have negative attitudes toward reading. It also suggests why a highly participatory activity such as drama or creative activities such as visual art, used in conjunction with the reading of particular stories, might help them to experience stories in the highly satisfying way of engaged readers.

Most of the research regarding remedial or less proficient reading focuses on word identification and provides little insight into the obstacles and operational difficulties experienced by these readers. The studies that have been conducted strongly suggest that these readers do not make use of a productive conception of reading or the strategies necessary to consummate the sort of reader/text relationship that allows for an "aesthetic" (Rosenblatt, 1978) literary transaction and experience. So, I found myself asking, how can classroom activity help students to take on this kind of active reading role and to rethink the nature of the reading act?

Less proficient readers have been shown to read more slowly and less accurately than better readers. They read in local, piecemeal ways and do not make use of either extratextual information such as their personal experiences, known as schematic knowledge, or larger units of intratextual information, such as a sense of textual configuration and coherence (Cromer, 1970; Daneman & Carpenter, 1980; Perfetti & Lesgold, 1979). Yet the use of extratextual information to create global meanings is a process necessary to the creation and sustaining of what Edmiston (1991) calls "a drama world," which suggests that drama would be one way of helping students to bring their background experiences, schema knowledge, interests, desires, and questions to bear on the reading act.

Johnston (1985) has posited that reading problems result from a combination of negative attitudes, conceptual difficulties, and self-defeating strategies. I thought this was true of many of my own students. Gambrell and Bales (1986) found further that lower-ability readers did not "spontaneously employ mental imagery as a strategy," therefore depriving them of full evocation and participation in a story world. And less proficient readers studied by Purcell-Gates (1991) were also at a loss for strategies for stepping into and sustaining "envisionments." They did not make use of strategies for creating meaning by building relationships with characters, taking their perspectives, and imagining and visualizing secondary worlds.

## Turning Reading into an Active Process

These studies imply that less proficient readers tend to conceive of reading as a decoding process rather than as active meaning-making (Gambrell & Heathington, 1981), an attitude that is certainly reinforced by traditional questioning and discussion patterns regarding literature. Less engaged readers' approach to reading is passive; the text itself is regarded as expressing meaning to be received, instead of constructed (Johnston & Winograd, 1983). This was certainly the case of many of my own student readers, as evidenced by their initial reading attitude inventories.

As I began to think about using new classroom techniques to support the notion of reading as the active construction of meaning, I found that the use of dramatic and artistic activity to help readers both experience and learn from text is supported by a wide variety of research in language, literacy, learning, and cognition throughout various content areas (Barnes, 1986; Knapp, Stearns, John, & Zucker, 1988; Rosenblatt, 1978; Vygotsky, 1978; Wade, 1983). Active, participatory experiences enhance motivation and concept attainment (Bransford, 1979; Reid, 1988). Active participation, such as that incorporated in the creation of drama and visual art, creates a context for more sophisticated comprehension and the creation of elaborated meanings made with text because background schemata are necessarily activated and created, a foundational aspect of proficient reading (Hansen, 1981; Langer, 1984).

Rosenblatt (1978, 1982) has repeatedly stressed that "response" to literature is not something a text may "do" to a reader, but is instead a highly complex production of meaning. Rosenblatt (1978) points out the difference between the text, made up of words on a page, and the aesthetic experience, or "lived-through evocation," of the literary work. A reader's reflection on those experiences is what is organized into an interpretation (pp. 69–70). Further, Rosenblatt (1982) emphasizes that reading is an experience and that as teachers "our initial function is to deepen the experience . . . to return to, relive, savor, the experience" (p. 275).

Less proficient and less engaged readers must learn to think differently about the reading act and learn how to participate in the experience of literature and construction of literary meaning. My own classroom experience told me that this engagement will not occur spontaneously, but that it might be taught through the modeling of expert reading strategies and the use of participatory literary activities. As I wrote in my journal:

> It's becoming clear to me that reading is one of the creative arts. The reader has to develop and use artistic tools to create people and pictures. But how can I convince my students of this; give them this experience of reading as artistic creation? Maybe by using activities such as drama and art that encourage and scaffold active response? And that can show, right out in the open, what the reader is doing and the meaning that has been created? (October 1992)

Semiotic theory based on Pierce (1931/1958) argues that artistic sign systems have similar potential to linguistic ones in their power to represent knowledge, facilitate learning, and form new experiences and concepts; and that artistic representations are used by readers creating and responding to "story worlds" involved with transactions with texts (cf. Smagorinsky & Coppock, 1994). According to this view, readers construct a reality rather than discover it, and can construct it only through signs and in contexts that validate the use of the signs. Pierce is particularly insistent on the vital role of the icon, or concrete image, in all thought and communication, arguing that "The only way of directly communicating an idea is by means of an icon; and every indirect method of communicating an idea must depend for its establishment upon the use of an icon" (vol. 2, p. 158). In other words, if I say the word "apple," it means nothing unless you picture an apple in your mind. The word is a symbol that evokes an icon, or concrete image. If the word doesn't evoke a picture, no meaning has been made.

If iconic response is prerequisite to other forms of response, then reluctant readers might benefit from learning to project concrete, iconic representations of stories such as those achieved through activities such as drama and visual art. They then might be able to sustain or extend these representations in their mind, and use them as objects to think with.

So it was that 12 weeks into the school year, my students and I set off on an exploratory journey to investigate the extent to which drama might help less proficient readers to engage in the activities of more proficient readers, and to reconceive of the act of reading and of themselves as readers.

The questions driving this classroom study included:

- How might drama guide and scaffold student readers' development of the productive response of more expert readers, as defined by the activities of Cora, Ron, and Joanne?
- How might dramatic activity guide and support student efforts to fill textual gaps and to elaborate on and move around in textual worlds?
- How might drama engender reflection about the reading experience and the students' conceptions of the reading act itself?

## THE STUDENTS: KEVIN, MARVIN, AND LIBBY

The drama study involved all of my students enrolled in the two reading/language arts classes that mainstreamed the school's EEN (exceptional educational needs) population of students labeled both LD (Learning Disabled) and ED (Emotionally Disturbed). All students participated in the pre- and postdrama evaluation procedures and were observed throughout the project. Both classes included students who regarded themselves as nonreaders, who were regarded by teachers as less proficient readers, and who expressed in various ways their lack of motivation and resistance to reading.

For the purpose of collecting and analyzing a manageable set of data, I chose three case study students (from my original set of nine case study students) to help me tell a coherent story about drama as a way of entering and responding to literature. These three were students for whom drama seemed to work in powerful ways, and that is why I have chosen to tell their stories.

The first student, Kevin, was a regular education student considered to be a less proficient and unmotivated reader both by himself and his previous teachers; the second student, Marvin, was labeled both LD and ED; and the third student, Libby, was labeled LD but differed from many of her classmates because she enjoyed reading on her own. The students were selected on the basis of how well they represented a cross-section of students having some difficulty with their reading and response, and on their availability for interviews during my one free period.

Kevin was fairly representative of approximately 40 percent of the regu-

lar education students in the two study classes who indicated on the
prestudy survey that they were "nonreaders," that they read "rarely," and
that they regarded reading solely as a "school activity."

A small, wiry, and very pleasant boy, Kevin could not seem to sit still.
Several of his past and present teachers indicated that he could be ADHD
(Attention Deficit/Hyperactivity Disorder), but a formal referral had not yet
been made. He wore flannel shirts and a hunting jacket with a tag flapping
on the back. He owned a game farm at home, which he ran by himself, and
demonstrated complete devotion to hunting. He expressed that reading was
"a boring waste of time," though his test results on the Analytical Reading
Inventory (Woods & Moe, 1989) placed him on the seventh grade level for
Word Recognition and the fifth grade level for Independent Comprehension. Kevin was described by another teacher as "fairly average, at best" and
by another as "a squirrely kid, never serious . . . a pain in the butt."

In his initial interview, Kevin indicated that he "never read stories. I
mean, what for?" but that he did sometimes read "to learn things, you know.
Like about hunting and fishing or raising animals." His only extracurricular
reading was *Field and Stream* magazine.

Marvin (who was introduced at the beginning of Chapter One) was
fairly representative of the EEN (exceptional educational needs) students,
most of whom indicated that they were "poor readers," that they "never"
read, and that they regarded reading solely as a "school activity" that should
be avoided or faked whenever possible. Marvin was a big boy for his age,
both heftier and taller than his teachers, and was a very low ability reader.
He liked to wear black Metallica t-shirts and unlaced black Nike high-top
basketball shoes. His test results indicated a second grade level for Word
Recognition and a first grade level for Independent Comprehension. His
scores were approximately one to two grade levels below his LD classmates.

Marvin was often in trouble for hitting and pushing other students, and
for constantly requesting hall passes to go the restroom. A former teacher
told me: "He can't read. He'll never be a reader." Early in the year, one
of Marvin's most frequently invoked expressions was: "Reading is stupid!"
Marvin stated that he "never" read outside school. In fact, according to all
of his teachers, he rarely read in school, usually bothering other students,
acting out, or staring into space when given reading time. Marvin went so
far as to state: "It's not like I'm missing something [by not reading]."

Libby was a very small and slightly built girl with long, straight brown
hair. She was very serious and shy and seemed to blend inconspicuously
into the class, never drawing attention to herself. She preferred t-shirts and
jeans, often wearing subdued colors such as watery yellows or greens. The
Analytical Reading Inventory indicated that she could read independently
and recognize words on the fifth grade level.

Libby represented an entirely different kettle of fish, for despite her LD label, she indicated that "I like reading" and was often seen carrying and reading books. However, she felt that she was not a good reader because she had trouble answering questions about what she had read and performed poorly on quizzes and tests regarding her reading. She reported that she liked "stories about girls like me," but that she had trouble understanding stories "where the characters aren't like me." She disliked most of the reading she did for school except "when I get to choose." She particularly liked series of books such as the American Girls, Baby-sitters Club, and Nancy Drew. She told me that she disliked school because "all you do is sit, sit, sit and write, write, write . . . you never get to do anything. . . . I don't like school 'cause you can't do what you want. School blocks you from what you like to do." She told me that she could learn more staying at home and "reading what I want." She liked only the social aspect of school: "I like to see my friends." Her favorite activity was horseback riding, which she did once a week at a local farm. "I like working in a horse barn. In the barn I get to do and learn things."

## BEFORE DRAMA

For the 12 weeks prior to the use of drama as an intervention, I collected information and coded student response to stories into 10 dimensions, as described previously in the chapter about Ron, Joanne, and Cora. In contrast to the rich response data revealed by these three engaged readers, Kevin, Marvin, and Libby related little codable data about what they did as readers to evoke and reflect on story worlds.

### Literal Reading: But It Doesn't Say

Libby was by far the most active reader of the three, and did indicate some awareness of her reading strategies and could report on seeing story worlds and relating to characters in particular kinds of stories. In conversation and her literary letters about her free-choice reading, Libby was able to discuss characters' appearances and settings. She almost always did so by comparing characters to people she knew—usually her sister or her friend Jenna. Nearly all characters looked like and reminded her of a small group of people she knew and liked. However, when reading a story in class that was less familiar to her than the stock characters and situations of her favorite series, she often looked surprised and was unable to answer questions about character and setting. "It's really hard to tell," she'd report, "the book really doesn't say much stuff about how things are." She often told me that the stories we read in class were "kind of plain." When I pressed her on what she meant by this, she told me that "It's the characters. I don't feel like they're like me. I don't get the story. It's just kind of plain. Nothing is happening. I don't feel like I know anybody so I don't like it very much."

Though she was able to evoke characters and story worlds in particular kinds of books, Libby had great difficulty in doing so with unfamiliar material. She recognized the differences in her various reading experiences, but she seemed at a loss about how to engage with unfamiliar stories in the same way as she did with her favorite books, which she liked because "you get to know the same characters over and over again, or new ones kind of like people you really know." Reading was better for her, she told me, "when I don't work so hard on the words because I already know stuff about the people and places." (This demonstrates the importance of previous life experience and the activation of this prior knowledge, or "schema," to reading.)

Then there was Marvin. On one occasion during this first part of the year, I was reading a baseball story with Marvin. He read aloud that "Jack slid into second and kuh-nocked his kuh-nee," pronouncing both silent k's. When asked what a "kuh-nee" could possibly be, Marvin shrugged. "I just told you what it says. How should I know what it means?" Marvin often indicated that it was the reader's job to pronounce words, but not to make meaning. When asked if he could "see" what was happening in the story, Marvin replied, "No." Marvin offered that he had both played baseball and been a spectator at baseball games. So he was asked what body parts one was likely to injure when sliding into second base. Eventually, Marvin acknowledged that the "kuh-nee" was probably a "knee."

Later in the story I asked Marvin who was behind the plate calling balls and strikes. "It doesn't say," he informed me, which was true in the literal sense.

"But Marvin," I asked, "you play baseball. Who calls balls and strikes?"

"The umpire," he replied. "But it doesn't say who's doing it here!" When I pursued the issue, he pushed the story across the desk to me and said, "Okay, you find it. Go ahead. You find it then!"

Marvin was not creating or visualizing a story world in his head, nor was he bringing his life to literature to construct a meaningful experience with the text. Further, he expected everything of importance to be clearly stated in the text.

I had a similar experience with Kevin as the class began reading *The Incredible Journey*. I asked Kevin what Mrs. Oakes looked like. "It doesn't say," he answered.

"But what do we know about her?" I persisted.

Kevin became cautious. "Well, it says she's middle-aged . . . she cleans

and cooks . . . sort of a maid . . . she lives down the road with her husband . . ."

"So," I asked triumphantly, springing the trap, "what might she look
like? What clothes will she wear to the house? What color hair? Do you think
she likes the animals?"

Now Kevin was exasperated. "It doesn't SAY," he replied testily. Later
during our conference he told me, "I know what the story says. It's not fair
for you to ask me what it doesn't say."

As an experiment, I asked several less proficient readers, including
Kevin and Marvin, to select a Mrs. Oakes lookalike from several photographs cut out of magazines. One photograph was of a young, stylishly
dressed career woman in high heels, carrying a briefcase. Another was of
an older, grandmotherly type baking bread, and so on. The students were
unwilling to make a choice. "We really don't know what she looks like," one
student complained. "There are no pictures of her in the book," another
told me by way of explaining why he was not sure. Oddly enough, the book
had included an engraved picture of Mrs. Oakes that neither student had
noticed or processed.

That next Monday I asked another group of less engaged readers, including Libby, to read an Eskimo legend. The story was short, economically
told, and highly suggestive. After reading it, the students were asked to describe the landscape of the story, the houses, what the people looked like,
and how they dressed. Their primary response, despite the fact that they
knew it was an Eskimo story: "It doesn't say." Libby told me that there was
"nothing there to get. It [the story] made me feel kind of dumb."

I asked the students about the landscape near the Arctic Circle, and
together they could describe it beautifully, with tundra adorned by wolves
and icebergs dotted with seals and polar bears. References were made to the
scenery in the movies *White Fang* and *Never Cry Wolf*.

The students knew what Eskimos looked like and about igloos and even
eating whale blubber. But they used none of this information to build a
story world, however, because the text did not include the information and
the students did not instantiate it. "It doesn't really say anything," Libby
told me. She, like her classmates, did not seem to recognize the inferential
and elaborative work that the story was asking her to do.

## Passive Reading: Tell Me What It Says

Like many of their classmates, neither Kevin nor Marvin played an
active role in creating meaning with text. Neither brought his life to literature nor took a literary experience back to his life. Neither indicated in any
way that he had "experienced" literature at all. Both conceived of reading

as the decoding of words. Marvin did not expect reading to be meaningful, and if he had a goal it was to identify individual words successfully; for Kevin, if meaning existed it was "in there," inside the text waiting to be discovered. Successful reading was being able to answer factual questions about text to the teacher's satisfaction.

Though Libby had a different idea about reading that she did for herself, she too seemed trapped by the idea that good reading—for school, anyway—was answering someone else's questions. And she seemed very tied to textual details, failing to build on these details and elaborate textual suggestions or possibilities.

Marvin revealed that the whole of his reading instruction over the past several years had been exposure to DISTAR (Direct Instructional System for Teaching Reading, Engelmann & Osborn, 1976), a method in which students repetitively identify letters and words, and that he had rarely read stories or been read to. He had no memory of reading picture books or having enjoyed or completely read a book. When I once asked him what he could "see" as he read a particular passage, Marvin replied, "See? I don't see anything, man, nothin' but words!" For Marvin, reading certainly was "stupid," as meaningless as lists of nonsense words like "kuh-nocked" and "kuh-nees."

Kevin offered that he had read "lots of stories, mostly from the big book [anthology] they give you in English." For him, successful reading was "being able to answer the questions at the end . . . to know characters' names and what happened to them and stuff . . . basically you have to tell the teacher what it says."

For Kevin, stories were particularly "dumb. They're confusing and you can't really learn much stuff from them. Not like from a magazine." For Kevin, a story didn't provide information efficiently, and he had no sense that there was an experience to be created and valued through reading.

For Libby, enjoyable reading experiences were about "something you know about"; the power of literature to provide new experiences and to help the reader enter new perspectives seemed inaccessible to her.

These students' past reading experiences and schooling appear to have given them a reductionist, information-transmission view of reading. For Marvin, reading had consisted of words, and he did not expect that the words would work together to express any meaningful message. Reading, for students like Kevin and Marvin, was not creating and imagining meanings (Enciso, 1990), completing the openness of the text (Eco, 1978), filling gaps (Iser, 1978), or reading along indices (Barthes, 1986), to build up meanings throughout the course of a reading. What Bruner (1986) calls the "landscape of consciousness" never entered into the reading they or Libby did. The experience of reading was, at best, the passive reception and then the retelling of what, according to Kevin, "some book is telling you, or trying to tell you."

This flies in the face of current reader-response theory, whether from schema-theoretic, psycholinguistic, or developmental orientations, which has come to view reading as a transaction between reader and text that constitutes an "experience" (Rosenblatt, 1978), as a purposeful meaning-making activity (Goodman, 1982), and as a "heightened sensory activity that imagines meanings" (Enciso, 1992). Reader-response theory argues that personal involvement and imaginative evocation of a text are necessary to the experience of a secondary world. This experience is the purpose of "aesthetic," or literary reading, and is a prerequisite to any interpretation and reflection upon that world. Without such an evocation, there is no experience, and therefore nothing to think about. Reading, in Marvin's words, must indeed be impossibly "stupid" for those readers who do not know how to evoke and enter a secondary world.

Throughout the first 12 weeks of the school year, neither Kevin nor Marvin demonstrated any sense that this meaning-making was what reading was really about. Though Libby created meaning as she read, she did not seem to create new meanings, but rather revived old ones. Neither boy showed the ability or inclination to enter or evoke a story, or any sense that they might control strategies that would allow them to do so. Libby did not seem to see or experience new kinds of stories, and I had little evidence that she reflected on stories or used them to think with. I presumed that all three possessed the cognitive ability to evoke a secondary world and to consider and reflect upon the meaning of such a world. I had observed that they were, after all, quite adept at engaging with television shows and inferring character or mood in real life. Kevin, a student in my first-hour class, liked to make announcements as I entered the room such as "He's in a bad mood today!" based on casual observation (when he made such pronouncements, he was usually right).

Through various techniques of story drama, I hoped to provide these readers with procedures that would enable them to evoke story worlds, to help them make inferences about characters and their situations, and thus find reading literature to be a rewarding experience.

## DRAMATIC HAPPENINGS

At this point the drama phase of the project began; for approximately eight weeks the students engaged in a variety of drama activities directly connected to the stories they were reading.

For my classroom purposes, I used both techniques of story theater, by which I mean the enactment of described story events, and techniques of "story drama." For the story drama activities, I used Heathcote's (1984, 1990) definition of drama. Heathcote advocates isolating moments or details from stories to create dramatic encounters that will require entry into that story moment, elaboration of it, the taking on of other perspectives, and, consequently, a challenge to the students' own current ways of thinking. Heathcote (1984) argues that "Drama is human beings confronted by situations which change them because of what they must face in dealing with those challenges" (p. 48). In drama you "put yourself into other people's shoes and by using personal experience to help you to understand their point of view you may discover more than you knew when you started" (p. 44). What is called "story drama" in this study is any activity that requires entering a character's point of view or attitude and enacting a situation or conflict that involves it. These activities were suggested by the stories we read, but were not bound by them.

All of my students first participated in several drama activities that were tied to a class reading of Sheila Burnsford's (1960) novel *The Incredible Journey* and later to class readings of various short stories and some nonfiction pieces regarding particular issues such as animal rights.

Story theater activities were used to play out the text of the story. Story drama activities were used to express, explore, and elaborate story understandings and possibilities. The story drama activities described in the following list were largely inspired by the work of Edmiston (1991). Brian Edmiston was also personally quite helpful as he discussed the use of such activities with me and helped with preliminary coding of videotaped sequences of students involved in the drama. The first, revolving role drama, was a daily activity; the others were used once or sometimes twice during these eight weeks of intense dramatic activity.

1. *Revolving Role Drama.* The staple of our drama activity was the daily use of a revolving role drama. Each day we took on character roles and enacted particular scenes that were suggested by the story. We did the drama before reading the parallel scenes in the text so that we could bring our own experience with the characters' problems and dilemmas to our reading. In each activity the students were asked to take on another perspective, usually that of a story character, and to visualize the story world and enact movement and interaction within that world. The students acted out their scenes in pairs, subsequently switching their roles and partners once or twice during each class. See Appendix B for a set of lesson plans using revolving role drama to explore our class reading of *The Incredible Journey.*
2. *Dramatic Play.* Students were given a prompt or situation to be used as

a stimulus for imagining and filling out a story event. The prompt usually came from the story itself, as students were asked to take on the roles of story characters imagining and enacting the psychological and physical activities that would follow a particular stimulus.

3. *Guided Imagery.* Students were asked to imagine scenes, often along with the guide of my visual description or musical accompaniment, and to subsequently write about or visually depict their conceptions of these particular scenes as they mentally experienced them. Some of the visual depictions were used as "tableaux" or as "sets" for role-playing scenes.

4. *Snapshot and Tableaux Dramas.* Students were asked to physically or artistically depict the "freezing" of particular scenes as moments in time that showed physical or emotional relationships, and displayed character gestures, expressions, and activities. When a scene had been frozen I usually asked them to provide a headline or caption for the picture, and sometimes to explain how and why they had created it. Students also drew such "snapshots" or series of such snapshots in a technique called "tableaux drama," which is the visual depiction of a story sequence through the use of several pictures and accompanying captions or scripts.

5. *Analogy Dramas.* Students were asked to write and perform dramatic vignettes that in some way paralleled a story situation. I asked them to imagine a similar situation in their own lives, or in the life of someone else they knew, and to play out what would happen.

6. *To Tell the Truth Game.* Based on the old TV game show, several students at a time played the parts of characters. These characters were interrogated about their story lives by judges who decided who had most convincingly "become" that character.

7. *Correspondence.* Students wrote and responded to diaries, postcards, letters, and advertisements in the role of story characters.

8. *Missing Scene Scripts.* After identifying scenes that were suggested but left out of the text, students wrote and produced vignettes that filled these gaps, elaborated on story events, or explored alternate story possibilities.

9. *Newscast.* Students produced a videotaped news show about *The Incredible Journey* that involved interviewing characters, reporting on their activities, and editorializing on particular actions and decisions.

## THE MOVES THEY MADE

In contrast to the first 12 weeks of school, once we began these drama activities, Kevin, Marvin, Libby, and many others began to make new moves to create story worlds, to connect to these worlds, and to reflect upon them. I used some of the dimensions of response gleaned from Ron, Cora, and

Joanne (see Chapter Three) to code and organize the emerging new reading activities of these three less engaged readers.

### Entering the Story World

Langer (1989) has argued that readers must "enter an envisionment" as a prerequisite to experiencing text. Blunt (1977) and Thomson (1987), in their respective developmental models, place "entering the text" as the first developmental stage of response. Like many of my other students, Libby, Kevin, and Marvin demonstrated difficulty in entering story worlds. During a prestudy interview, Kevin told me that he had read the first few pages of over 10 books in the past three weeks. "I just can't seem to get into any of them," he complained. "I try, but it's just words." After reading Chapter 1 of *The Incredible Journey,* Marvin's nightly literary letter was simple: "This story is boring. I hat [hate] animels." Libby reported that "it's kind of confusing. I don't really get it."

While the students were reading Chapter 2 of *The Incredible Journey,* I asked them to enact and role-play various excerpts from the book, such as this one:

> Twenty minutes passed and no move was made; then suddenly the young dog rose, stretched himself, and stood looking intently down the drive. He remained like this for several minutes, while the cat watched closely, one leg still pointing upwards; then slowly the Labrador walked down the driveway and stood at the curve, looking back as though inviting the others to come. The old dog rose too, now, somewhat stiffly, and followed. Together they turned the corner, out of sight. (p. 21)

When the three case study students were asked to relate what had happened in this passage and what it signified, they had no reply. The passage was reread while three student volunteers slowly acted out the animals' parts. Three LD students from Marvin's class did a wonderful reenactment. Dan (as Luath the labrador) gestured to Brad, poking him. Brad (as the comfortable Bodger, the old bull terrier) brushed him off and settled himself back into a beanbag chair as if to go to sleep. Dan continued to dance around Brad, heading toward the door, returning, and gesturing to Brad.

Suddenly the student audience came to life. "The big dog [Dan] wants to leave!" Marvin practically shouted.

At a similar point in Kevin's class, Kevin had explained that "The old dog sort of wants to go, but he's lazy. My buffalo [from his game farm] is that way, the cows will all leave for the pasture and he goofs around and bellows but when they don't come back he gets up and follows them." This analogy was the first indication that Kevin had made connections from his own life to help create the life of a story. In her class, Libby role-played this scene with two friends. "It was cool," she said. "I could kind of see and feel what was happening." I asked her to describe what she was feeling more exactly. "It was like the dog saying, 'Let's be adventurous, let's do something.'"

What Benton (1983) calls a "secondary world" had been made accessible to these readers through the dramatic reenactment, and with it meanings came alive.

The three animals were then interviewed at a postchapter news conference, with the class playing the part of reporters. Students spontaneously stood as they peppered the animals with questions: Why were they leaving? How did they feel about their departure? Did they think they were prepared? What did they expect from the trip? What would have been said in this scene if they could talk? The questions showed the students retrospecting and predicting, visualizing, and empathizing, operating on the landscapes of action and of consciousness. In addition, students elaborated on the story, filling textual gaps and imagining possibilities. As they did so, they overtly modeled different types of productive, meaning-creating response for their classmates.

That night, Marvin wrote me his longest literary letter to date: "I like the dogs and the cat becaus they are nice. I think they will like to do things together and that they will make the 250 miles to be home. I hope so."

Kevin wrote, "I think they will have to hunt to stay alive. It will be a hard trip for dogs and a cat. Maybe this will be a good book."

Throughout the study, dramatic activities regarding a story helped students to enter the story world, and this ability to enter a particular story was sustained through succeeding chapters involving the same characters without further reenactments and through rereadings not accompanied by drama.

Other information from these students (in the form of video tapes, literary letters, journals, my own observations, and running assessments of each student) also indicated that by the end of the study these students and their classmates were "entering" more stories more readily, and could more easily identify when they did not, sometimes articulating particular reasons why the entry was difficult.

### Seeing the Story World

Before beginning Chapter 3 I asked the students to engage in dramatic play in order to visualize the secondary world of the story.

"We are the animals," I prompted the students. "Where are we?"

"In the woods," someone answered.

"Okay. It's morning. We had a hard day yesterday. How do we feel waking up after the first day of a hard journey? What do we see? What are we planning to do next?"

After a short episode of dramatic play, the students were asked to write the diary entry of one of the animals, and then to share those entries. Kevin wrote in his response journal: "I'm hungry. I can see the sun rising through the trees. I'm stiff from sleeping on the ground and my shoulders hurt. I'm excited to get going, and do some hunting."

When I spoke to Kevin, he indicated that he was comparing an experience he had had camping out during a hunting trip to the animals' experience in the book. He concluded our conversation by saying, "This is really getting good." To which he added, "Sometimes I do like reading, you know."

Libby wrote that "It's pretty dark under all the pine trees and so we slept pretty late we were so tired. I think we need to find the old road again." Libby told me that "It reminded me of being in the woods. . . . When I read best I guess I feel like I'm in a drama. I make up surroundings and make up scenes. I understand it better." A bit later she advised me that "Writing and reading is easier if you are a character. It's harder to write if you're not somebody. You should let us do more of that." (This points out that drama, in which you have to become somebody and take a perspective, can help students write as well as read.)

Throughout the study, my students indicated that they consciously brought their experience and knowledge of the world to the drama world.

"You have to," one boy told me, "you have to think when did I feel like that or when did I see something like that . . . otherwise you can't get started [with the drama]." This reference to their own experiences was something Kevin, Marvin, and many other students did not indicate doing while reading before we began to use drama, and that Libby had difficulty doing with new material.

Individual checksheets indicated that students who did not report visualizing a story world before the study regularly did so in both the four weeks after using drama and throughout the remaining semester of the school year. Anecdotal evidence indicated that this change came about at least partly because of the dramatic activities themselves, and partly because of the sharing of response that drama engendered. Late in the school year one girl revealed that she couldn't "get over the idea" that she should be in a play or a movie as she read. She also said that she referred to dramatic activities experienced several months earlier when she reflected upon the experience of the story. Some students, like Libby, made an explicit connection between the experience of reading and participation in drama.

## Seeing What's Happening

As we continued our reading, I occasionally asked different students to perform "snapshot dramas," freezing their bodies into particular scenes at a moment in story time, showing the physical relationships of characters to each other, and displaying their gestures, expressions, and activities.

On one occasion I asked students to "freeze the movie in your head" and to sketch out or make notes about what they saw. Next, I asked students to create visual "tableaux"—or poster-size pictures—illustrating a sequence of events, and to share these, in character, with a group interested in their adventures. Many students had difficulty with this task, wondering how to portray the setting. I told them the author had left it up to them to "fill in" details that had been left out of the text. As the students made their tableaux, I encouraged them to fill the pictures with weather, artifacts, and other items that would fit the story world of that particular scene.

At the end of Chapter 9, I asked students to become Tao the cat or one of the two dogs, Luath or Bodger. I then asked them, as characters, to create postcards of three scenes from the story that were most important and meaningful to them. They were to write a note to their owners on the reverse side, commenting on the scene displayed on the postcard. Groups of three were formed of the different characters. Postcards were then shared and discussed, in character, in the groups.

On one of Marvin's postcards he had a picture of a raging river. It was almost completely water, with one tree on a far bank. The note read:

*Dear Elizabeth,*

*I never should of swum across this raging river. But I did and my head go bashed in by a log. I didnt know what hit me. A little girl took care of me cuz I couldnt hear. She remind me of you so I hurryed to catch up with the dogs so I could get home.*

*Sined, Toa.*

Here Marvin demonstrates empathy with the cat, her feelings of regret about crossing the river, feelings about missing her owner, and her motivation for continuing the journey—as well as composing the longest piece of writing that any of his present or previous year's teachers had seen from him.

## Relating to Characters

Before reading the final chapter, I arranged for students to play a variation of the old "To Tell the Truth" game. Four students at a time played the part of one character. Their job was to do the best possible job of becoming the character, thereby convincing the "expert panel" that he or she was the most credible "real" character.

A second set of students played the part of this "expert panel," which would judge which student responded most like the character, thereby earning their votes. The rest of the students were other characters from the book who asked questions of the four students claiming to be Bodger, Tao, Luath, or one of the minor characters.

In this way students had the opportunity both to become a character and to play the part of an expert reader, testing elaborated ideas of what a character was like. This role-playing required a building of information throughout the reading of the text, a reading along what Barthes calls "indices."

When Marvin was on the expert panel, he asked those students posing as Tao: "What would you have done if you hadn't got your hearing back?"

Marvin was posing an elaboration on the story, a "What If" question, because in the story Tao does recover her hearing and then leaves the isolated Nurmi family to find the dogs and continue their journey homeward. This elaboration was a clear demonstration of Marvin's engagement, that he was "playing" the text and making it "go," as Barthes would put it.

During a different round of the game, Kevin explained why he did not choose Contestant Number Three as Bodger. "He said he looked healthier than when he left. But everybody here knows Bodger got hurt by the bear and he was in the fight with the collie so he musta had scars and stuff so he couldn't of looked all that good." All this from the reader who couldn't make any guesses about Mrs. Oakes's appearance from the available details. Acting out the scenes with the bear and the collie appears to have helped Kevin to see the scene, to enter the story world, and to see the consequences of those actions in his mind.

Reports of empathy for the main characters were very high throughout the study, both during dramatic activity and in readings of the same story that followed the activity. Students who never reported experiencing relationships to characters before the use of drama later reported engaging in a variety of relationships: becoming a friend or confidant, merging with the character, and inhabiting a parallel universe to the character. The drama activities appear to have made characters come alive for them to the degree that they recognized story characters as people to understand and have relationships with.

Interestingly, each day when we would role-play some scenes that had happened or that anticipated what would be happening to the animals during that day's reading, Libby would immediately pair up with her friend Jenna. Jenna seemed to invite Libby into the drama world and to make particular moves within the world. When I talked to the girls about this, Libby told me that "Jenna helps me to become a character and to figure out how they're going to act then I can go from there." When I asked how Jenna helped her, she said that "In the drama, I try to do what she does. I don't call her by her name but by the character's name. She asks me questions and I try to answer them. . . . She listens to me. . . . I allow her to express her thoughts and feelings. I try to make her feel happy if she's sad and I react the way I should. Maybe she'll help me to solve problems, maybe say, 'What do you think we should do?' or 'Remember when you did such and such?'"

Libby told me during a different interview that during her reading of the story "I felt like I was like Tao [the cat] . . . quiet, shy, can do stuff for myself even though people think I need help. OK on my own but I like to be around my friends." She reported that at the beginning of the book, she had "trouble understanding the characters . . . but now I can see the animals are just like people." When I asked her how she came to understand the animals, she said, "By being them with my body. I got to do things and make decisions and things with my body when I was imagining I was them so I felt like them."

For Libby much more than for the other students, using her body to do things was an important part of the dramatic experience. "I can get it because I'm doing and shaping things. Drama is like writing a story with your body." She also liked drama because "other people have to listen to you when you are a character or they won't know what to do. . . . You have to do things together." This was in contrast to most of school, during which Libby told me "everyone works alone and they don't listen to each other."

## Elaborating on the Story World

As we were reading Chapter 7, in which the little Finnish girl, Helvi Nurmi, cares for Tao, a student asked me what was happening to the dogs during the same time period. I seized this as a dramatic opportunity to demonstrate how readers are asked to fill textual gaps.

"Authors leave the reader many gaps," I told the students, "which they expect the reader to fill in. Sometimes these gaps are details, like what people are wearing or might be thinking, but sometimes they can be whole scenes, or years' worth of time which we have to create in our mind in some way consistent with the cues from the story."

I then asked the students to write out the scene they felt might be transpiring with the dogs during the same time frame when Tao's experiences with Helvi are recounted. What happened to the dogs during this time?

How are the dogs feeling and acting? What does the author expect us to know about what is happening to the dogs, and how do we know this?

Kevin wrote the following scene:

*(Night in the forest.)*
Bodger: *I sure do miss that cat.*
Luath: *You sure do miss eating the food he gets for you.*
Bodger: *Yup. That too. But I sure do miss that cat.*
Luath: *Shut up, Bodger. (wipes his eyes) (a wolf howls in the distance)*
Bodger: *I sure just felt better when she was around.*
Luath: *Me too. I wanted us all to come home together. It won't be the way I wanted it now. Maybe we should just keep going. I don't feel much like sleeping or talking tonight.*
Bodger: *Maybe we should leave a clear trail, you know, so she can follow us.*

During the "To Tell the Truth" game, Libby wrote down several questions for Tao, all of which were inference questions regarding Tao's feelings and motivations during different times in the story: "Why did you fight the MacKenzies' cats and how did you feel about it?" "How did you feel about Helvi and do you miss her?" "How would you have felt if Bodger died?"

When I observed that all of her questions were about feelings that weren't reported in the actual text, she told me that "I think reading is really about feelings, about seeing and feeling things. . . . That's what I like about the drama, in a regular class you can't share your feelings."

Though there were no indications that the less proficient readers in the study elaborated on story facts before our use of drama, they were entirely capable of doing so in the context of dramatic activity. Few students spontaneously employed such elaborative activity on their own after the study, but they did seem to recognize it as an element in a reader's repertoire, naturally elaborating when coming upon a situation that required it.

## Connecting Literature to Life

After the class had completed their reading of the book, I structured several activities, which I called analogy dramas, designed to help the students compare their lives to the story and the story world back to their lives. The first activity was called "Two-Sided Story." Students were asked to act out a scene from their lives (real or projected) that in some way paralleled a scene from the book. A second activity, "In Through the Mirror," required the animal characters to leave the story world and enter our classroom. They used what they had learned from their journey to deal with new situations and challenges.

A third activity was called "Scrooge Looking Down." Students imagined that they were being taken back in time to view scenes from their personal histories. Applying what they had learned from the experience of reading the book, they were asked how they might have lived differently or what they understood about the situation now that they had not understood at the time. Students then met as part of an "Out of Body" seminar to share and converse about their experiences.

In Kevin's scene he was looking down on himself on his first rabbit hunt. "Kevin," he said, "don't leave those other guys behind just because they're slower and noisier. Stick together. That's one thing I learned from Luath. It's just better to do things together, and you never know when you might need someone else . . ."

In such activities students often made statements about the significance of particular events, a story's central focus or meaning, and sometimes about the relationship of events to each other and how this sense of configuration or coherence helped make a rich experience for them. Though this reflective activity was not spontaneously occurring after the study, it was recognized and referred to by the students as a readerly activity, showing up continuously throughout the year in their work, and being then recorded on students' individual response checksheets. Further, when students were asked to reflect upon a story, they sometimes reported "imagining" themselves to be characters or to be in particular situations in a type of individual dramatic play.

## READING AS PLEASURE: "YOU HAVE TO LIVE THE STORY"

During a conference with Kevin, I was highlighting and describing the expert engagement strategies he had used while reading a "free choice" book. After I told Kevin that he was doing "lots of things that expert readers do," he excitedly turned to me and said, "Hey, maybe I can get good at this!"

This expression of reader agency revealed precisely the attitude I wished to engender in all my students. I didn't have much evidence of this kind that Kevin had rethought reading or himself as a reader until later in the semester. A student doing a report on Canada asked me if I knew of any stories from Canada. "I'll take him to the library," Kevin offered. "I know where all those stories are."

"Really?"

"Yeah, I checked out some of them about the gold rush in the Yukon and one on duck hunting."

Kevin, who had earlier reported that he never read stories, had been motivated to read other stories about Canada because "I liked the book [*The Incredible Journey*]."

Libby told me after the study that "I feel more equal in a drama. People listen to me more," and that "Reading after a drama is different. . . . I can see things better and I feel like I have more choices, just like in the drama." When I asked her how reading was different from drama, she revealed that "Reading is different because it's alone—but it's the same because you have to pretend you're a character and that other people are there." Libby then went on at length about how she and Jenna were using drama together as a strategy to evoke and enjoy their free reading. "We'll talk on the phone and pretend we are the characters and are solving their problems." She reported reading a book called *Me, Addy* about the Underground Railroad and that she and Jenna "played the parts" to help "us understand and think about what's happening."

Marvin's case of thinking about the act of reading is also dramatic. After validating strategies he was using to evoke text, and encouraging those strategies I saw used throughout our reading and response to *The Incredible Journey*, Marvin's attitude toward reading underwent a clear sea-change. The ED teacher (resource teacher for the emotionally disturbed) said that Marvin came into the ED resource room for three days running, announced he was going to read, and proceeded to do it for the whole period. When he was finished, he proudly announced that this "is the first book I ever read by myself." (Interestingly, it was entitled *Raging River.*) He then turned to his teacher and said, "I liked it, and I don't want anybody to ask me any questions about it."

Marvin was stating that his enjoyment and experience of the book was sufficient, and should suffice for the teacher too.

A few months after the study, when he was no longer in my class, I asked Kevin what he had learned from our story dramas.

"You have to live the story, Mr. Wilhelm," he told me. "You have to be the book." Now, when I see Kevin in the hallways, he greets me with the hang-ten sign and sometimes cries out, "Be the book!" And he is almost always carrying one.

"What story are you living now?" I'll call after him as he's jostled away by the swarming students.

It is a conversation that would have been unthinkable without our involvement with drama, which helped us to share our inner experiences of reading.

## EPILOGUE: THE POTENTIAL OF DRAMA

Kevin, Marvin, and Libby had a history of reading characterized by what Michael Smith (1992) calls "submission": They expected to receive meaning, passively, from the text. They and many of their classmates seemed to learn for the first time, through the use of story-related classroom drama, to exert "control" over the strategies and processes of meaning-construction with text. They began to see the text as a springboard for imagined possibilities.

To do so, these readers had to first achieve what I propose to call "entry" or "merging" with text. Drama, throughout this study, proved to be an effective technique for achieving entry into a textual world. Further, it provided a meaningful mode for moving around in that textual world, making meaning of it and in it, and of observing and reflecting on the world and its meaning. Drama enabled these readers to see that reading is an activity of constructing meaning, and that readers build and own this meaning.

All of these students seemed happy using drama as a response to literature, and they now seem happier about themselves as readers. Since the study, they have continued to talk about reading differently, and do more of it more profitably. They now exhibit the idea that reading is something "in the reader" and that it involves what Libby called "making choices" and "doing things," versus their previous attitude that reading was something "in the text" or "out there."

For them, reading literature has become something that needs to be created and constructed and enlivened. For the boys, reading literature has for the first time become an experience that holds out the promise of enjoyment. Even if they did not become passionate readers during the course of the study, this change of attitude had already made many things possible, such as Kevin's interest in reading wilderness stories in his free time, Marvin's pride in reading his first book, and Libby's use of drama with her friends to help her understand unfamiliar pieces of literature.

These readers seemed to suffer most from a passive view of reading and a concomitant lack of literary experiences that required their participation. Drama, by its nature an active, participatory experience, helped the students to experience a story world, sustain that experience as they continued to read, and eventually to indicate that they had reconceived the nature of reading. Drama seemed to make story language more accessible to students such as Marvin who had clear language difficulties, perhaps by generating interest and activating the necessary schemata. Drama also allowed for the sharing of response activities and for the "trying on" of more proficient readers' moves and strategies, such as when Libby mimicked the moves of her friend Jenna. This involvement, in turn, may eventually help them to become more engaged and powerful readers.

This classroom study suggests that though less proficient readers may have difficulties decoding words and processing figurative language and implicit meanings, the real problem may reside within the reader's view—and resultant process—of reading. These readers may have been taught or have interpreted instruction in such a way that they attended only to surface features of local text and had therefore never learned to create unified worlds and meanings by using the text more globally as a guide or "blueprint." Teachers such as myself may help such students enormously as we come to more fully understand actual processes of making meaning through reading.

In any event, the use of drama helped less proficient readers overcome their local-level decoding problems and enjoy the experience of literature. It aided them in responding on many of the sophisticated dimensions used by more expert readers of their age. Using new strategies to produce meanings helped them to also rethink the act of reading and themselves and their roles as readers.

The success of this exploration leads to other, more specific and focused questions that are worth researching. Do specific types of dramatic activity encourage activity on particular dimensions of response? Is drama useful in developing and extending the response of all readers, including those who are already highly engaged? Is drama an effective prewriting technique for reflective essays about issues the students may not have personally experienced?

Other creative artistic activities may also hold promise for changing student attitudes toward reading and their conceptions of the reading act, and for developing previously unexplored dimensions of response. I believe these questions and others are worth the attention of classroom teachers and teacher-researchers. The possibilities are dramatic.

# CHAPTER FIVE

# Reading Is Seeing

I used to work with a woman whose husband did the hiring for a nationally recognized investment firm. At a party, I asked him what kind of profile he used when he filled sales positions at his company. "It's easy," he told me. "I only hire teachers."

"Why?" I asked.

"Think about it," he replied. "Teachers are selling something that their clients really don't think they want, and they're doing it to groups of 30 or more five or six times a day. To be successful, they have to be very organized, very enthusiastic, and they have to make one helluva sales pitch.

"So I hire them and I ask them to sell something *everybody* wants *one* time a day to a group that usually averages about *fifteen*. They do a fantastic job." Then he winked at me. "And I pay them a lot more, so they're happy as clams in the summer sand."

I don't tell this story because I'd like to leave teaching to sell investments. I'm already selling the greatest futures investment there is: the education of our children. Besides, I'm about as happy as a teaching clam can be (especially in the summer!). I do tell the story to highlight that classrooms are very complex and intensely human places. Teachers deal with nearly 30 different individuals' needs several times throughout the day. In this context, it often seems that there are no unqualified successes; our successes are ephemeral, invisible, and intensely human. They can't be captured by bar graphs and percentages and numbers of happy customers. And it seems that every teaching story and every success is fraught with some disappointments.

## STILL STRUGGLING: TOMMY, WALTER, AND KAE

Even as most of my students and I were excitedly pursuing drama and finding it a powerful way to engage with and share our reading, there were a few students who seemed reluctant participants, and who continued to struggle and be frustrated by their reading and by our classroom work. As a result, I continued to struggle to help them, and I was beginning to be frustrated too. Notable among this group were two LD-labeled students, Tommy and Walter, and an ESL student named Kae.

Not entirely to my credit, I vented my frustration in my journal in the following way:

> Tommy and Walter are conspiring to give me a headache. Not just any old headache, but the pounding, throbbing, EXCEDRIN inducing, pain piercing right through to the back of your pedagogical eyeballs sort of headache. . . . They don't want to read. I'm working hard to help them, to provide them with fun and supportive things to do as they read, and they don't *even want to try*! (October 1992)

If the truth be told, there were some other seventh grade students who were providing them with considerable help in the headache induction department, but I mostly blamed Tommy and Walter. After all, they were both in my last class of the day—ninth period—and they could be the most unreasonable, resistant, class-sabotaging students of the day. These were basically good kids, and I liked them. I knew they had had trouble in school over the past few years, and that Walter had transferred into our school from a parochial school to get the extra help his parents thought he needed. They could be pleasant and likable as well as negative in their behavior.

Their frustration with school and with reading class was almost palpable by the end of the day. Some days it was as if they walked into class with a giant force field of rage or gloom hanging around their bodies. I wanted badly to help them, to create openings for literacy opportunities that they could enjoy and participate in and grow from. But sometimes I just found myself out and out frustrated. There were days when I gave up and let them just sit there. I wrote that "If we had prizes for 'Frontal Lobe Headache Maker of the Day,' Walter and Tommy would get my vote every single election" (October 1992).

Another student who concerned me was Kae. Kae was from the Hmong culture and had come to us from Laos, via Thailand and Chicago. She had arrived in the latter part of the previous school year with very limited English language skills. Kae seemed painfully shy and would not orally respond in class. I was impressed by her diligent struggles to pay attention and to complete her written work, which I was generally able to decipher and understand. She seemed to have little interaction with other students, ate lunch with other Hmong students, and seemed—to be honest—to be at least a little sad and out of place.

Of my 120-plus students who had participated in the dramatic activities during our study of *The Incredible Journey*, only 8 had written negative evaluations of the experience. Of these eight, only four had been consistently passive participants in the dramas. None had been actively resistant, instead choosing to not respond to others in the drama, or to drop out of the drama world and just act like themselves. All of these four had occasionally participated in some fashion, however muted. Nonetheless, these four students had certainly resisted full participation in the dramas. There was little evidence that they had been helped to grow as readers through the dramatic intervention. They had even indicated that they would prefer to not participate in future dramas. Of these four, of course two were Walter and Tommy. And they weren't just resistant to drama; it seemed they were resistant to everything in school except lunch and the bus ride home.

Kae, however, indicated that the drama activities were "OK" and told me that there were a few other students who had invited her in and helped her to take part in the dramas. Still, I had often observed her during the dramas to be at a loss for something to do or say; whether because she didn't understand what was going on or could not think what to do next, I just didn't know.

Kae was labeled an ESL student and participated in our ESL program. This was the first time that she had been mainstreamed into language arts classes. She told me that her family had fled from Laos to Thailand, where she lived in a camp, and that she had spent most of her time there "drawing in the sand." More than a year earlier her family had arrived in Chicago, where, she confided, she didn't like school. Kae was very small and very quiet.

When I addressed her in class she would hang her head, turning from me as if trying to hide. When I spoke to her personally, before or after class, she would always give me a very big smile of gleaming white teeth, though she would say little. When I talked to her she usually answered with pat replies. "How is it going?" She would answer, "Good." "Do you understand what we're doing?" "Pretty much. I trying." I did not give Kae an Analytical Reading Inventory, but her word recognition and comprehension seemed on a par with some of the LD students. Because the typical homework assignment each night throughout the year was for students to free-read for 20 minutes, choosing material of interest to them, Kae took the opportunity to read almost exclusively from her brother's extensive comic book collection. She did not seem to discriminate between different kinds of comics and told me simply that they were "easy to understand." She read mostly about superheroes. She told me that she liked "the pictures" and that they helped her "to understand story." Later in the year she read other comic books such as *Classics Illustrated,* which I provided, and then stories with illustrations, such as *Little House in the Big Woods.* She also pursued other reading in English, reading some of the American Girls series and short romances, which she seemed to especially enjoy. She revealed that she sometimes read in Hmong at home.

With some struggles and difficulties, she seemed to achieve some literal understanding of her reading, as evidenced by literary letters and reading logs. But she seemed to be working hard and had difficulty achieving and expressing other forms of response. Most clearly, she seemed estranged from the classroom community and had trouble taking an active part in many of our language activities. She was obviously bright and diligent. I hoped that I could find a way for her to enter into the life of the classroom and to help her improve as a speaker and listener, as well as a reader and writer.

I had also noticed that Kae liked to draw pictures; she seemed highly artistic. A few early literary letters were spontaneously accompanied by illustrations that she smilingly shared with her reading partner. On one occasion, she pointed to an illustrated letter and told me, "She understand it!"

Both Tommy and Walter were labeled LD (learning disabled) students. Both were small for their age, fragile looking. Tommy was olive-skinned, with stringy black hair swept across his forehead, and liked to wear camouflage clothing. His friends called him "The Camo Man," and his dream was to buy a car and cover it with camouflage paint. Walter had wispy blondish hair hanging in bangs in front of his eyes. Every single day, no matter what the heat, he wore a gray hooded sweatshirt, jeans, and beat-up Reebok sneakers. His moniker was "The Ninja." He made ninja stars out of paper and threatened to impale people with them.

"These are two kids we're probably just not going to get. They just don't like to read. They just refuse to," the LD teacher told me. Her description, to my mind, was fairly accurate. On the ARI (Analytical Reading Inventory, Woods & Moe, 1989), Tommy and Walter both scored on the second grade level for Independent Reading. Their scores for vocabulary and comprehension were similar—second grade—and their Instructional Reading level was only about a grade level higher—slightly above third grade. But in class, no matter how carefully I chose the material to match their abilities and interests, they refused to read. Tommy would often just sit in his desk staring straight ahead. He would become extremely angry and agitated if disturbed from his trance. No amount of coaxing or cajoling would convince him to read. "I can't do it," he'd say. "You can," I would reply. "CAN'T. Never Could. Never Will," he'd say with finality. Even when he had chosen his own book for free reading, he wouldn't crack it, or would crack it to draw pictures inside. Tommy, in fact, spent most of his active classtime drawing pictures, sequences of them such as cartoon stories, pictures of faces and animals, and ornate etchings of exotic settings and monsters and amazing machines.

Walter's reluctance to read was also interesting. He would carefully set aside the assignment and, usually, begin to "read" a book of his own. His chosen book was always filled with photographs, pictures, or drawings. He especially favored *Calvin and Hobbes* or *The Far Side* and could often be seen quietly chuckling, head down on the book. Walter did quite well on the free-reading component of the course, which made up about 40 percent of class time—for free reading itself, response to it, and sharing. But on shared readings and projects he refused to take part. "I can't read that stuff," he snarled at me on one occasion. "Why not?" I asked. "I don't know. I just CAN'T!" Walter, normally quiet and almost mousy, typically friendly and polite, would explode when pressed on this issue, the ninja side of his personality rising to the surface. On two occasions when the LD teacher gently tried to cajole him to read the assigned text for the day, or offered to help him to read along with his classmates, he threw books, once yelled an obscenity, and stormed out of the classroom.

I was agitated myself. How could I encourage these boys to read more widely, or at all? How could I convince them that reading literature was an experience worth pursuing and enjoying?

## SEEING THE VISUAL POSSIBILITY

Much of what these students revealed to me made me begin to believe that these students did not "see" anything when they read, and that therefore they could not experience and think about what they had read. They had no ownership over the process, and no sense that it could work for them in personally meaningful ways. Tommy and Walter seemed to have very low expectations of print and no sense of what to do as readers to make their print experiences meaningful. And Kae seemed to struggle with her language difficulties and not get beyond the meanings of words to see the world of a story.

I knew that visualization was considered to be an important part of reading and that it has been shown in various ways that the use of mental imagery has various powerful positive effects for readers. It has been demonstrated that visual imaging encourages students to access and apply their prior knowledge as they read, increases comprehension, and improves the ability to predict, infer, and remember what has been read (Gambrell, 1981; Gambrell & Bales, 1986; Pressley, 1977; Sadoski, 1985). Gambrell and Jawitz (1993) have also shown that the use of visual imagery while reading helps students to monitor their comprehension. Jacob (1976), in a review of imagery, has emphasized that the ability to use imagery is a central difference between good and poor readers. Yet Belcher (1981) has reported that teacher's guides designed for use with basals and anthologies rarely mention the use of mental imagery, and never as a strategy for experiencing text and improving reading ability.

So despite compelling evidence of its importance, neither teachers nor materials seem to emphasize visualization in reading as an important element of active reading, comprehension, comprehension monitoring, and response. And the need for such instruction has been demonstrated: Gambrell and Bales (1986) found that lower-ability readers did not "spontaneously employ mental imagery as a strategy," therefore depriving them of full evocation and participation in a story world. Less proficient readers studied by Purcell-Gates (1991) were also at a loss for strategies for stepping into and sustaining envisionments by building relationships with characters, taking their perspectives, and imagining and visualizing secondary worlds.

I wrote in my journal:

I'm beginning to believe that students who do not "see" what they read won't be able to do so just because I ask or tell them to! Telling them to "see what you read" just doesn't work—they don't know how to do it. I wonder whether letting them create visual art as a response to their reading would help them to start seeing how to build visual meanings from text, reinforce the importance of this, and interest them in participating more actively in class. (November 1992)

The confluence of three events helped me decide to use visual art as a classroom intervention and to pursue a study about how art might influence and help develop student response and discourse about what they had read.

First, I was interviewing Ron, whom I had decided to use for a case study early in the year. Ron had enlisted his friend Chris to read some Tom Clancy books together with him, for the purpose of "talking about it" and "doing a project together." "It's a funny thing," Ron told me. "Sometimes we'll be silently reading the same part of the book, and I'll be laughing and snorting and practically rolling on the ground, and Chris won't be giving any reaction at all." When I asked Ron why he thought that was, he replied, "I guess . . . he must not see the story the same way I do. He can't be, because for me a part might be hilarious and it doesn't affect him. He can't be seeing what I'm seeing." Later in the interview, Ron told me, "It's like he can tell me what's happened, so he knows that, but it's like he hasn't, like lived it like I have. It's not like . . . there for him or something." I found this idea of "seeing" the work in order to experience it fully a compelling idea that was corroborated by a lot of other student data that I had collected.

Later that same day I was interviewing Tommy about a one-page story called "The Dinner Party" that involves a cobra that is found underneath the table during dinner. Tommy insisted that he had experienced nothing by reading the story. When I began to poke around, asking different questions about the reading and what he thought about it, even disliked about it, he exploded: "I can't think about it, talk about it, do anything about it, if I can't see it!"

This made me pause and think. A few minutes later I was doing a cued protocol story response with Walter and the story "Larceny and Old Lace" (Arthur, 1960). At every cue he gave either no or very thin indications of what he was doing. "Nope, nothing here." When I asked what the two protagonists looked like, he indicated that "They're women, you know . . ." When pressed he indicated that they had blonde hair, red dresses, looked pretty much, he guessed, like "Mrs. Kirst," Walter's young and very athletic science teacher. I then elicited from him that he knew that the characters were former schoolteachers and were retired, and that he knew at what age people typically retired. But he had not translated this knowledge into a picture of what they might look and act like. He had not seen the world and characters of the text. At the end of the story, Walter indicated that he "didn't get it." And that the story had "done nothin' for me. Sorta boring."

The interview completed, Walter hurried back to his seat, opened *Calvin and Hobbes,* and immediately began chuckling. It was then that I experienced a teacher's epiphany. Walter enjoyed the humor of *Calvin and Hobbes,* which was often quite sophisticated, at least partly because he was helped to see and therefore experience the imagined world of the story through the cartoon pictures!

I then remembered two separate occasions when I had experienced and discussed the enthusiastic and powerful reading of two deaf children. Apparently, profoundly deaf children typically do not learn to read beyond the second or third grade level (Allen, 1986). There was a constant factor in both cases, however: both children, one a boy and one a girl, had been inveterate readers of comic books. The girl's mother told me that her daughter had "consumed" the series of comics called *Classics Illustrated* and *Classics Junior.* The boy was more typically interested in *Superman* and *Spiderman* adventure comics. My hypothesis began to develop: the pictures, paired with words, helped less engaged readers to visualize the action of a story and to understand how words suggest various characters, settings, and activities.

One of the powerful lessons my case study students taught me was later recorded in my journal:

Listen to your students! If you want to know how to teach your students, get to know them! If you want to know how to help them, look at what they can do and build from it! If you want to know what they are thinking, ask them! . . . It's almost as if Libby and Kae, Tommy and Walter and so many others have been demonstrating to me how I could help and encourage them, but it just didn't register. . . . Libby's dramatic play with Jenna in the hallway and Tommy and Walter's constant doodling . . . why not pick up on it and use it? So many kids just seem to love using the arts for any purpose, it's personal and meaningful and fun for them . . . and now it seems that visual art is helping them to understand their reading and to participate in class. (January 1993)

Eisner (1992) asserts, "We cannot know through language what we cannot imagine. The image—visual, tactile, auditory—plays a crucial role in the construction of meaning through text. Those who cannot imagine cannot read" (p. 125). And, according to my classroom experience, don't want to.

## THE VISUALIZATION PROJECT: ART IN THE CLASSROOM

So I began a second study project that ran as a sort of mini-theme through the last two and a half quarters of the school year. Though the project included all of my classes, I emphasized it most heavily in my two LD mainstreamed classes. The project was designed to convince reluctant readers that reading involved seeing, and to find ways that would scaffold and support that sort of "readerly" visualizing and image-making for the students.

The "aesthetic experience" of a textual world was first described by Rosenblatt in *Literature as Exploration* (1983) and in *The Reader, the Text, the Poem* (1978). She has stressed the difference between the "text," made up of words on a page, and the "aesthetic experience," the reader's lived-through evocation of the text as it is imagined and visualized and experienced in the mind's eye. Rosenblatt insists that reading must be seen as an experience and that teachers must help students to actualize the potential experiences of texts by helping develop their repertoire of reading strategies.

By looking back at the literacy histories I had collected from my most reluctant readers, including Tommy and Walter, I noticed that none had recalled being read to much, nor did they have any memory of ever reading picture books. I wondered if they had ever learned to "experience" literature, to evoke and "see" textual worlds in their minds. In any case, it was my job to help them do so in more vital and meaningful ways, and I set out to use their penchant for creating visual art to help them do so.

Talking to Tommy and Walter, I asked them if they had ever been able to use their artistic skills in the classroom. "Usually we get in trouble for it," Walter offered. They did remember a poster contest in science, drawing maps in social studies, and making a life-size drawing of the body's internal organs in health. Neither had yet had the opportunity to enroll in an art class. "We pretty much had to draw what we were told to," Tommy commented on these projects, "when we do what we're thinking about we pretty much get in trouble." They then proceeded to recount some of these misadventures, which often involved both of them. This was the first time that I realized that Tommy and Walter were friendly, and that they exchanged and talked about their drawings in exactly the way I was trying to encourage students to share their responses to reading.

When I talked to Kae, she said that creating art was "easier" for her than writing or talking, and that she liked to "do it when I can." She felt that people "understand my drawing" better than they understood her when she spoke and wrote. She said that reading and writing took a lot of her time and energy and that she wished there were other ways, such as art, for her to do schoolwork.

Eisner (1992) cites three critically significant aims of arts education: 1) to increase the variety and depth of meaning people can secure in their lives, 2) to develop cognitive potential, which is achieved only through the exercise of various opportunities, and 3) to achieve educational equity. These aims had certainly not been met for Tommy and Walter, nor for Kae. School had limited the variety and depth of meaning they could secure through their drawing. They were not encouraged to use their artistic strengths to develop cognitive potential in related areas, such as reading. They had been educated against the very grain of the way they liked to think about and know things. This can hardly be considered educationally equitable.

Representing ways of knowing is discovering or inventing a private world and then making it public. Tommy and Walter did not know how to invent and enter the "secondary world" (Benton, 1983; Tolkien, 1964) good readers experience when they transact with text. Kae had difficulty doing so in English and difficulty communicating about her reading with others. Visualization activities regarding literature, I was sure, could help them to do so. Representation stabilizes thought, serving what Eisner (1992) calls "a place holding function." This conception can then be shared with others, and tested, negotiated, and revised communally. The drawings of these students, I hoped, could help their responses to literature be part of our classroom community. It could then lead to the refinement of their own individual responses and reading processes, and those of the class-room community.

I had been tracking the response of all students, including these three, throughout the first quarter of the school year and then through the drama study. I continued to track their response on different dimensions as they participated in the following activities making use of visual art.

## Symbolic Story Representations

The SRI, described earlier, involves creating cutouts for characters, the reader, the author, and any props, settings, ideas, or forces that played a part in the student's reading. The students then used the cutouts, explaining them and moving them around to describe the action of the story and how the story had been read and experienced by the reader. The SRI seemed to provide a natural bridge between the drama and visualization projects. Students were necessarily representing essential story elements visually as they dramatized a story for their classmates. Their reading, made visible, could be talked about, critiqued, manipulated, and revised. New moves and elements could be added and experimented with.

## Visual Protocols

During the classroom use of visualization techniques, students were asked to read a story and to stop whenever they had formed a strong visual impression and draw a picture of that impression. Some students began to stop and draw when they felt the need to get a visual impression clear in their minds, and they were encouraged to do so. Though some students participated in cued protocols, during which they were asked to either de-scribe or draw their visual impressions at particular points in a story, Kae, Walter, and Tommy participated only in uncued protocols, so they drew pictures only when they indicated that they wanted to.

## Reading Illustrated Books

During the first part of the project, in mid-December, I brought a book cart of picture books into the classroom. Each day, I would share one of these books as a companion piece to another nonillustrated reading. We discussed how the picture books worked: how the pictures worked with the words to contribute to our experience of story. We then discussed the type of pictures the nonillustrated story might have, the sort of pictures we could imagine in our minds that would fit the story, how using different types of pictures (different color schemes, techniques, photos versus drawings, foldout, pop-up, highlighting different scenes or moods) would affect the reader's experience.

After Christmas I brought in sets of the complete series of *Asterix* and *Tintin* comic books, some copies of *Classics Illustrated,* and two copies of the illustrated Holocaust tale *Maus.* There was a stampede for these books, and it continued for months, on the part of the less proficient readers. Many of these students read nothing else but comic books for their free reading for the rest of the year. On the other hand, these illustrated books were pretty much ignored, with one or two exceptions, by the more proficient readers. (An exception was Art Spiegelman's Holocaust stories *Maus* and *Maus II,* which were read and traded by several very proficient readers and discussed at length among themselves and with both myself and the social studies teacher.)

Kae had been reading comic books since the beginning of the year and was now reading other sorts of books as well. Tommy, over the course of the next two quarters, read every single *Tintin* book and most of the *Asterix* series and did some library research to see if there were other such series of books. This activity was from a boy who had refused to read on his own for 10 weeks. Walter read most of the *Tintin* books while continuing to read his own comic books involving various superheroes. Walter also began to branch out to books with a few illustrations, such as *Scary Stories,* which had an illustration at the beginning of each story, and one or two embedded in the text. Though Tommy remained fairly reticent, Walter would often excitedly discuss the illustrations in comics and books with me, coming into class with his finger holding his page and exclaiming, "Look at this, Mr. W!"

One of their classmates and friends, a boy named Jeremy, after reading *Maus* and running to the bookstore to buy and read *Maus II,* exclaimed, "Why don't they write more books like this?" These students, I observed, enjoyed reading such books, finding something engaging, supportive, and helpful about them. Once students were introduced to picture books and encouraged to read them, they did so vigorously. I wrote in my journal that "I just have to wonder if school conveys a very limited view of literature that does not include picture books and comics, and if this limited view of literature contributes to how bummed out and distanced many of my student readers become from literature and the literary experience. School denigrates what experience is accessible to them, and denigrates how they read. Could it be?" At the same time, I wrote that, "It's amazing to me how much I enjoy reading the comics. I've spent several free-reading periods that I had intended to conference with students reading *Tintin.* So there's something in it for me too!" (January 1993).

Interestingly, the German teacher and I spoke about this phenomenon and she gave me several comic books in German, which I read with gusto.

I wrote in my journal that "Reading comic books in a foreign language gives me a little insight into why it is so supportive for kids who have trouble reading. It's much easier to figure out words from context and to follow the story line. It's a lot of fun too!" (January 1993).

## Illustrating Books

In the next stage of the project, taken up just before Christmas and continuing into the next calendar year, students were asked to illustrate nonillustrated stories that we read as a class, and then to write and illustrate their own picture books with original stories, or adaptations of stories they knew or had read. During an integrated unit with social studies, each student (as part of a learning group) performed a tableau drama of at least four poster-sized drawings. The tableaux helped to share an important myth or fable from the studied culture, and were accompanied by narrative as they were presented to the class.

## Picture Mapping

Picture mapping is a way of note-making with pictures. Students were asked to visually depict the key details of particular texts, usually nonfiction, in the most efficient way possible. Students were encouraged to draw reminders of the key details any way that they liked, and to combine several details into one drawing if they chose. It was emphasized that there was no right or wrong way to depict ideas, it simply had "to work" for the student. Students were also encouraged to graphically show how the key ideas related to each other. The picture map took the place of summarizing and note-taking, and students were allowed to use their maps to complete other assignments that required them to use information from the text.

## Collages

In this project, students were asked to create poetry and story collages that would represent their response to a particular piece of literature, usually a song or poem of their choice. The completed collage was then used as part of a presentation about their response to the literary selection, guiding the sharing of their literary response with classmates.

## THE ART OF READING

The art these students created and discussed as a response to literature typically encompassed two or three dimensions at a time, centering primarily on the dimensions of entering and seeing the story world. But once they had achieved these reading milestones, I was excited to see that they began to make moves on other response dimensions, such as considering the significance of details and how various details work together to create meaning.

## Entering and Seeing the Story World

The first thing that struck me about student response using the SRI was how naturally students of various abilities made use of it.

> After my brief presentation modeling the SRI it was like everyone knew exactly what I was talking about . . . showing what the story was about was easy for them to grasp, symbolically representing characters, settings, even ideas or forces—which I had worried would be difficult for them—did not cause the anticipated confusion. Even creating cut-outs of themselves as readers caused no consternation; everyone did it though not everyone made use of this cut-out in their presentations. Overall, I was astounded by how richly the students recounted their scenes, and especially by how they discussed how they actually read the scenes and what they [the scenes] meant to them. I hadn't expected this level of discussion on the first try—if ever. Another thing that really psyched me was how students were trying out new ideas and moves as they made their cut-outs and presented their scenes, and how they responded to each others' presentations. All in all it resulted in tremendously rich small group discussions, group after group after group, such as I have rarely seen in my career. . . . Conversations leading to new moves, deeper understanding, sharing and discussion—it was truly a great success. Can't wait to try it again, maybe with a new wrinkle . . . (December 1992)

When creating his first SRI, Tommy asked if he could use the story as a reference. Of course, I told him. He constantly referred to the story as he created his cutouts, studying it in an intense and interested way that I had never witnessed in him before. Though many students made highly symbolic cutouts, or used icons that related to characters (e.g., a gun or helmet for a soldier, a crutch for a crippled person), Tommy created very detailed and literal pictures. Typically they consisted of pencil or ink drawings on typing paper, cut out and mounted on construction paper. He also liked for the cutouts to stand up, and in later SRIs he sometimes created 3-D scenes such as a basketball court with upright standards in which the cutouts, like chessmen, could move around.

He had gone over this story carefully, he told me, so he could be sure he'd "got it right." Tommy had never much cared before about getting answers to quiz or test questions right, so I asked him what the difference was here. He stopped short of scoffing at me. "I'm *making* this," he told me, "and other people are gonna see it." I asked Walter about the care he took with his cutouts and he simply replied, "It's fun to do."

Walter's cutouts were also quite literal, though usually less ornate and more colorful. Walter also created scenes for his cutouts to move around in, though his were usually flat.

This creation of scenes during an SRI proved to be an exception throughout the use of this technique by the class. Some students used cutouts of props to indicate a scene (e.g., a tree meant the scene was in the forest, a bed indicated a hospital room), but only a very few students continually created elaborate "stages" for their SRI presentations as Tommy and Walter did.

I asked Walter about his use of the elaborate scenes and he told me:

*It's like when I see the people then all of a sudden I'm seeing where they are too. . . . It's kinda weird . . . it's like I don't see much but I start to make the thing [cutout] for a person and before I'm done doing it I can see exactly where they're at and that's just got to be part of it [the SRI] then.*

Tommy simply asserted that "You're not telling the story [through the SRI] unless you have where it happened. . . . I don't care about these other ones [from other students], we [Walter and I] got it right and theirs aren't as good." This feeling of doing superior work was an important step for Tommy and one that I encouraged him to make as I told him, "Let it all hang out. Show the other kids what they could do too if they wanted their SRIs to be better." Tommy nodded and said, "Okay." I wrote in my journal that this was "an incredibly positive step. I suggested that he had something to teach other students and he agreed!" (January 1993).

During their initial SRIs of scenes from "Pandora's Box," both Walter and Tommy dramatized complete summaries of the action that their respective groups found totally complete and understandable. Tommy did little in the way of explicitly discussing what he had noticed and done as a reader, but his emphasis on the turmoil of Dorie in deciding how to classify Max during triage ("She was thinking will he hate me when he doesn't have a leg and I could have let him die?") and Max's subsequently amputated leg indicated his involvement all the same.

Walter discussed his involvement as a reader with more awareness. "Here I was feeling like I was him and would I want to die and be a cripple? But then I wasn't him anymore."

Kae's initial SRI recounted the story action and little else. Her cutouts were highly stylized and artistic, and she spoke confidently to her group when giving her presentation. She was very excited by her work with the SRI, telling me, "This is so good!" and that the other students "could see what I see!" Kae drew very elaborate characters, props, and sets onto cutout shapes of paper. She told me that "When I draw I just draw, I don't really think. . . . I kind of discover and think what person look like when I draw." She explained that she usually had a very sketchy idea of what people and places in a story looked like until she drew them. "I kind of just do it and draw dresses and faces which I did not really know but then I know what they look like and be like and feel like." She felt strongly that she saw and understood a story better. "I see the hospital and people now."

I wrote in my journal:

> Kae really seemed to enjoy class and participate fully for the first time. . . . I think that making the cutouts required her to go beyond the words of the story to think about what they mean and to start creating a highly visual model of the story in her head. From what she said it was almost as if making the artwork was what made her discover the story. . . . The SRIs helped Tommy and Walter to enter and merge themselves into the story—not immediately as we expect students to do, but over time as they created the SRI—and the creation and performance of the scenes made them want to do that. . . . I have never seen them so motivated or involved in response to a story. I've never seen them be so much a part of the class. (December 1992)

## Relating to Characters

Kae, who often expressed romantic sentiments while reading, indicated that she had come to know and understand some of the characters in "Pandora's Box" when she said, "I think they kind of love each other" when referring to Dorie and Max. "I think she really love him all years. That's why she so sad," she explained, inferring unstated relationships and emotions not explicitly stated in the text. This move excited me, and I wrote that "Kae is finally moving beyond her struggle with word meanings to create a textual world that is personally meaningful to her!"

Walter, too, demonstrated that he had come to know and understand the characters in this first SRI. In response to a question, Walter said that Max "didn't know what he was talking about" when he said he'd rather die than be crippled. "That's stupid!" he almost ranted, then pointed to his head and said, "Think about it, man!" He was evaluating Max and his beliefs, but he backed off a little, saying, "I guess it would be hard to know." Walter then commented that his own leg "hurt" when Max had to have his leg amputated. He clutched his right thigh as he made the comment. "You just can't imagine it," he repeated. When I asked him to explain, he just said, "You can never know." Though it is unclear exactly what Walter was thinking, he was certainly putting himself in Max's situation, trying to know and understand him. And he certainly felt for Max and his situation. He ended the interview by saying, "I'd be really P.O.'ed if she [Dorie] hadn't of saved him! Really P.O.'ed!" It struck me that "the story was something *real* to him—this is something I haven't seen before! Big step!" (December 1992).

While watching another student perform an SRI for the nonfiction piece "Swish" (Robinson, 1991), about a boy who can make half-court baskets with his back to the basket, Walter twice started to interrupt the presentation. When the student was finished, Walter took issue with the student's interpretation of the story.

"You said he wanted to be good at basketball," Walter pointed out, "but he didn't—he already got cut from the team. He wanted to be good at anything!"

When other members of his group wanted an explanation, the normally taciturn Walter went full steam ahead. He explained that the boy's sister was a basketball star and that he wanted to be, too. He explained how this probably really "killed him" that his sister was a star at something he wanted to be good at but wasn't. Finally, he concluded that:

> *He just wanted to be good at something. Shooting baskets that way ain't being good at basketball—it's just being good at something! If he could have been good at something else and got attention he would of done that.*

This was a subtle point Walter had made, and he had made it by trying to know and understand the position of the character. It was also the most thorough response Walter had ever given to another student's response. His comment stimulated some discussion in his group.

Tommy demonstrated activity on these dimensions of knowing and understanding characters less often, but the visualizing activities seemed to scaffold his own preliminary efforts on these dimensions. After Max's amputation, for example, he commented, "That would really suck." When the story was over, he indicated that "it [the story] kind of makes you feel sorry for everybody."

Kae's artwork continued to help her operate on this dimension of response, and to think about characters long after she had read a story. A few days after her SRI of "Pandora's Box" she said, "Now I know nurses and how they sad."

During our reading of *The Incredible Journey* she became very excited by our postcard exchange. She drew a scene of Tao being washed down the river with the other animals helplessly watching. "Now I know how everybody feel," she said. "They so scared and so sad." She then went on a slight tangent as she talked about how sad her owner Elizabeth was that Tao was washed down the river. When I told her Elizabeth was still in England and didn't know Tao was missing, she said, "Oh, then she will be sad if she knows."

When I asked her how drawing the postcard worked for her, she said, "If I draw a person I know them. I know their feelings." She also said that drawing the postcard had helped her "see things in my head."

Kae's tour de force was a symbolic story representation of a Hmong cultural tale, orally told in her family, called "The Seven Daughters," which she presented to part of the class during an integrated unit on cultures that we pursued with the social studies classes. Kae's elaborate performance lasted nearly twenty-five minutes and held her listeners enthralled. It was a love story about a prince from a valley town and his beloved, a princess who lived high on a mountaintop.

The story begins with the prince befriending a man by killing a dragon who lives on his lake. The man gives the prince three magic arrows. The story was very nuanced and involved, with several subplots about the theme of love, but the basic plot is this: The prince and princess fall in love. Before they can get the proper parental approvals to be married, he must go off to war. His parents are then turned against the match by an evil crow. In interesting subplots the princess uses two of the magic arrows to save other girls in the town who eventually find love and happiness. But the princess then begins to die slowly of a curse from the crow and is saved through magic by her father, who takes her back to his mountain kingdom.

The prince returns to find the princess gone. He rebukes his parents for not taking care of his love and goes off on a journey to find her. He finds a magic horse and is able to overcome several supernatural obstacles, such as stone elephants trying to keep him from the Mountain Kingdom. The crow makes a last-ditch effort to stop him with snakes and fire, but the prince overcomes them. He reaches the palace and uses a handmaid to communicate with and then meet with his love, but the king won't consent to the marriage because of the problems his daughter has suffered. The prince must prove his worthiness, which he does by shooting the final magic arrow through the princess's crown. Kae ended her presentation with a flourish. "So the king think, 'Maybe he strong enough to marry her,' and so they get married. Then they try to get the evil bird and shoot it with same arrow. Then they very happy."

Kae used a white cutout of herself as the reader, because "I feel like a ghost, go everywhere, see everything, but no one see me." She often positioned this reader cutout to show how she was relating to the characters. She placed this cutout near the Mountain King and said, "I really see the king and queens. They very sad about their daughter and wonder what to do."

During the princess's great troubles under the curse, she placed the princess cutout over the cutout of herself as reader and said, "I cared about princess the most. She did nothing wrong. Why do they want to burn her up and stuff? I feel like I her and I feel very sad. She not understand why everyone so mean to her." She then placed the reader cutout over that of the crow and said, "I hate him. He evil. I want to cover him up." At the end of the story she again overlaid the princess cutout on her own, and said, "I am like princess the most. I love her the most. I want to be strong like her."

At the end of the story she placed her reader cutout right next to the prince and princess and said, "I like prince and princess. They have really strong relationship."

As we talked after her performance, she said, "It [the SRI] helped me to see the story and show it to other people. . . . It helped me know the people and they feeling." She told me that she had drawn some of the cutouts several times, until she thought the cutouts really "look and feel like people in story."

## Considering Significance

At the end of her SRI performance of "The Seven Daughters," Kae told her group that the story was meant for Hmong parents, and was a warning to them not to stand in the way of their children's romantic desires. "Parents shouldn't try to always be boss. They should listen to story and see what happens when they don't listen to child." She explained that if the prince's parents had respected their son's love for the princess, all of the trials and tribulations could have been avoided.

She then made an explicit connection from the story to her own life by telling a story of her cousin and his girlfriend and how his parents would not approve of the girl, thereby destroying their hopes to be married. She ended by saying, "My parents doesn't do that," and commented:

> *I want to be Hmong but I don't want stuff to happen to me like what happens to other Hmong girls. I want to finish high school or college before I get married. I want to find good man and have his parents approve me. I will take care of them but I want them to take care of me too.*

Here Kae explicitly reflects on the meaning of the story and connects it to her own life.

Throughout the visualization project, Tommy, Kae, and Walter were interviewed about their reading, and were asked to complete periodic "visual protocols." Sometimes we read the stories aloud together, but usually they read the stories silently on their own. During the protocols, the students were asked to stop and draw a picture or to verbally describe what they were seeing whenever they had formed a strong image, or felt the need to get a sense of one. Many students involved in the studies chose to verbally describe what they were seeing. Notably, Tommy, Kae, and Walter always chose to draw. If they discussed what they had seen as they read, it was by discussing the drawing.

The first protocol selection used with Tommy and Walter was Liam O'Flaherty's "The Sniper" (1923), a story set during the Easter uprising in Dublin, Ireland. The second protocol was completed with Donald West-lake's "The Winner" (1970), the futuristic story of the poet Revell, who is imprisoned for the expression of personal and individualistic views considered inappropriate by the state. He is in a model prison without walls or fences, imprisoned by a "black box" implanted in his body that will make him reel in pain when he wanders more than a 100 yards from the prison compound. Despite the intense pain, Revell continues to try to escape, because if he stops doing so, "They would have made me stop being me." A third protocol was completed with "The Little Boy Whose Friend Died on Him" by Ana Maria Matute (1968). This story involves a little boy whose best friend dies in the night. The boy can't believe it because all the toys they played with are still in the yard. He will not eat or sleep. The next morning he proclaims the toys worthless, throws them away, and goes home. His mother exclaims, "How this child has grown. My God, how this child has grown!"

In the first two protocols, Tommy and Walter chose to stop twice to draw pictures. On their own initiative, they independently stopped to draw a third picture after the story was over. On each occasion, the first picture was drawn after reading the first few paragraphs. In these protocols, Tommy and Walter separately stopped to draw within two sentences of each other, Walter stopping first on each occasion. The boys were eager to make the drawings, Walter calling out "I've gotta stop here," and Tommy murmuring, "Wait, I need to draw now . . ."

The first drawing was used in both cases to situate the story world. From it, the boys could recount who the characters were, the conflict, how the conflict involved these characters, and a somewhat elaborated view of the setting the characters found themselves in. Tommy explained drawing at this point as "figuring out what's going on," and Walter as "getting it like, set in your head." The actual act of drawing itself seemed to help them to enter into the "secondary world" and to imagine and get this story world set in their minds.

The second pictures involved the climaxes of the stories. Tommy twice drew a climax earlier than Walter. In "The Sniper," Tommy drew it at the point when the sniper dropped his rifle over the building's edge to trick the other sniper into thinking he was dead.

Walter, on the other hand, waited until the sniper actually shot his enemy. Both readers seemed eager to stop at those points and then to finish the drawing once they had decided to do so. When asked why they drew at this point, Tommy said, "because it's important"; Walter said, "now he's won . . . he's safe now." Both indicated that they felt the drawn event was climactic and important to pay attention to.

Both readers also chose to draw a picture after the story was read. The purpose seemed to be to reflect on the ending of the story. In contrast to the previous two drawings, which were quick sketches, both students took their time with these drawings, sometimes staring into space for periods of time before continuing to sketch. In "The Sniper," Walter drew the sniper springing to the side of the dead enemy to turn him over. "That's the last thing he did." Since this action was not stated in the text, the drawing seems to have helped Walter to fill in textual gaps, imagining how they should be filled.

Tommy's final picture moved back into the story to the point at which the sniper shot his enemy. "That's the big thing in this story," he said. "If he had missed—KER-BLAM—he's dead, man, and the other guy's turnin' *him* over." Tommy did not reflect on the ending as much as rethink the climax of the story and how it affected the ending.

Their visual responses to "The Winner" were similar to those created for "The Sniper." Both figured out that Revell was a prisoner and identified with him, but had trouble figuring out what he was imprisoned for. Tommy dismissed this problem; Walter thought about it until he decided that "Somebody doesn't like him." Tommy's climax was when Revell crawled into the woods, "escaping" from the warden's sight and defying his prediction that Revell couldn't make it that far; Walter drew later, when Revell and the doctor were arrested at the doctor's office. Tommy's final drawing was of the doctor being arrested. He observed that "They [Revell and the doctor] can't get away with it. Ever." Walter's final drawing was of the doctor and Revell in prison together. "Now there's two of them going to try and escape."

In "The Little Boy . . ." both Tommy and Walter drew one picture, to set the story world at the beginning. They did not draw further pictures, commenting instead on what they perceived to be the stupidity of the story.

"Nothin' happened!" Walter complained. Tommy, in his protocol, sneered, "What a stupid story!"

In the first two protocols, these two boys used their drawings to set the story world, set and reflect on the climax, and set and reflect on what they considered to be the resolution—in the form of a resolving action. Bruner's (1986) conception of the "landscape of action" and the "landscape of consciousness" is useful here, I think. Tommy seems to operate almost solely on the landscape of action; Walter makes moves into the landscape of consciousness somewhat only at the very end, after absorbing all of the story's action. In this final story, which has little action, operating instead almost exclusively in the consciousness of the boy and his mother, these readers did not experience nor visualize a complete story world. It was not a story to them at all.

Kae completed three visual protocols with different stories. She always drew three pictures. One typical visual protocol was for a science fiction story called "Human Frailty." In this story, the captain of a space ship overrides the computer and has a rescue ship save his young female apprentice instead of himself. At the end of the story, this decision is explained by the computer as being due to "human frailty." Kae drew a first picture five paragraphs into the story "to tell me what I seeing and where I am." The second picture was drawn toward the middle of the story, "because I want to know for sure what happening." At the end she drew a third picture, "to help me think about story." Her final picture was of the captain drifting off through space as the spaceship disappeared in the other direction. "I guess he really love her. That's all," Kae said of the ending.

Kae seemed to draw her pictures less to record what she was seeing and more to actually work out her visualization of the story. Like the boys, Kae also seemed to use her first drawings to set herself inside the story. She used the second to understand story action, and the third to operate on the landscape of consciousness to understand the story's meaning. "After I draw," she said, "I can think about what story mean. That's hard when I just read." On another occasion she had told me that "Art and computer [hypermedia] help me to understand what I learn and how to work with other people. It help me know what to do and I get to know things. . . . Without pictures it hard to know what things mean."

## Remembering

In addition to helping these students enter the story world, see people and places, and get the "story" set in their minds, the visualization activities seemed to enhance their memories of the stories they had read. Earlier in

the school year, for example, while reading *The Incredible Journey,* Tommy
and Walter could often not comprehend story sequences, nor remember
what they had read the day before. In contrast, they could discuss in detail
the scenes they had responded to through the SRI or through drawings,
sometimes weeks after the reading and response.

A particularly striking example of this phenomenon was with the picture map these students completed with David Quammen's "Republic of
Cockroaches," a nonfiction tale of the cockroach, framed by why it will
probably inherit the earth.

With the Quammen piece, all three students picked out and drew key
details of the tale. Kae's and Tommy's pictures corresponded to key details
on a one-to-one basis; Walter had one picture that expressed two key details
and another that expressed three. The picture maps were completed before
Christmas; I produced them again in May. All three students could tell me
exactly and correctly what each picture expressed about the cockroach, including Walter identifying the multiple meanings of his two pictures! Drawing the pictures was a powerful memory prod for these students that was
not fulfilled by note-taking or other conventional study techniques.

The boys indicated during this session that drawing helped them to
read, understand, and, as Walter put it, "to talk about, you know, what you
read." They were amazed at how the pictures helped them to remember and
think about stories. Kae indicated that she already drew pictures as part of
the notes she made in school. Walter indicated that he would now take notes
for other classes, "in pictures, as much as I can . . . it works better for me."
This indicates a tremendous amount of metacognitive awareness about how
he best learns and responds, and a new willingness to use it to his advantage.

Five weeks after her initial SRI of "The Seven Daughters," I asked Kae
to do it again for me. I had kept her cutouts and gave them to her from my
filing cabinet. Without any review, she launched into a full twenty-three-
minute rendition of the story, complete with comments about how she read
and felt about the story. When I told her how amazed I was at her memory,
she told me, "When I make it, I remember it."

The SRIs and drawings also seemed to help these students build up an
awareness of intertextual connections, and the ability to remember and
draw upon these connections. After reading "The Sniper," Walter commented that his reading of this story was similar to that of "Pandora's Box,"
"because they're both war stories and the people wonder if they did the
right things." Kae compared "The Seven Daughters" to the Greek myth of
Perseus that another student performed through symbolic story representation. "He [Perseus] love this girl and magic help him to get her."

Kae, as mentioned earlier, quite often used her artwork created around
a story to talk about incidents that occurred or that she thought about from

her own life. After her second SRI of "The Seven Daughters" she said, "Sometimes I look at the stars and wonder what going to happen to me. I want to get marry and be happy too, but without all the troubles."

## MOVING TOWARD A REFLECTIVE RESPONSE: "THE BOOK SAID ALL THAT"

As if unleashed by the "go-ahead" to respond artistically to their reading, these students, especially Tommy and Walter, submitted a continual stream of artwork to their classmates and teachers (myself, their LD teacher, and occasionally to the social studies teacher). In Tommy's case, much of the artwork did not reflect what I would consider to be full or rich readings in that they sometimes missed, subverted, or violated important textual details. But at least he was doing some sort of reading, often doing it enthusiastically, and creating and sharing his responses to that literature. He had become a member of the classroom community.

When given a choice among various activities introduced in the class that would incorporate artistic response, Kae almost always stuck with small drawings that corresponded on a one-to-one basis with story scenes and ideas. Throughout the year, after making a drawing she often made the move of explaining how the pictured scene or idea was important to the story, and why the author had put it there. Tommy and Walter usually stuck with simple one-page drawings, usually drawing one scene or event from a book. They almost always chose to spurn more complex uses of visual art that required more interpretive or reflective artwork. Throughout, Tommy's drawings got bigger and on occasion more colorful, taking on a mural-like quality. At the end of a class reading of *Roll of Thunder, Hear My Cry*, Tommy made an action-packed drawing of the fight between the Wallaces and Mr. Morrison on the Vicksburg road, complete with Papa's broken leg and head wound, gushing blood, gunshots, Kaleb's broken back, a muddy road, the red pickup and its shining headlamps, and the dark rain of the night. Walter made a series of pencil drawings of major scenes: the sabotage of the bus, the fight with the Wallaces, and the fire at the end of the book. In their discussions of the pictures, these two boys pointed out what had happened in the scene, how they had seen it—sometimes referring to textual clues that helped them to see it that way, and on one or two occasions, to what the scene meant to the story. For example, when explaining one drawing to his learning group, Walter had this to say: "So they dug the hole to wreck the bus because they were always getting crapped on and they wanted to get back. . . . I put them in the woods all covered with mud and laughing because the book said all that."

Particularly effective for helping these students organize and share their personal experiences and responses to literature was the collage project. The process of making the collage both motivated and scaffolded their attempts to understand the meaning of the poem or song in question, and the presentation of it scaffolded their move from nonverbal to verbal expression. Both Tommy and Walter found it much easier to talk about their collages and what they did to make them than to struggle with the often abstract and suggestive nature of the literary works to which they were responding.

Tommy's collage was of John Ciardi's poem "The Shark," which we had read in class. In the poem, the shark is described as having only one thought, which he thinks constantly, "of something, anywhere, somehow to eat." At the end of the poem, the speaker says, "Be careful where you swim, my sweet."

In Tommy's collage, there was an interesting pattern of three separate levels of drawings mixed with photographs cut from magazines.

On the middle level were drawings and photographs of sharks, whipping and swirling through the water with snarling faces. The drawn sharks had gaping jaws and huge teeth trailing thin streams of blood. Above the sharks was a top level that included mostly photographs of food: hams, turkeys, gourmet meals, a McDonald's hamburger, and much more. Tommy drew a thought bubble containing a single chicken drumstick from the head of one shark. This, he explained, corresponded to the line in the poem that the shark "has only one thought, but he thinks it a lot."

On the lowest level was a fatherly figure wagging an index finger in the face of a young woman. This was a father "warning his kid not to go swimmin'." Tommy further explained that the whole poem "was this guy talking to his kid about how dangerous it is to swim where there's sharks." He indicated that the scenes of the sharks and foods that were placed above these two characters' heads were "what they were thinkin' about in their minds as they were talking. Mostly the dad, but then the girl too as she thinks about what he's sayin' . . . except she thinks about herself getting chomped—like the girl in *Jaws*."

Tommy has done some very sophisticated literary reading here. He knows that on one level the poem is about the dangers of the food-obsessed shark and was able to visually depict this and explain it to his discussion group. He has recognized a speaker and an implied audience within the poem, and has spectated as a reader upon the scene that transpired between them. He has participated in the drama of the shark's appetite and has expected that the two characters also participated in this imaginary experience. He articulates that the collage is a created evocation of the text that he imagined as he read, and that he expects characters implied by the poem to imagine things when they speak and listen to that same text. This, in my estimation, was the high point of Tommy's response during this school year. He did not create it spontaneously, however. The final line of the poem, "Be careful where you swim, my sweet!" gave him fits. "I don't get it!" he told his reading partner and then me. "It don't fit!" I was quick to point out that he was right—it didn't fit, and that I was pleased he had recognized that. "It introduces something new," I told him, "and you have to figure out what that is." Tommy cared enough about his collage that he undertook to canvass other readers about the final line until he was satisfied that he had a coherent and complete understanding of the poem.

Significantly, after his presentation his group proceeded to discuss how the poem could be about the many dangers and consequences of single-mindedness, and the danger of encountering people who, as one student put it, "only want to use you." Tommy did not make this thematic generalization himself. But the group's discussion of this point was stimulated and scaffolded by his artistic rendering of the poem. The group was helped by his picture of a father and daughter and by the notion of advice-giving and warning as they came to a general understanding of the poem's thematic implications. "It can't be about sharks," one boy remarked. "What dad goes around making a big deal of sharks?" This began a discussion about what parents did make a big deal of. As the group discussed these possibilities, Tommy could be seen shaking his head in agreement, and once said, "Yeah, that's it!"

## EPILOGUE: OPENING DOORS WITH ART

The artwork considered in this study helped me as the teacher, and helped the students themselves, to see the various ways in which one text could be evoked and the various possibilities that it held to be read in different and potentially richer ways.

Tommy and Walter, for example, practiced reading much in the way described by the phenomonologist Georges Poulet (1969). For Poulet, reading is a passive submission to the world of the text, which assumes a life of its own. Textual details are submitted to in order to "concretize" a world defined by the text. Readers, in Michael Smith's (1992) terms, "surrender" to the text, creating as closely as possible the world it suggests. In Poulet's terms, preconceptions and assumptions are "bracketed out" so that the reader can engage with the text's ways of perceiving. Tommy and Walter were attempting to understand exactly what it was the text was saying. At least when their reading would serve as the basis for an artistic project, they wanted to "discover" the textual world, and "get it set." This was very difficult for them, and artistic activities helped them to do so.

As such, their readings were what Vipond and Hunt (1984) call "information-driven": the questions they asked themselves and the subsequent evocations of the secondary world that they created had to do with information "Right There" (Raphael, 1982) in the text. They seemed preoccupied with what Peter Rabinowitz (1987) calls rules of notice and signification, asking themselves, What details should we pay attention to, and what do they mean? This was true of Kae as well, though as her language and reading proficiency grew, she moved beyond this.

Perhaps this is a necessary starting point for unengaged readers. It is a starting point from which other, more creative forms of reading may be launched.

The use and discussion of artwork with other students began to move Walter beyond this rather passive way of reading into more productive and participatory dimensions, anticipating the more active roles of filling gaps and adding meaning to text that were exhibited by other readers in the class. Tommy's artwork involved him in discussions and interchanges where other readers were doing this sort of elaborating and connecting with literary works. During these discussions they were able to involve him as a member of the literary club, and perhaps, in time, these exchanges could help him to become a more active reader as well. Kae quickly used stories as a way of telling other stories, stories about her family, her life in Laos, and herself. She introduced herself to others through her art and built up relationships with them.

The greatest recommendation for including artistic response in the language arts classroom is that it encouraged very different readers to respond in natural ways, to share that response with each other, and to extend and develop it in unforeseen, socially supported, and personally validating and exciting ways.

The idea of "art for art's sake" can be replaced by that of "art for the reader's sake." That is an idea that my readers and I found quite compelling.

## Individual and Democratic Response

The experiences we had together suggest that artistic response activities may help less proficient and less engaged readers to respond on various dimensions to enter, evoke, comprehend, and sometimes elaborate and reflect upon the experience of reading. Further, art may provide a means for experiencing what it means for a reader to enter, create, and participate in a story world, especially for readers who may not naturally see and experience what they read, whether because of operative reading difficulties or because of limited language proficiency.

It is a central tenet of reader response theories that a reading is an experience created by the reader. The use of art as response stresses the individual's control in creating, organizing, and constructing experience and knowledge. Using art is also a way to get children both to move beyond simple comprehension and to do the work of responding, instead of having it done for them. Since art requires drawing on personal experience of the world, it reinforces how prior experience is the raw material we bring to a transaction of text to create a literary experience with it, and encourages students to connect what they read back to their own life.

Visual response is a very democratic form of response not only because it is useful in different ways to different students, but because it validates a form of knowing and exploring not normally made use of in core academic classes; it offers perspectives not usually considered in the classroom. And art, unlike traditional forms of response, is not perceived by students to be "correct" or "incorrect." It may therefore open doors for readers who have become resistant to contributing in class because they have been so often told they are wrong, or because their response has been in some way devalued. Artistic response encourages risk-taking because it is traditionally freer from judgment than the answering of authority-generated questions about a reading.

Art encourages and celebrates spirited thinking. It therefore has possibilities for building self-esteem and the belief that the reader "can do it" and can "contribute" to the grand conversation about literature. The use of art in my own classes, I believe, helped to express the attitude that every student can respond to literature in unique ways, and that each response adds to everyone else's experience. Because it encouraged risk-taking, it was a way for students to attempt and perhaps fail at something difficult but interesting, such as when Walter believed that his depiction of important scenes from *Roll of Thunder* did not quite "get" or capture his experience of the book. He then began to consider how more of the experience "could be got."

This sort of controlled floundering is what education should be about. Walter knew he was doing something difficult, he was critical about the process and product of doing it, yet he felt entirely capable of taking on the challenge and considering what to do next.

The use of artistic response as a springboard for literary discussions decentered the teacher as the authority, and foregrounded the students as conversants and generators of discourse. That the students often explored and developed their private visions as they created their artistic renderings, and that these visions continued to be negotiated and developed during small group sharing, allowed the readers to experience themselves as productive theorizers of an evolving literary landscape and meaning. The use of small group sharing encouraged every student to become part of a meaning-making community; the sharing of artistic response enhanced both individual and group understanding. In the case of Kae, the use of art brought her into classroom conversation for the first time and provided her with a way of communicating and sharing with other students in a way that she valued and they appreciated.

Artistic response reinforces the reader's role in the reading transaction precisely because students immediately see that they are dealing with their own private visions and experiences. It is interesting to them to share the visions of others, and they know it is unlikely that such a vision could be considered "wrong."

As Tommy told me, "I don't usually like to talk in class, but I didn't mind talking about my pictures because people seemed interested and nobody was telling me that what I did was wrong." Tommy also used art to include himself as a valuable member of collaborative groups. "I used to not want to work with other guys, but now they know they can give me the drawings and stuff like that to do." During the making of a mural of the civil rights movement, in fact, Tommy was drafted by a group of students who normally operated as an exclusive clique because they valued his artistic ability. He responded with two highly elaborate and complicated panoramas reminiscent of the confusion and texture of Bosch's *Garden of Earthly Delights* or the social vitality of a Breughel scene, with layers of people involved in different individual activities. One was of the March on Washington, and the other of the Watts riots in Los Angeles.

In an art class, such risk-taking is rewarded. Divergent views are "interesting" rather than incorrect. Students are prodded to explore and express their visions and understanding, not simply to justify them. By bringing art into the reading classroom we open the doors to these same possibilities with literary response.

### Engaging Multiple Intelligences

The artistic activities were not universally embraced by all of my students. Though no student refused to attempt them, many students selected other options when given a choice. Some students indicated that they did not really feel that they possessed "artistic talent" and chose to respond in different modes when given an option, and by cutting and pasting photographs rather than drawing when required to create something visual. Still, the use of such activities may convince some students who feel less compelled by visual activities that artistic response may work for them in some way, and it may enhance or become a part of their response repertoire. And using such activities as a choice among several options opens wide doors for many previously disenfranchised students such as Tommy and Walter, or students trying to find a way into the classroom such as Kae.

The artistic activities did include new members in the conversation about literature, and seemed to encourage students such as Tommy and Walter to think of themselves as readers with private visions worth sharing. Other students, such as Kae, were able to extend and develop their thought about literary works, and to converse more fully and fruitfully about their response through the use of art. A few very proficient readers seemed enabled to explore tangential worlds and visions through their art, and were able to share these visions with others in ways not normally encouraged.

Howard Gardner's work (1983) with multiple intelligences has helped to debunk the notion that there is one way of learning, or that there is such a thing as a fixed IQ. Gardner suggests that instead of asking "How smart are you?" we should ask "How are you smart?" School should be a place where students are encouraged to use their natural talents and aptitudes. So language arts classes become a place where student strengths and interests are called on. If they are not, students will be unrecognized, bored, and unhappy. Gardner suggests that every child is gifted. By providing various opportunities and choices, we help students to develop their own unique combinations of talents.

Researchers working on the problem of how the brain works and learns have corroborated Gardner's ideas. Hart (1984), Ornstein (1990), and others have shown that all learning is auditory, visual, or kinesthetic in nature. None of these researchers' work has been disputed by any other. So we have fairly good information that certain types of brains and learning styles privilege certain ways of learning. Yet almost all classroom experience is auditory. This excludes many students from using their preference to learn in kinesthetic (like Libby, who wanted to learn by "doing things with my body") or visual ways (like Tommy, Kae, and Walter). And it precludes auditory learners from expanding their own repertoires.

When we use a wider variety of techniques and emphases in our teaching of reading and response to literature, we create richer possibilities for exploring, experiencing, and knowing through literature. We provide more opportunity for engagement, and higher expectations from print.

It is, I think, the job of the teacher to encourage students to use their natural talents and aptitudes as they construct meaning. It is the teacher's job to call on children's individual strengths and to build upon these. The use of various meaning-making activities such as drama and art helps us to reach the various strengths and multiple intelligences of our various individual students.

## Art as a Metacognitive Tool

The creation of artwork provides students with concrete tools and experiences to think with, talk about, and share

My team teaching colleague Paul, upon hearing one group share and discuss their artwork with each other, told me: "This artwork is as sweet a piece of metacognition as you can imagine. The kids are seeing how they think and seeing how other kids' minds work. They can actually be let into their heads and see what others see when they read!" (March 1993).

Students have a concrete reference as they ask themselves and each other: Why did you do that? What else can you do? Possibilities can be considered, widened, and narrowed as students ask themselves such questions.

The artwork can then lead to more reflective response on more abstract levels, once these students have a concrete reference and anchor point from which to engage in more risky explorations.

# CHAPTER SIX

# Expanding Concepts of Reading, Response, and Literature

Through this school year of studying literary response with my students, the focus of class became reoriented. We came to focus on the *how* and the *why* of using various reading responses and strategies instead of just the *what* of that response. With this as the focus, students were given time to create and share responses to literature. "What was most exciting," I wrote, "is that they then began to learn from each other, evaluating and trying on each other's response moves" (June 1993). I also came to believe in the importance of providing time for both individual and group readings so that students could compare their response to the same story, and bring their own unique contributions and responses to the class. Our class became a study of self and world and response, instead of an exercise devoted to curricularly defined content, and this proved to be motivating and interesting for the students. Making the *process* of reading a major subject of the class and emphasizing the sharing of moves and strategies helped the students to rethink of reading as a personally meaningful, productive, and creative activity.

Studying response with my students allowed me to get to know my students as people and as readers. It allowed me to validate who the students were and what they did as readers, and gave me the possibility to develop, build on, and extend these abilities.

I came to see that research techniques such as the protocol and the symbolic representation interview could be adapted for the instructional purpose of helping students to see what they did as readers, to extend and develop their use of these moves, to share and learn from each other, and to set their own goals. The research methods, when used by the students, helped them to gain more awareness and ownership over their own reading strategies.

For teachers interested in practicing reader response theory and natural language learning in their classrooms, the stories I've told here may have some informing power. My work with student readers has impressed the following points upon me with particular force.

## READING AS ENGAGEMENT

First, I found that thinking about literary reading as engagement was a powerful move for me as a teacher, and for my students as readers. Engagement means that the reader uses a variety of moves and strategies to enter and involve herself intensely in worlds of meaning. In these "story worlds," the reader interprets characters, setting, events, and thematic possibilities through her interaction with and movement through that world. Adopting this perspective helped me to implement reader response theory into my classroom, to get to know my students as readers, and to provide opportunities and activities that helped develop them as readers in both their abilities and attitudes. This development was especially notable in the cases of many learning disabled students and reluctant readers.

The notion of reading as engagement, in turn, expanded my view of what constituted reading and response. I found that truly engaged readers responded to texts in a variety of creative and productive ways that were not encouraged or privileged by my own typical classroom activities. As I came to know my student readers through the research procedures that we used together in class, I was very surprised at what individual readers could and could not do. The variety, intensity, and often stunning sophistication of the most engaged readers' responses was an amazing contrast to the virtual nonexistence of available moves and expressed response on the part of the less engaged readers. Even among the most engaged readers, response was highly individual and idiosyncratic, their response on each of the 10 different dimensions drawing on the personal experience, interests, and even mood of the reader.

I realized that the response of engaged readers is intensely visual, empathic, and emotional. By focusing in class on the importance of these evocative responses, that is, entering the story world, visualizing people and places, and taking up relationships to characters, less engaged readers were given strategies for experiencing texts and were helped to rethink reading. As a result, many were helped to become more enthusiastic readers. These less engaged readers' use of insufficient or impoverished strategies were then used as a springboard to richer and more reflective response.

I think it was an important finding that none of the less engaged readers ever responded on the connective or reflective response dimensions unless they had first fully evoked and experienced the world of the story. This indicates that teachers might well begin to privilege the development of evocative response before asking students to reflect on their experience of a text. This creation of a textual world or a "mental model" (such as we did through drama and art) is an activity that is almost completely neglected by classroom instruction and curriculum guides in reading, and yet every other kind of response and thought about reading depends on this.

## ALTERNATE TEXTS AS LITERATURE

In the context of expanding my notion of response, I also began to adopt a wider and more inclusive view of what constitutes literature. I began to encourage readers to read young adult novels, picture books, comic books, illustrated books, organic nonfiction pieces, and student writing— and to respond and share all of these works as literature. This invited more students to become readers, composers of literary response, and conversants about literary experience.

As the word suggests, *canon* is a holy word, and there are many teachers and parents who think that there is a particular set of texts so culturally important that every student needs to know them. This becomes the job of schools. I think, though, that we need to ask what our purposes are as teachers: to teach texts, or to develop readers who can and will want to engage with and know texts in personally powerful ways throughout their lives?

A colleague of mine once told me that "we have to teach Shakespeare or the kids will never have read him." He later told me that his own students didn't enjoy his Shakespeare unit, but "it was for their own good." As a teacher who loves Shakespeare (and who thinks his work can be taught in a way that connects to students' current lives), I thought this was pretty cynical. In my experience, when someone says something is for your own good, it's not; it furthers his own agenda. My response to him was, "Do we want to stuff Shakespeare down their throats like castor oil so they'll hate it and never want to read him, or do we want to develop readers who love story and language and who will want to read and go to Shakespearean plays in the future?"

A transactional view of literature makes the case that any intense and personally fulfilling experience with text is an aesthetic literary experience. Readers who know the power of the literary experience will return to it throughout their lives. These are the kinds of readers we should be working to develop in our classrooms.

## USING STUDENT EXPERIENCES:
## ART AND DRAMA ACTIVITIES

Developing a richer vision of the reader's response repertoire also led to expanding my teaching repertoire. Now I try to encourage student growth along what I came to see as various dimensions of response. For example, a relatively new move for me as a teacher is working hard to help students enter story worlds, to see these worlds and move around in them, and to take on various relationships with characters. Two major techniques that were shown in the studies to develop these student response strategies *and* more positive reading attitudes were the use of story drama and visual art activities. When used in conjunction with particular reading selections, these activities worked particularly well for many reluctant and learning disabled readers.

I found that these reluctant readers possessed a passive, text-bound view of reading, in which they submitted themselves to texts. Drama activities were motivating and helped them to enter and merge with texts, and to begin to exert control over their reading and to see reading as a constructive, meaning-making activity. The use of drama with reading also helped these students decode words and process implicit meanings.

The use of visual art was also powerful for many students, including some few who were not engaged by the dramas. Art, as in the case of drama, helped reluctant readers to enter texts and respond on new, untried dimensions, opening up their notions of reading as well as their repertoires. Art and drama both reinforced the necessity of drawing on the reader's prior experience to create meaning. Art also helped the students both to explore and create new meanings, and to "set" and place-hold what they had come to know. As such, art became a powerful metacognitive tool for many students.

Taken together, the studies reported here show the possibilities of considering and encouraging the use of multiple intelligences in the reading classroom. New ways of thinking can be engendered and developed. Spirited thinking, response, and risk-taking can be encouraged. Different ways of knowing can be validated, and more students can be included in conversations about literature.

## THE ROLE OF THE TEACHER

For me, pursuing and completing these studies wrought a personal change that provided a larger context in which to understand my own role as a teacher and as a researcher. This political realization of a new role and position has become another result of my year of teacher research. As I wrote in my journal:

> I've come to realize that I have a political agenda as a teacher. I have to work towards valuing my different students' abilities and perspectives. I have to work towards changing school so that many students,

who really are downtrodden in some sense, can feel they have a place in the school, that they have a say and choice in what happens to them here and out there in the world. I think it all has to do with conversation. Conversation means I engage other viewpoints and value them. I have to do that with other teachers to work towards change. I have to do it with students to grant them some authority and respect. If they can't pursue their own reading and learning and creating, then can they ever be said to really be learning? (June 1993)

I have therefore chosen to conclude this book with a discussion of the teacher's role as a highly professional educator who creates learning environments and researches learning *with* students.

I believe that what I discovered about readers and reading will have implications for other teachers in the field and that these findings would be generally true in other instances. However, what I found was certainly particular in many ways to my own community, classroom, and students. So, more importantly, I want to argue that teachers should take a look at their own classrooms with students, and create new learning environments along with them.

## Testing Situations

At a faculty meeting earlier this year, we were doing a "postmortem" on the recent two-week period of standardized testing for the seventh grade.

It was at this point that I asked the question: "Why is it that we give a week of standardized tests anyway?" I was told, rather frostily, that the testing committee had chosen this test as the one that best fit our curriculum.

I had been on that committee. The first question I had asked was whether giving up standardized tests was an option for our district, if we could find an alternative assessment procedure. The answer was the unceasing monosyllable: NO. In effect, I said, we had been free to choose the "best-tasting poison."

The frosty atmosphere became positively polar at this point.

"Do you want to be a scientific educator, or are you satisfied with practicing voodoo?" I was asked.

"What do you mean?"

"If you are a professional educator, then you had better want to evaluate whether students have learned what you have taught them!"

"Oh, I agree, wholeheartedly," I replied, "that we should evaluate student learning. I just don't think that a standardized test is the best way to do that. I think teachers and students should work together to demonstrate what has been learned. I think we should be turning to teachers for assessment, not to the faceless tyranny of testing companies! Then the teachers and the students might have some control over their own learning, and they might get some benefit and learn something from the assessment."

I really hadn't intended to be a gadfly, much less a full-fledged nuisance, but the atmosphere was getting pretty thick with tension.

"Do you really think that a teacher's evaluation of student learning would have any objective validity?" an administrator asked.

I was less astonished by this barb than by the total lack of response from the rest of the faculty. There was complete silence. No one took issue with their supposed incompetence to assess student learning.

It was hard to know what to say—the room didn't feel cool to me anymore—instead, I was feeling the room heat up like a hot air balloon ready to explode.

"Do you mean to tell me," I questioned, measuring my words out carefully before giving way, like a weakened levee, to a flood of emotions and words, "that one kid fills in circle B because he's guessing and it turns out to be right, and the next student fills in circle C because she has several reasons to believe it and she turns out to be wrong, and you mean to tell me that you believe we have learned something about what students know, how they think and how they learn? Are you going to tell me that these tests are not curriculum-altering and mind-altering devices? That the kids don't know they're being labeled as one of these or one of those? Are you suggesting these tests actually measure the many sorts of complex learning we try to engender in our classrooms? Do you mean to tell me that taking these tests is good for the kids, or good for educating them?"

My voice echoed in the silent room. I was breathing hard and sweating by now. I heard a brief spasm of dry, humorless laughter—like the sound of a rattlesnake.

Then the edict was made clear, with careful pronunciation of each word: "The issue of whether we will give standardized tests is not under discussion. The board has decided that we will give standardized tests to evaluate student learning and progress. We will do so to compare our success to other schools."

Punto. Period. End of meeting.

And there I sat, feeling some warmth in my face and shakiness in my knees, wondering why educators agree to this situation.

### What Counts?

There are some pretty big issues at stake here:

- What are the purposes of education? How do curriculum and evaluation contribute to these purposes?

- What is the role of the teacher? Are teachers simply people who deliver prepackaged curricula, who teach to premade tests? Or are they individuals who create learning environments based on individual students' present needs, desires, interests, and abilities? Are we simply technicians painting by numbers, or are we educational adventurers guiding our students on their personal paths of learning?
- What measures, in what situations, best capture the sorts of learning we hope for in a school? How do these measurements help our students to be better, more empowered and more 'wide-awake' learners, and to feel better about themselves?
- What is the role of the teacher in shaping curriculum and assessing learning?
- Most of all, what sort of research and evaluation "count" in school settings?

All of these issues are tied to the issue of teacher professionalism, and as a corollary, to that of the teacher as researcher.

They have much to do with what I see as the personal and professional implications of pursuing and reporting the research projects I have described in this book.

Knoblauch and Brannon (1993), in their work *Critical Teaching and the Idea of Literacy,* make the same point as my faculty meeting story: that power resides with those who name and define what education should do and how to do it, and that these people are not teachers.

These commentators' view of critical teaching is that it values difference and attentively fights subordination. Its purpose is to consider how education will help students to "address inequities and renegotiate the terms of their lives" (p. 97). Critical teaching is visionary; it is about offering possibilities and ways of pursuing these possibilities. This work must be pursued "in the pragmatic terms of stubborn advocacy, continuing conversation, and small gains" (p. 23).

Teachers can help to develop their own critical literacy and that of their students when they engage in teacher research. They can observe what is, pose problems and solutions, converse with students and other members of the community, implement change, and observe whether students are actually enlivened and empowered by the changes. By assuming responsibility for constructing our professional lives, we help students assume responsibility for constructing their own, and we give them ways of doing so.

In my own case, I attempted to observe and analyze what my most proficient readers did to engage deeply with literature. I then asked what my other, less engaged readers were doing, what they might be able to do next, and how I might help guide and support that new, creative readerly

activity. I asked: "What might my students be and do as readers? What possibilities can be made accessible, or be realized for them through the reading
of literature? How can I help these possibilities to become real?"

My role as a teacher depended upon what I found out about my students: the readers, therefore the teacher.

As a teacher, I left behind the role of curriculum delivery boy and became a dealer in what might be possible for my students. My new role was
that of co-researcher, collaborator, mentor, information broker, attention-
payer, success celebrator, encourager of experiments, and believer that every
single student could read in more satisfying ways, and share that reading for
the benefit of the classroom community. Instead of taking on the job of
teaching solely for myself, I became one who enlisted students to help each
other, and who used the community and the computer, paints and music,
video camera and microphone, and the possibilities of drama and art to aid
students in their development as readers.

## THE TEACHER AS RESEARCHER

Teacher research is really about evaluation: an evaluation of what kids
have learned; how they learned it; and what stances, methods, and situations are most empowering for the learning.

Teachers are necessarily researchers. They are continually evaluating,
interpreting, and making decisions—or they wouldn't survive two minutes
in a classroom. Teachers must deal with numerous kids' individual needs
for some five or six different hours a day. Is Joanie too upset to do her work?
Does Max understand the lesson? What can I do differently to help Shana?
Why didn't Joe do his homework? Does Tommy really have to go to the
bathroom? Why won't Tanya read?

Little questions and big questions, moment-to-moment survival, and a
constant conversation of theory with classroom practice—these are the sorts
of research and evaluation teachers engage in each day.

In my own classroom, I began to notice the gaping difference between
my attitudes toward reading and those of many of my students. I began to
compare the experience of many "expert" and highly engaged readers (myself, my wife, my friends, my daughter, and many of my students) with that
of the reluctant and resistant readers whom I taught. This became a driving
question behind my teaching. How could I uncover what readers "do" when
they are engaged? And what could be done in the classroom to encourage
the activity and attitudes of those who love to read? Because I was interested
in transforming my classroom in order to better teach my students and de-

velop them as readers, teacher research was the most potent instrument at my disposal.

Just as I had a relatively unformed view of what readers do until I studied it in my own classroom, my view of teacher research was similarly vague until I found myself undertaking it. Teacher research has helped me to re-imagine my role as that of a democratic worker: reading and learning with my students in collaborative fashion; helping to establish a community where we listen to, value, and learn from each other; and establishing democratic values and processes as we read and learn and work toward better ways of being, understanding, and acting both as individuals and as a community.

My experience has brought me to the position that the educational research and evaluation conducted by or with teachers needs to be highly valued. It tells real stories and is highly informative for classroom practice and student learning. Conducting teacher research in conversation with the field's theorists and professional researchers can have powerful consequences in awakening teachers and students to as yet unrealized possibilities.

## TOWARD A CRITICAL LITERACY

Perhaps it is necessary to step back and ask a set of more fundamental questions that we do not often attempt to answer: Why do we teach the language arts? What do we hope to achieve for our students and for ourselves through this enterprise? How will it make their lives better and their living more powerful?

Such questions as these require a look at the framing issue of literacy itself, what it is and what it can achieve. And what it can achieve, I believe, is the ability, first, to look inward to define the self; second, to imagine and enter the selfhood and perspectives of others; and third, to look outward to critically read and converse with the world. Such a conversation allows the reader a sense of agency, and the ability to "rewrite" and help transform the world. Being literate, that pursuit of reading and conversing with the world's many "texts," continually develops those three abilities that I would call "self-definition," "social imagination," and "critical literacy."

Knoblauch and Brannon (1993) also frame critical literacy in these terms when they argue that it is a commitment to understanding language use and its relationship to power in order to use "language for self-realization, social critique and cultural transformation" (p. 152).

Literacy is both the willingness and the ability to evoke, conceive of, express, receive, reflect on, share, evaluate, and negotiate meanings, in the various forms that meanings may take. In this view, literacy is not limited to proficiency with written and oral language, but extends to the making of meaning with other sign systems: music, art, drama, physical movement. In my own work, I found that if students' work with one sign system was valued and encouraged, they could use this work as a springboard to operating in other systems.

Literacy is both a private and a public phenomenon. As a private act, it helps the reader in the process of self-discovery and definition, in that continual odyssey of "self-realizedness." (Such as when Kevin realizes that "maybe I could get good at this," or when Kae dreams about her future and how she wants to define it differently than it has been planned for her.)

But such a process, though it has private moments, is really only enacted communally. Johnston (1993) calls the capacity to value and explore multiple perspectives a "social imagination"; this includes the ability to imagine the worlds and possible worlds of others different from ourselves. Literacy is a window into the social world, where it empowers and emancipates the reader, helping us to become social by understanding other perspectives and to develop a personal sense of agency in the world (versus just in the classroom). Literacy, in this sense, is both social and political; it allows one to secure satisfactions in the world and impinge upon that world in an effort to make it more satisfactory for the self and for others.

For those students who have been outside the conversation, ways must be provided to include and value their voices, to make them a part of the meaning-making community. Drama was a way in which Kevin, Libby, and Marvin came to value their voices and contribute to class; visual art was a bridge for Kae, Tommy, and Walter.

Literacy is the ability to traffic in meanings, which allows the reader to participate in democratic meaning-making with others. Without such participation, literacy loses its ethical and democratic edge. Literacy should be helping students, much as Giroux (1987) and Boomer (1987) argue, to become aware and attentive to realities, penetrating and interpreting what is happening to them; and to possibilities, to the means in which the world can be transformed. This "critical literacy" includes a sense of "wide-awakeness," as Maxine Greene (1978) describes it, that is necessary to a sense of agency. Giroux argues that this kind of literacy is a "project of possibility."

Essential to this teaching for the possible is what Simon highlights as a "moment of transformation," during which students think critically, make choices, and "believe they can make a difference in the world" (cited by Giroux, 1987, p. 179). Both writers stress the need for students to be supported in becoming "agents." Giroux proposes that the purpose of education is not to foster "functional literacy," that is, to train workers, operating as an adjunct of corporations, but to operate "as vital sites for the development of democracy," developing critical citizens who have "civic courage," who see possibilities and act as agents.

> Democracy requires citizens who can think, challenge, and exhibit long-term thought. This means that public schools need to become places that provide the opportunity for literate occasions, that is, opportunities for students to share their experiences, work in social relations that emphasize care and concern for others, and be introduced to forms of knowledge that provide them with the opportunity to take risks and fight for a quality of life in which all human beings benefit. (Giroux, 1987, p. 181)

Being literate in this sense means that the student can make conscious choices, see possibilities, and judge and evaluate the truth and usefulness and limits of what is read, heard, and experienced. Critical literacy includes knowing the worlds of a particular writer, and being able to explore and judge why he wrote in a particular way.

When Tommy suggests that the class respond to a story by making a collaborative mural, he has seen a possibility. When the class agrees, we have made him a member of the community who can help to set its agenda. When he judges the completed mural to see if it "works," he is evaluating its possibilities for entering the world of another's experience. When the mural helps him to enter a conversation about the way the world is and might be, he is entering the grandest of literary conversations: about the ways that he and his classmates might envision and find of being human in the world.

Literacy, for myself and for the profession at large, used to mean the mastering of basic sets of skills to "correctly" extract other people's meanings from text. This set of meanings is the body of knowledge that curriculum lays out for us. This is the set of facts standardized tests can measure. This may be part of being educated, but it is not all of what we most want for our students, or what education should really be about.

As a result of my learning with students, I have come to know something new about literacy: that it requires readers who bring personal meaning to bear on a dynamic and critical interaction with texts, *and* with the world, in order to "outgrow our current selves" (Hanssen, Harste, & Short, 1990), to augment our knowledge base, and to revise our theory of the world.

Susan Hynds (1990) argues that literate behaviors are only engendered in situations that move beyond skill-building to provide opportunities to make and judge meanings. This is what promotes the actual experience of being literate and thus the desire to become literate. So it was that Kevin began to read on his own, visiting the library to find stories from the far north of Canada, and creating "movies in my mind" after the drama project empowered him to make meanings with texts that were rooted in his own experience. Thus it was that Tommy and Walter began to create and share cartoon versions of stories they had read when their way of knowing and exploring meaning through their drawing became valued.

How we teach literacy is of great importance if students are to understand the acts of reading and writing as productive and evaluative pursuits, and if they are to become empowered as lifelong readers and writers. As Anne Dyson (1984) has pointed out, and as many of my own students quite articulately confirmed, children and young adults see the difference between reading for school and reading for the self. In classrooms, they learn to "do school," developing a "pragmatic sense" of how to demonstrate competence according to the idiosyncratic demands of the school situation. School reading revolves around what is discrete and testable; personal reading revolves around a powerful experience that is organic, personally meaningful, and satisfying. Teachers must move beyond teaching skills and testing for comprehension, if students are to embrace a new way of being literate. If we do not, students like Libby, Marvin, Tommy, and Walter will trudge through school days filled with frustration and failure, without the possibility of discovering how reading can be a unique, personal, and powerful way to both experience and know themselves and the world. And students like Ron, Cora, and Joanne will complete their schoolwork in perfunctory fashion, never bringing what they know to be the vital private experience of reading into the classroom, where it can be shared and extended with others.

This sort of program to embrace a new classroom agenda of literacy can only be undertaken by teachers with their particular students; their year of sharing and growing and keeping track together is research at its best.

This is not to argue that traditional research cannot be useful to the teacher. It is only to insist that it must be complemented by a body of teacher research that builds upon what is known: that explores what the data might mean, how it might inform instruction, and how it will be played out in classrooms full of learners so that it can improve real lives.

When I became interested in "what readers do," as I referred to it in my journal, I searched the professional literature for theories of reading and literature that focused on the reader's role; for studies about the engagement, moves, strategies, and activities of individual readers; and for stories of classroom practices that would help develop these activities.

This professional reading was then, and continues to be, invaluable to me as I think about reading, and pursue researching the reading act with my students. Still, I found that there were great gaps in the literature. Literary theory looked at model readers instead of real ones; theories of expertise focused on adults. The very few studies that looked at the moves of individual student readers focused on both younger and older students than I taught. And no study looked at how a theory of reading as "engagement"— as the deployment of various strategies to construct and imagine meanings, to live and move around inside the world of a book—could be played out in a real classroom. Such a study, or series of studies, that would address the concerns of myself and my students was left to me to undertake.

When these stories are shared, as I have tried to do here and by participating in round-table discussions at schools and conferences, they will provide a unique angle to the thinking of teachers about reading education, an angle that can only be provided by a practicing classroom teacher-researcher working with his or her particular students.

I don't believe that the abilities of self-definition, social imagination, and critical literacy can be developed or measured through set, fact-based curricula or standardized tests. I do believe that these abilities can be developed through knowledge of students, celebration of what they can do, and the use of creative activities such as reading and writing, drama and art, sharing and discussion that build upon, extend, and develop what students already know.

Such a project requires a teacher who embodies a wide-awake agency through a clearly articulated theory of the purposes and processes of learning and, as I have stressed, of reading.

Such a project requires a community of teachers who listen to children, and who make critical readings of their own theories and practices of teaching. We need to share teacher views and stories about children and learn to listen to them, "so that we can come to imagine those perspectives ourselves—developing social imagination. Imagining two different interpretations gives us both depth of vision and the grounds for self-correction" (Johnston, 1993, p. 428).

If we can work together with our colleagues and our students, sharing stories and meanings and building upon these, we can help our students to become the caring, involved, empowered citizens necessary to a democracy made up of diverse people and voices.

Education is experience in how to learn; it is an exploration and an expansion of what it means to be human in the world. It is practice in the construction of meanings with others.

As I make my way with my students, I try to equip them and guide them through the first few stages of an educational journey that I hope will be neverending. I am a teacher-researcher because if I improve instruction, the lives of those I teach can be enhanced. The meaning of our work, as Hu[] (1993) reminds us, is in the lives it enables others to lead.

# Questions and Activities for the Ten Dimensions of Reader Response

## 1. ENTERING THE STORY WORLD

### What the Readers Do

Express "excitement": "want" to read, "think about" what reading will be like

Anticipate pleasure; generate enthusiasm

Willing to read, and to help create an aesthetic experience under the guidance of the text

Activate linguistic capacities and strategies needed to comprehend the text's guidance

Bring personal experience to help enter and build up a story world

Activate necessary schema for genre, topic, and theme

### Questions to Ask (Tell me . . .)

When you first saw the book, what kind of book did you think it was going to be? What made you think this? What were your feelings? How might your feelings influence your reading?

Tell me anything that caught your attention about the book: the cover, the book itself, layout, pictures, anything else.

What will the book be about? What do you know about this topic/text/ author/type of story? How will this influence how you read? What would you like to know about the topic or about X, Y, Z? How will this influence how you read?

How will the story be told or organized? Have you ever read other stories/books/poems like this? What sticks in your memory most vividly about these types of books? What will you want to know right away?

Many questions that appear in Appendix A come from Chambers (1985) and Iser (1978)

## Possible Activities to Aid Story Entry

Book talks or previews to get students interested

Simulations or drama activities that connect to or foreshadow events and scenarios that will occur in the reading

Look over the book, make predictions

Brainstorm what is known about the topic of the reading

K-W-L: students list what they *know* about the topic, what they *want* to know, and (as they read) what they are *learning*

Prereading activities that focus attention on topics or themes to be explored in reading: surveys, opinionaires, anticipation guides, rankings, case studies, autobiographical writing

Activities to build necessary background knowledge for reading: expert speaker, demonstrations of activities or ideas from reading, constructing a timeline or museum exhibit, sequence texts so that students build background knowledge text by text, review texts previously read that were of a similar genre, style, or topic

As part of literature circle or reading group activity, have students describe when and how they entered the story

## 2. SHOWING INTEREST IN THE STORY ACTION

### What the Readers Do

Begin to "get into" or "enter" the story world

Comprehend literal meanings: "I understand"

Make an undifferentiated response—"It's good because I like it." Decide to go on with reading.

May summarize, giving a brief description of the event, or a condensed version of a whole section

Predict and anticipate what might happen next, in the short term: "I think," "I predict"

Form expectations: "This will be good/interest me"

Begin construction of a story world

Create rudimentary mental images, usually stereotypes from film and television

Recognize some "rules of notice" to make contact with the text. Accept the game devised by the author, though reader may not show understanding of all basic conventions of this "game."

May be confused or tentative. May express lack of background knowledge, too narrow a response, indifference. Could give up on story at this point.

## Questions to Ask (Tell me . . .)

Did the first pages meet your expectations? What has caught your attention?

What is happening in your head as you read the first paragraphs?

What do you think the author wants you to notice? How is your attention drawn to these items? What is the text signaling you to notice?

What do you know that is helping you to understand the story? What might you need to know more about to understand more of the story?

What type of story will this be? What characteristics will it have?

Are you asking yourself or the text any questions?

What are you imagining might happen next?

How do you think the story might develop?

How did these present circumstances arise?

What do you think will happen next, or what will happen when or if X occurs?

How do you think it will all end? How would you like it to end?

## Possible Activities

Students write telegrams summarizing the beginning of a story

Prediction games

Ask students to make a personal statement about what they are noticing, what is catching their attention, what kind of book they think this will be

## 3. RELATING TO CHARACTERS

### What the Readers Do

Create character and expectations about characters: "I think/hope she will"

Feel emotions in relation to character activities and situations: "I'm scared/excited/worried/happy for X"

Become a presence in the story world, as "character," "friend," close observer, distant observer, "in the midst"; may use "spy" tool to see, hear, and move around in story world, e.g., peephole

Make judgments about character and character actions

Project self and personal knowledge of people into the story world; life brought to literature

Identify, empathize, or merge ("become") character, jumping into character's head

Role-play—how would I feel if/what would I do if I were in character's situation?

Enact: physically become or represent character

Achieve parallel focus (Enciso, 1990): refer to friends as characters, or imagine scenarios that seem parallel to story

Become agent: may desire to act on character's behalf

Define frame: designate a relationship between self and character.

## Questions to Ask (Tell me . . .)

What clues do we have to the character's personality?

Do you like the character? For what reasons?

What do you think the character will do? What problems will she have?

What are the character's problems? How are they solved? Are any not solved? What would you do differently?

What feelings are you experiencing as you read? How did you feel when X happened to the character? Are you feeling pleased or irritated with the character? How would it feel to be one or more of the characters?

What personal experience have you had that helps you to better understand these characters? (*Note:* Different from connecting because there is no reverse analogy from character to understanding one's own life)

What do you feel about this character? setting? incident?

What character interests you most? Is that character the most important character? Or is the story really about someone else?

Which characters didn't you like? Which bored you? Did any character remind you of someone you know? Has anything like this ever happened to you? Did you feel the same as the people in the story?

Did we ever get to know what the characters were thinking about? Did you agree with what character X thought about Y?

When you were reading the story did you feel it was happening now? Or did you feel it was happening in the past and was being remembered?

What in the writing made you feel that way? Did you feel that things were happening to you? As if you were the character? Or were you an observer? If so, where were you watching from? From different places? Can you tell me where in the book you felt a particular way?

## Possible Activities

All drama activities (See Chapter Four)
Retell episodes from different perspectives
Write character diaries
Discuss characters in terms of whether you would like to know, meet, or be that person
Write a letter to a character; a classmate could answer the letter as the character
Write a story about the character if she were in your town today

## 4. SEEING THE STORY WORLD

### What the Readers Do

Notice cues for visualizing a "secondary world"
Create and sustain a "secondary world" in the mind
Create visual pictures of characters, physical features, physical gestures, placements, settings, situations, and mental images of affect

### Questions to Ask (Tell me . . .)

What impressions are you forming in your mind of people and places in the story? What pictures do you have in your mind's eye?
Are you able to see in your mind the characters and the places where the events take place? Do you see pictures in the text? All of the text? Or only in some parts? What in the text helps you see a picture? How and when does the clarity of your visualization change? Where are you seeing the story from? What sort of vantage point or perspective do you seem to have?
As you read this story, do you see it happening in your imagination? Are you unaware of images, but seem to have a sense that you are "seeing" in another way? Can you describe that way?
What kind of details in the story help you see it most clearly? Can you tell me some of those details? What do they suggest to you? How do they connect to your experience?
Where did the story happen? What was it like there?
Did it matter where it happened, or could it have happened anywhere? What did you think about the setting as you were reading?
Where are characters placed in relationship to each other? To important objects?

What is the setting like? Can you describe it? If you were going to take a picture or make a movie of this scene, where would you do it? What would you include? What sort of music would be playing?

## Possible Activities

All visual art activities (See Chapter Five)

Describe an important setting or scene from the book

Draw a floor plan or map of an important setting

Write about how the story would be different if it happened in your town

Make a character book or yearbook including drawings and descriptions of characters. Cutouts from magazines could be used.

Create a hypermedia version of the story, or a hypermedia scrapbook of important elements

## 5. ELABORATING ON THE STORY WORLD

### What the Readers Do

Build meaning through accumulated clues: "I added X and Y," "X made me remember Y"

Recognize openness of the text

Draw on repertoire of personal experiences both as a reader and as a person to extend and develop the story

Begin to play "detective"; actively fill out textual cues and gaps in creating a secondary world

"Imagine" new situations, characters, settings, and episodes

Imagine alternate or parallel endings or consequences

Ask "What if?"

Elaborate: imagining details, situation, character qualities, conversations, and actions not apparent in text alone, but still consistent with experience of the story world

Generate expectations about alternatives and possible long-term outcomes; extend and hypothesize, taking character and events beyond time and frame of the story

### Questions to Ask (Tell me . . .)

What episodes or information did the author leave out? How did you fill them in?

What if X had not happened? What if Y happened? What if character Z were different, or the setting or situation or timing were different? What other adventures might these characters have? What would be an alternate ending for this story? A sequel to this story? What was left out of the story that you wish had been included? How would you include it? How would the story be different/better/worse if the author had included these changes?

What other books have you read that the story you are reading reminds you of? Have you ever read other books, stories, or poems like this one? Tell me about them: What sticks in your mind most vividly about them? How are these two works alike? different? How could this book be made more similar or different to that one? What characters from this book might fit in a previous book? How would they behave differently from the characters in this book?

What will you tell your friends about this book? What won't you tell them because it might spoil the story or be misleading?

## Possible Activities

Keep a detective's log of clues regarding important questions you have or patterns you notice

Write a new ending

Compose a flow chart of cause-and-effect relationships; change the resolution of one major conflict and trace how it changes the rest of the story; or create a Choose Your Own Adventure flow chart of the book, showing what other alternatives could have eventuated and what would have happened next

## 6. CONNECTING LITERATURE TO LIFE

### What the Readers Do

Make explicit connections between personal experiences and the character's experiences; between story experience and own life; use intertextual references: "I connected/compared/related"

Take a perspective: may consider what someone else might be seeing, thinking, or feeling; consideration of most likely experiences and interpretations others would have in a situation; may switch or coordinate various perspectives, e.g., mutual perspective-taking (Selman & Byrne, 1974); take third-party view to reconcile two other perspectives (Note. Perspective taking differs from empathy in that it requires contemplation of other's feeling, and this depends upon projecting own experiences, attitudes, and feelings)

## Questions to Ask (Tell me . . .)

Tell me what things have happened in your life that are similar to some of the things that are happening to characters in the story.

Do any of the characters remind you of people you know? Does knowing the characters help you to understand the people you know who have similar qualities or situations? Tell how so.

How does what is happening in the book make you more aware of your own life? How does it inform how you think about your own life and identity?

Have you learned anything important about other people? Has your understanding of others increased? Have you learned anything new about the world? others? yourself?

Has the book influenced what you believe in, what you think is right or true? Has it helped you think how you might behave in some future situation? Or helped you to think how you could have done things differently in a past one?

## Possible Activities

Many drama activities (see Chapter Four)

Create a Life's Little Instruction Calendar of Ideas or Suggestions for better living that were found in the book

Two-column notes comparing situations and problems in book to situations and problems in your life

Cast your friends in various roles for the movie version of the story

## 7. CONSIDERING SIGNIFICANCE

### What the Readers Do

Establish significance

"Know": state with conviction that they have knowledge about something in the story, historical period, character's thoughts, author

Ask "how did the text work?"; ask how experience fits together

"Remember"/retrospect: refer to earlier parts of story to make sense of the present

Perceive changes—shifts in reading experience, changes in character or plot, diction or setting, style or tone

May express wonder or surprise, implying reader expectations about what would occur, and wondering why it did not

Formulate puzzles, enigmas, accept (or reject) "hermeneutic challenges" (Iser, 1978), "I wondered why," "I tried to figure out"

Apply rules of signification, and elaborate upon possible meanings

Begin to consider matters of coherence, and how separate elements fit together to indicate meanings

Compare (character's view to own), classify, critique (communicating what is of value, enjoyable, interesting)

## Questions to Ask (Tell me . . .)

Tell me about the parts of the story you liked the most/the least. What parts excited you? Bored you? If you stopped reading, what stopped you?

What is the connection between events that are seemingly unrelated? What is the point of a particular event or description? What did the author leave for you to explain or fill in? Why was a certain character or passage included in the story?

What patterns of meaning are being created by you and the author?

Was there anything that puzzled you? Things you thought were strange? That took you by surprise? Did the author try to do these things to you purposefully? For what reason? What was the author expecting of you in these situations?

What idea was the author exploring through this story? What comments or generalization would the author make about that idea?

If you were filming the story, when would lighting and music change? Why? When would characters change? How would you capture this in costumes, gestures, looks? What changes in feeling or tone would be captured by these changes?

## Possible Activities

Radio or news show in which you discuss or debate what you think the book reveals about people and their lives

Share one new idea about people and their lives that you realized after reading this piece

Dramatic interview or debate with author in which you disagree with at least one of his ideas

Create a main idea book or a picture book version of the story that captures all major scenes and ideas

Write a script for and videotape a part of the story to capture its mood and meaning

## 8. RECOGNIZING LITERARY CONVENTIONS

### What the Readers Do

"I noticed" a change, shift, literal meaning that author "couldn't have really meant" or that "didn't make sense"

Recognize literary event as a highly conventionalized and socially constructed experience

Recognize highly sophisticated rules of signification involving the subversion or undercutting of literal or usual expression, e.g., story inversions, prolepsis, analepsis, symbolism, irony, unreliable narrators

Draw on literary and cultural repertoires to construct implied meaning: "I thought about Dad/Mom/movie/previously read story when X didn't make sense"

### Questions to Ask (Tell me . . .)

How long did it take for the story to happen? Was the story told in the order that it happened? Why or why not? What effect did the changes have on you as the reader?

What information did the author know that she withheld? Have you ever withheld information while telling a story? For what purpose?

Who was telling the story? Do we know? How does this make a difference?

Are there parts of the story that took a long time to happen but are told quickly? Are there parts of the story that took a short time but take a long time to tell? Are there events that happened once, but are repeated in the telling? Events that reoccurred but are told only once? Why did the author change the actual time and order of events when she told it? Have you ever done such things when you have told stories? For what purposes?

How do you recognize when X device is being used? What subtle clues are you given to be alert? How do you feel about the use of this particular device for telling this story? In what ways does it change or add to the story? Were you surprised when it became clear that the surface story could not be taken literally? Do you think you were meant to be surprised? For what purpose?

### Possible Activities

Assignment sequences (see Michael Smith, 1986, 1991) to develop student problem-solving strategies for recognizing and using conventions

Have students write their own Ripley's Believe It or Not that displays irony

Have students rewrite stories from other perspectives, with new time sequences, or with new elements and discuss how the story is different

## 9. RECOGNIZING READING AS A TRANSACTION

### What the Readers Do

Question significance: step back from ongoing experience to see how that experience fits together

Refer to how story is told; may critique authorial choices

Recognize implied author

Generalize; concerned with understanding the world through the literary work

Interrogate text and the author as a presence shining through the text in order to evaluate author's construction of meaning and to match the author's representation of the world with one's own

Apply rules of configuration and coherence in an attempt to understand author's expressed vision

Accept, reject, or resist (parts of) the author's vision

### Questions to Ask (Tell me . . .)

What kind of person is the author?

Did you find her to be someone you could like or not? For what reasons?

What values or attitudes does the author want you to affirm or question? What ideas of the author's did you respond to with a "Yes, she's right!" or "No, that couldn't happen/could never be," etc.?

Do you agree with how the author sees the world? In what ways?

Did you notice things in the story that made a pattern? (Could play "I Spy" game with students, asking them to cite striking elements. List and see if patterns are formed.) Why did the author create the patterns that she did in the story? Why did she write the story in the way she did?

How do you feel about the way the story is told? Is there anything you enjoyed or were irritated with about the way the book is written?

What do you feel is the most significant word/passage/event from the story?

If the author asked you what could be improved in the story, what would you say?

## Possible Activities

Dramatic interview or debate with the author

Create the author's yearbook page or a scrapbook page

Write a letter to the author explaining your reactions and asking questions

Brainstorm what authors you would most want to invite to a dinner party, to be with you on a deserted island, etc.; discuss why

## 10. EVALUATING AN AUTHOR, AND THE SELF AS READER

### What the Readers Do

Recognize implied reader, and relationship between implied author and implied reader

Acceptance/resistance/rejection of assigned role as implied reader or as member of reading community

Apply rules of coherence and exercise awareness of process of meaning-making undergone in concert with author and text; Aware of how process worked or did not work for them in this case

Recognize text as socially constructed and role of reader as part of literary community

Exercise reflexiveness, leading to an understanding of textual ideology, personal identity, and one's own reading and learning processes

### Questions to Ask (Tell me . . .)

What kind of reader was the book written for? What kind of person do you think the author imagined in his mind's eye? Are you that reader? Could you become that reader? To what degree?

Did you sympathize with the author's worldview? Did any of her attitudes or opinions make the book difficult, enjoyable, reassuring, or annoying?

Would you like to get to know this author?

How did your experience as a person and as a reader guide your reading?

Where were you as you were reading? When you read, do you hear the words being said in your head? Whose voice was it you hear?

What was your reading rate? Did it vary? When and for what reasons?

How did "meaning" happen? Were you conscious of the text's language? Did you note unusual words, images, style? Did you reread certain sections? For what purposes? With what results?

Would you read the story again? If so, would you read it differently?

How has your reading helped you understand yourself any better?

If you read the story before, was it different this time? What did you notice that you didn't notice the first time? Did you enjoy it more or less? Because of your experience, would you recommend that others read it again as well?

We've listened to each other's thoughts about the story, and heard all sorts of things about what we've noticed. Are you surprised by anything someone else said? Has anything been said that changed your mind? Helped you enjoy the story more? Understand it better? What struck you most about what others said?

Now, after all we've said, what is the most important thing about the story for you? Should you give the book to others? Who? How? Should it be read aloud, or should it be read silently? What would be best for the story? For the reader?

How do you feel now that the reading experience is over? What would help you to reflect further? What might distract you?

What will you do differently the next time you read? What are your goals for the next time you read?

## Possible Activities

Nominate the book for an award based on what it did for you as a reader

Write a letter to your librarian explaining why the book should or should not be purchased based on what the book expects of a reader

# Revolving Role Drama Lesson Plans for *The Incredible Journey*

### Day One (Before Beginning Reading)

The revolving role drama project will be explained to the students in the context of our purpose of learning how to enter and experience "story worlds." It will be explained that each day we will enter an imaginary "drama world" that will anticipate and parallel the "story world" of the book we are reading.

The class will engage in a few warm-up exercises. imagining we are in class on a hot day, at the North Pole, Christmas morning, the day of a test. We will discuss how we imagine and express our entry and experience in these imagined worlds. Concerns will be discussed.

We will then, as a class, enter a drama world, via guided imagery. The teacher will explain that at the end of school one day we were escorted to a bus without windows. We were taken on a long trip. No one explained where we were going. After about 14 hours we finally stopped and were allowed off the bus. We were then put on a plane and flown over the wilderness, finally landing on a remote lake, and left at what appears to be an old hunting lodge.

Within the drama world, students will be asked to share their feelings and concerns about our current situation.

For several weeks we are well cared for, but also carefully guarded by several friendly guards, none of whom seem to be able to communicate with us or tell us why we are here or how long we must stay. We are in the middle of a wilderness area, and all we can see from the top of the house we stay in are lakes and trees—for as far as the eye can see.

One day, we awake and find we have been left alone. We call a town meeting to address the following questions: Why are we here? Should we try to find our way home, now that we have the chance? What preparations must we make if we are to journey across the wilderness? As a group, what problems do we foresee and what rules do we wish to make for our group? The students will conduct the town meeting.

## Day Three (Parallels Reading of Chapters 2 and 3)

It is the second day of the animals' journey. Today students will be assigned to play the roles of an A or a B. They will find a person playing the other role to enact the story drama in pairs. After 2 to 3 minutes of role-playing, students will be asked to switch partners.

### Role-Play #1

We are still in the wilderness. We have no idea where we are and have seen no people or travelled roads. We have been out for a whole week. Role A has some food but is still quite hungry. Role A has had some limited success hunting and fishing.

The students in Role B, however, are weak and starving—having not eaten since the first day of the journey. The person in Role B finds the person in Role A and asks for some food. Role-play the drama.

### Role-Play #2

Role A finds a new Role B partner. Role B2 is a friend of the person who role played B1. You are worried about B1. You think that your friend will die if some situation is not worked out to find and share food. Try to work out a situation. Role-play the drama.

### Role-Play #3

Role A finds a new Role B partner. Role B3 is a friend of B1. You tried to wake up B1 this morning and you cannot do so. B1 is totally unconscious, but is still breathing. B1's lips are cracked and bleeding, cheeks sunken, skin a greyish color. Talk to Role A about what to do. Role-play the drama.

### Reflection

Write short diary entries that explore your reaction to today's role drama. Tell how you felt as each character in each situation, etc.

## Day Four (Parallels Reading of Chapter 5)

We are now 10 days out on our journey. Tonight we can see lights up in the sky ahead. We decide that we are perhaps only two days' walk from some sort of town. Unfortunately, we are camped on the bank of a wide and torrential river filled with rocks and white water. There is no easy place to cross as far as we can see.

### Role-Play #1

Role A does not want to cross the river, at least not at this particular place. Role B does want to cross the river, right here and right now. The two roles must give their reasons, explore possible options, and come to some sort of conclusion.

### Role-Play #2

Find a new partner. Role A2 is a hermit who is slightly unbalanced and lives in a fantasy world. A2 has lived in the wilderness for many years. Role B2 has become separated from the group during the group's river crossing. What are your concerns? What can you do for each other? Role-play the scene.

### Role-Play #3

Find a new partner. Roles A3 and B3 are both group members who have just realized that one of the group members was lost during the river crossing about an hour ago. What should we do? Role-play the drama.

### Role-Play #4

Find a new partner. Role A4 is a park ranger who has just found the one person who was separated from the group, played by B4. What are your needs and concerns in each role? What must be done immediately, and what plans must be made? Role-play the drama.

## Day Five (Parallels Reading of Chapter 6)

### Option A

In pairs, students will write a scene about the two dogs that occurred when they were separated from Tao the cat. The scene should include some sort of adventure and a conversation about the cat. The dramas will then be rehearsed and performed for the class.

### Option B

In pairs, create a tableaux drama of "snapshots" of key episodes from the last three chapters (4–6). These tableaux will be presented to the class. Class members will guess what episode is depicted by each tableau.

## Day Seven (Parallels Reading of Chapter 8)

Students are members of the intact group. We are walking along a set of telephone poles and wires. We believe that we are very close to civilization and that we will reach a town in just a few miles. We have been underway now for over two weeks. We are tired, dirty, scarred, and sore. What other feelings do we have?

### Role-Play #1

Role A is a guard from the camp where all of us were originally held. Role B is a lost group member. You run into a cave and the guard refuses to come in. Role-play your conversation.

### Role-Play #2

Role A2 is a member of the intact group and a special friend of the group member B2, who is the lost group member. B2 is approaching the group and is reunited first with his friend A2. What will you say to each other? How will you greet each other? What are the first stories you will need to tell? Role-play the reunion.

### Role-Play #3

Role A3 is limping along with Role B3, behind the rest of the group and out of yelling distance. Role B3 falls into a hole and suffers a broken leg (parallels porcupine quills in Luath's mouth). What are you going to do? Role-play the scene.

## Day Nine (Parallels Reading of Chapter 10)

The group believes that they are close to civilization and that everyone should just try to make it there as quickly as they can, so that the slower and weaker members will not hold up the others any longer.

### Role-Play #1

Role A is a best friend of one of the group of missing people, and has spent the past few weeks very worried about her missing friend. You have just been informed that two of the missing group members have reached civilization, but there is no news of your friend. Role B is your mother or father. What are your feelings? What attitude should you take toward this news? What do you want to do?

### Role-Play #2

Role A2 is the local police chief in the town that the two group members have finally reached. Role B2 is a parent of one of the still-missing group members. How can you find the rest of them? What plans do you need to make?

## Day Ten (Parallels Reading of Chapter 11)

### Role-Play #1

Role A is a friend who thinks that all of the group members have survived. Role B is a friend who is sure that they did not. Role-play a discussion between you.

### Role-Play #2

Role A2 will write a letter from Bodger, Tao, or Luath, still away from home but pining for it, to your masters. Tell them the most important things they need to know about your trip and about your current feelings.

Role B2 is Elizabeth, Peter, or Mr. Hunter. You are worried and pining for your lost pet. Tell them what you would want them to know as they struggle through the wilderness—if they are still alive.

## Day Eleven (After Reading Chapter 11)

Throw your letters into a pile at the center of the classroom. Choose a letter from a Role A if you are a B, and vice versa. Choose a powerful word or phrase from the letter and circle it or write it down.

We will now create a choral montage for Group A. Before we start, we will decide who has a phrase that will serve as an appropriate opening and who has one for the ending. Then we will spontaneously read out our phrases to form a choral montage letter for the owners.

Then we will do the same for Group B to form a choral montage for the animals.

# References

Allen, T. E. (1986). Patterns of academic achievement among hearing-impaired students: 1974–1983. In A. Schildroth & M. Karchmer (Eds.), *Deaf children in America* (pp. 161–206). San Diego: College Hill Press.

Applebee, A. (1989). *The teaching of literature in programs with reputations for excellence in English.* Albany, NY: Center for the Learning and Teaching of Literature.

Atwell, N. (1987). *In the middle: Writing, reading and learning with adolescents.* Montclair, NJ: Boynton/Cook.

Barnes, D. (1986). *Language, the learner, and the school.* London: Routledge.

Barthes, R. (1986). *Image-music-text* (S. Heath, Trans.). New York: Hill and Wang.

Belcher, T. (1981). *Mental imagery in basal manuals.* Unpublished manuscript, University of Maryland.

Benton, M. (1983). Secondary worlds. *Journal of Research and Development in Education, 16*(3), 68–75.

Benton, M., & Fox, G. (1985). *Teaching literature, 9–14.* Oxford, UK: Oxford University Press.

Bissex, G. (1987). What is a teacher researcher? In G. Bissex & R. Bullock (Eds.), *Seeing for ourselves: Case-study research by teachers of writing* (pp. 3–5). Portsmouth, NH: Heinemann.

Bleich, D. (1975). *Readings and feelings: An introduction to subjective criticism.* Urbana, IL: National Council of Teachers of English.

Bleich, D. (1987). Gender interests in reading and language. In E. Flynn & P. Schweickart (Eds.), *Gender and reading: Essays on readers, texts and contexts* (pp. 234–266). Baltimore: Johns Hopkins University Press.

Blunt, J. (1977). Response to reading: How some young readers describe the process. *English in Education, 11*(3), 34–47.

Boomer, G. (1987). Addressing the problems of elsewhereness: A case for action research in schools. In D. Goswami & P. Stillman (Eds.), *Reclaiming the classroom: Teacher research as an agency for change* (pp. 4–13). Upper Montclair, NJ: Boynton/Cook.

Bransford, J. (1979). *Human cognition: Learning, understanding, and remembering.* Belmont, CA: Wadsworth.

Britton, J. (1984). Message and text in poetic utterance. In M. Meek & J. Miller (Eds.), *Changing English: Essays for Harold Rosen* (pp. 220–235). London: Heinemann.

Brown, R. (1991). *Schools of thought: How the politics of literacy shape thinking in the classroom.* San Francisco: Jossey-Bass.

Bruner, J. (1986). *Actual minds, possible worlds*. Cambridge, MA: Harvard University Press.

Carlsen, G. (1980). *Books and the teenage reader*. New York: Harper & Row.

Chambers, A. (1985). *Booktalk*. London: The Bodley Head.

Cromer, W. (1970). The difference model: A new explanation for some reading difficulties. *Journal of Educational Psychology, 61*(6, part 1), 471–483.

Culler, J. (1975). *Structuralist poetics: Structuralism, linguistics and the study of literature*. Ithaca, NY: Cornell University Press.

Daneman, M., & Carpenter, P. (1980). Individual differences in working memory and reading. *Journal of Verbal Learning and Verbal Behavior, 19*, 450–456.

Dole, J., Duffy, G., Roehler, L., & Pearson, P. (1991). Moving from the old to new: Research on reading comprehension instruction. *Review of Educational Research, 62*(2), 239–264.

Durkin, D. (1979). What classroom observations reveal about reading comprehension instruction. *Reading Research Quarterly, 14*(4), 481–533.

Dyson, A. (1984). Reading, writing, and language: Young children solving the written language puzzle. In J. Jensen (Ed.), *Composing and comprehending*. Urbana, IL: National Council of Teachers of English.

Eco, U. (1978). *The role of the reader*. Bloomington: Indiana University Press.

Edmiston, B. (1991). *What have you travelled? A teacher researcher study of structuring drama for reflection*. Unpublished doctoral dissertation, Ohio State University, Columbus.

Eisner, E. (1992). The misunderstood role of the arts in human development. *Phi Delta Kappan, 8*, 591–595.

Eisner, E. (1993). The education of vision. *Educational Horizons, 71*(2), 80–85.

Enciso, P. [nee Edmiston]. (1990). *The nature of engagement in reading: Profiles of three fifth graders' engagement strategies and stances*. Unpublished doctoral dissertation, Ohio State University, Columbus.

Enciso, P. (1992, December). *Accounting for engagement: Emerging principles for rethinking reading processes*. Paper presented at the annual meeting of the National Reading Conference, San Antonio, TX.

Engelmann, S., & Osborn, J. (1976). *DISTAR language: An instructional system*. Chicago: Science Research Associates.

Fish, S. (1980). *Is there a text in this class? The authority of interpretive communities*. Cambridge, MA: Harvard University Press.

Flower, L., & Hayes, J. (1981). A cognitive process theory of writing. *College Composition and Communication, 32*(4), 21–32.

Flynn, E. (1987). Gender and reading. In E. Flynn & P. Schweickart (Eds.), *Gender and reading: Essays on readers, texts and contexts* (pp. 267–288). Baltimore: Johns Hopkins University Press.

Galda, L. (1982). Assuming the spectator stance: An examination of the responses of three young readers. *Research in the Teaching of English, 16*(1), 1–20.

Gambrell, L. (1981). Induced mental imagery and the text prediction performance of first and third graders. In J. A. Niles and L. A. Harris (Eds.), *New inquiries in reading research and instruction. Thirty-first yearbook of the National Reading Conference* (pp. 131–135). Rochester, NY: National Reading Conference.

Gambrell, L., & Bales, R. J. (1986). Mental imagery and the comprehension-monitoring performance of fourth and fifth grade readers. *Reading Research Quarterly, 21*(4), 454–464.

Gambrell, L. B., & Heathington, B. S. (1981). Adult disabled readers' metacognitive awareness about reading tasks and strategies. *Journal of Reading Behavior, 13*(3), 215–222.

Gambrell, L., & Jawitz, P. (1993). Mental imagery, text illustrations and children's story comprehension and recall. *Reading Research Quarterly, 28*(3), 265–275.

Gardner, H. (1983). *Frames of mind.* New York: Basic Books.

Gilligan, C. (1982). *In a different voice: Psychological theory and women's development.* Cambridge, MA: Harvard University Press.

Giroux, H. (1987). Critical literacy and student empowerment: Donald Graves' approach to literacy. *Language Arts, 64*(2), 175–181.

Golden, J., & Guthrie, J. (1986). Convergence and divergence in reader response to literature. *Reading Research Quarterly, 21*(4), 408–421.

Goodman, K. (1982). *Language and literacy* (Vols. 1 and 2) (F. Gollasch, Ed.). London: Routledge and Kegan Paul.

Goodman, K. (1985). Unity in reading. In H. Singer & R. B. Ruddell (Eds.), *Theoretical processes and models of reading* (3rd ed.) (pp. 813–840). Newark, DE: International Reading Association.

Greene, M. (1978). *Landscapes of learning.* New York: Teachers College Press.

Hansen, J. (1981). The effects of inference training and practice on young children's reading comprehension. *Reading Research Quarterly, 16*(3), 391–417.

Hanssen, E., Harste, J., & Short, K. (1990). In conversation: Theory and instruction. In D. Bogdan & S. Shaw (Eds.), *Beyond communication: Reading comprehension and criticism.* Portsmouth, NH: Boynton/Cook–Heinemann.

Harding, D. W. (1937). The role of the onlooker. *Scrutiny, 6*(3), 247–258.

Harding, D. W. (1962). What happens when we read. *British Journal of Aesthetics, 2*(2), 133–147.

Hardy, B. (1977). Towards a poetics of fiction. In M. Meek et al. (Eds.), *The cool web.* London: The Bodley Head.

Hart, L. (1984). *Human brain and human learning.* White Plains, NY: Longman.

Healy, J. (1990). *Endangered minds: Why children don't think and what we can do about it.* New York: Touchstone.

Heathcote, D. (1984). *Dorothy Heathcote: Collected writings on drama and education* (L. Johnson & C. O'Neill, Eds.). London: Hutchinson.

Heathcote, D. (1990). *The fight for drama—The fight for education.* Newcastle upon Tyne, UK: National Association of Teachers of Drama/Printers Inc.

Hillocks, G. (1987). Literary texts in classrooms. In P. Jackson (Ed.), *From Socrates to software: The teacher as text and the text as teacher* (pp. 135–158). Chicago: National Society for the Study of Education.

Hynds, S. (1990). Reading as a social event: Comprehension and response in the text, classroom and world. In D. Bogdan & S. Shaw (Eds.), *Beyond communication: Reading comprehension and criticism.* Portsmouth, NH: Boynton/Cook–Heinemann.

Iser, W. (1978). *The act of reading: A theory of aesthetic response.* Baltimore, MD: Johns Hopkins University Press.

Jacob, S. (1976). Contexts and images in reading. *Reading World, 15*(3), 167–175.

Johnston, P. (1985). Understanding reading disability: A case study approach. *Harvard Education Review, 55*(2), 153–177.

Johnston, P. (1993). Assessment and literate development. *The Reading Teacher, 46*(5), 428–429.

Johnston, P., & Winograd, P. (1983, December). *Passive failure in reading.* Paper presented at the annual meeting of the National Reading Conference, Austin, TX.

Knapp, M., Stearns, M., John, M., & Zucker, A. (1988). Prospects for improving K–12 science education from the federal level. *Phi Delta Kappan, 69*(9), 677–683.

Knoblauch, C., & Brannon, L. (1993). *Critical teaching and the idea of literacy.* Portsmouth, NH: Heinemann.

Langer, J. (1984). Examining background information and text comprehension. *Reading Research Quarterly, 19*(4), 468–481.

Langer, J. (1989). *The process of understanding literature.* Albany, NY: Center for the Teaching and Learning of Literature.

Langer, J. (1990). The process of understanding: Reading for literary and informative purposes. *Research in the Teaching of English, 24*(3), 229–260.

Meek, M., Armstrong, S., Austerfield, V., Graham, J., & Plackett, E. (1983). *Achieving literacy: Longitudinal studies of adolescents learning to read.* London: Routledge and Kegan Paul.

Miller, J. B. (1976). *Towards a new psychology of women.* Boston: Beacon.

Nell, V. (1990). *Lost in a book: The psychology of reading for pleasure.* New Haven: Yale University Press.

Newell, G. (1984). Learning from writing in two content areas: A case study/protocol analysis. *Research in the Teaching of English, 18*(3), 265–287.

Newell, G. (1990). Exploring the relationships between writing and literary understanding: A language and learning perspective. In G. E. Mawisher and A. D. Soter (Eds.), *On literacy and its teaching: Issues in English education* (pp. 111–127). Albany: State University of New York.

Newell, G., MacAdams, P., & Spears-Burton, L. (1987, November). *Process approaches to writing about literary texts: Case studies of three classrooms.* Paper presented at the annual conference of the National Council of Teachers of English, Los Angeles.

Ornstein, A. (1990). The arts and the learning of high-risk individuals. *Design for Arts in Education, 92*(1), 15–28.

Perfetti, C. A., & Lesgold, A. M. (1979). Coding and comprehension in skilled reading and implications for instruction. In L. B. Resnick & P. A. Weaver (Eds.), *Cognitive processes in comprehension* (pp. 141–183). Hillsdale, NJ: Erlbaum.

Pierce, C. S. (1931/1958). *Collected papers of Charles Sanders Pierce.* (Vols. 1–6: C. Hartshorne & P. Weiss, Eds.; Vols. 7–8: A. W. Burks, Ed.). Cambridge, MA: Harvard University Press.

Poulet, G. (1969). Phenomenology of reading. *New Literary History, 1*, 53–68.

Pressley, M. (1977). Imagery and children's learning: Putting the picture in developmental perspective. *Review of Educational Research, 47*, 585–622.

Probst, R. (1988). *Response and analysis: Teaching literature in junior and senior high school.* Portsmouth, NH: Boynton/Cook.

Purcell-Gates, V. (1991). On the outside looking in: A study of remedial-readers' meaning-making while reading literature. *Journal of Reading Behavior, 23*(2), 235–254.

Purves, A. (1973). *Literature education in ten countries: An empirical study.* New York: Wiley.

Rabinowitz, P. (1987). *Before reading: Narrative conventions and the politics of interpretation.* Ithaca, NY: Cornell University Press.

Radway, J. (1984). *Reading the romance.* Chapel Hill: University of North Carolina Press.

Raphael, T. (1982). Question answering strategies for children. *Reading Teacher, 36*(2), 186–190.

Reid, D. K. (1988). *Teaching the learning disabled: A cognitive, developmental approach.* Boston: Allyn & Bacon.

Rogers, T. (1988). *Students as literary critics: The interpretive theories, processes and experiences of ninth grade students.* Unpublished doctoral dissertation, University of Illinois at Urbana-Champaign.

Rosenblatt, L. (1978). *The reader, the text, the poem: The transactional theory of the literary work.* Carbondale: Southern Illinois University Press.

Rosenblatt, L. (1982). The literary transaction: Evocation and response. *Theory into Practice, 21*(4).

Rosenblatt, L. (1983). *Literature as exploration.* New York: The Modern Language Association of America. (Original work published 1938)

Rumelhart, D. E. (1985). Toward an interactive model of reading. In H. Singer & R. B. Ruddell (Eds.), *Theoretical processes and models of reading* (3rd ed.) (pp. 722–750). Newark, DE: International Reading Association.

Sadoski, M. (1985). The natural use of imagery in story comprehension and recall: Replication and extension. *Reading Research Quarterly, 20*(5), 658–667.

Schank, R. (1990). *Tell me a story.* New York: Scribners.

Selman, R., & Byrne, D. (1974). A structural-developmental analysis of levels of role-taking in middle childhood. In *Child Development, 45*(81), 803–806.

Smagorinsky, P., & Coppock, J. (1994). Cultural tools and the classroom context: An exploration of an artistic response to literature. *Written Communication, 11*, 283–310.

Smith, F. (1978). *Understanding reading: A psycholinguistic analysis of reading and learning to read* (2nd ed.). New York: Holt, Rinehart and Winston.

Smith, F. (1988). *Joining the literacy club: Further essays into education.* Portsmouth, NH: Heinemann.

Smith, M. (1989). Teaching the interpretation of irony in poetry. *Research in the Teaching of English, 23*(3), 254–272.

Smith, M. (1991). *Understanding unreliable narrators.* Urbana, IL: National Council of Teachers of English.

Smith, M. (1992). Submission versus control in literary transactions. In J. Many &

C. Cox (Eds.), *Reader stance and literary understanding: Exploring the theories, research and practice.* Norwood, NJ: Ablex.

Squires, J., & Applebee, R. (1966). *A national study of English programs with a reputation for excellence in the teaching of literature.* Cooperative Research Project No. 1994, University of Illinois.

Tierney, R., & Pearson, P. (1983). Toward a composing model of reading. *Language Arts, 60(5),* 568–580.

Thomson, J. (1987). *Understanding teenagers' reading: Reading processes and the teaching of literature.* Maryborough: Australian Association of Teachers of English.

Tolkien, J. R. R. (1964). *Tree and leaf.* London: Allen and Unwin.

Vipond, D., & Hunt, R. (1984). Point-driven understanding: Pragmatic and cognitive dimensions of literary reading. *Poetics, 13,* 261–277.

Vygotsky, L. (1978). *Mind in society* (M. Cole, V. John-Steiner, S. Scribner, & E. Souberman, Eds.). Cambridge, MA: Harvard University Press.

Wade, S. (1983). A synthesis of the research for improving research in social sciences. *Review of Educational Research, 53*(4), 461–479.

Wilhelm, J. (1992). Literary theorists, hear my cry! *English Journal, 81*(7), 50–56.

Wilhelm, J. (1996). *Standards in practice, 6–8.* Champaign, IL: National Council of Teachers of English.

Woods, M. L., & Moe, A. J. (1989). *Analytical Reading Inventory* (4th ed.). Columbus, OH: Merrill.

# Stories and Poems Cited in the Text

Adams, R. (1974). *Watership down.* New York: Macmillan.

Aiken, J. (1992). Lob's Girl. In *A fit of shivers* (pp. 63–75). New York: Delacorte.

Alcott, L. M. (1982). *Little women.* Franklin Center, PA: Franklin Library.

Alexander, L. (1968). *The high king.* New York: Holt, Rinehart & Winston.

Arthur, R. (1960). Larceny and old lace. In O. Niles et al. (Eds.), *Skills for reading.* (pp. 91 97) Glenview, IL: Scott, Foresman.

Bemelmans, L. (1939). *Madeline.* New York: Viking.

Bemelmans, L. (1953). *Madeline's rescue.* New York: Viking.

Bemelmans, L. (1957). *Madeline and the bad hat.* New York: Viking.

Bloe, J (1990). *A gathering of days.* New York: MacMillan.

Blume, J. (1987). *Just as long as we're together.* New York: Orchard.

Burnett, F. (1987). *The secret garden.* Mahwah, NJ: Watermill.

Burnsford, S. (1960). *The incredible journey.* New York: Bantam Starfire.

Carroll, L. (1965). *Alice's adventures in Wonderland.* New York: Random House.

Ciardi, J. (1975). The shark. In *Fast and slow* (p. 10). New York: Houghton Mifflin.

Clancy, T. (1987). *Patriot games.* New York: Putnam.

Clancy, T. (1989). *A clear and present danger.* New York: Putnam.

Clancy, T. (1991). *The sum of all fears.* New York: Putnam.

Cole, B. (1989). *Celine.* New York: Farrar, Strauss, & Giroux.

Corbett, J. (1985). *Man eaters of Kumaon.* Oxford, UK: India Books.

De Marino, L. (1989). *The Odyssey project.* New York: Pageant Books.

Flanagan, T. (1979). *The year of the French.* New York: Holt, Rinehart, & Winston.

Frank, A. (1978). *Anne Frank: The diary of a young girl.* New York: Pocket Books.

Gage, N. (1983). *Eleni.* New York: Random House.

Gitlin, T. (1987). *The sixties: Years of hope, days of rage.* New York: Bantam.

Gourley, C. (1992). Pandora's box. *Read, 42*(5), 18–29.

Grahame, K. (1908). *The wind in the willows.* New York: Scribners.

Grisham, J. (1991). *The firm.* New York: Doubleday.

Grisham, J. (1992). *The pelican brief.* New York: Doubleday.

Hinton, S. E. (1971). *That was then, this is now.* New York: Viking.

Ishiguro, K. (1989). *The remains of the day.* New York: Knopf.

Lee, H. (1988). *To kill a mockingbird.* New York: Warner.

London, J. (1980). *White fang.* Mahwah, NJ: Watermill.

Longfellow, H. W. (1952). The wreck of Hesperus. In D. L. George (Ed.), *The family book of best-loved poems.* Garden City, NY: Hanover House.

Matute, A. (1968). The little boy whose friend died on him. In *Los ninos tontos* (p. 10). Spain: Ediciones Destino.

Montgomery, L. M. (1976). *Anne of Green Gables.* New York: Bantam.

O'Flaherty, L. (1923). The sniper. In E. J. O'Brien & J. Corimos (Eds.), *The best British short stories of 1923* (pp. 242–246). Boston: Small, Maynard & Co.

Paterson, K. (1978). *The great Gilly Hopkins.* New York: Harper & Row.

Paterson, K. (1988). *Park's quest.* New York: Puffin.

Paterson, K. (1991). *Lyddie.* New York: Dutton.

Paton, A. (1953). *Too late the phalarope.* New York: Scribners.

Quammen, D. (1985). The Republic of Cockroaches. In *Natural acts* (pp. 53–60). New York: Dell.

Robinson, G. (1991). Swish. *Read, 40*(10), 16–19.

Schwartz, A. (1992). High beams. In *Scary stories* (pp. 66–69). New York: HarperCollins.

Spiegelman, A. (1986). *Maus: My father fleeds history.* New York: Pantheon.

Spiegelman, A. (1991). *Maus II: A survivor's tale, and here my troubles began.* New York: Pantheon.

Taylor, M. (1976). *Roll of thunder, hear my cry.* New York: Dial.

Voight, C. (1986). *Come a stranger.* New York: MacMillan.

Walker, A. (1982). *The color purple.* New York: Harcourt, Brace, Jovanovich.

Westlake, D. (1970). The winner. In H. Harrison (Ed.), *Nova 1* (pp. 44–48). London: Knox, Burger Associates, Ltd.

White, R. (1973). *Deathwatch.* New York: Dell.

Wilder, L. I. (1981). *Little house in the big woods.* New York: Harper & Row.

Wilhelm, H. (1988). *Waldo goes to the zoo.* Reinbak: Carlsen Verlag.

# Index

# About the Author

**Jeffrey Wilhelm** has been a teacher of reading and the language arts at the middle and secondary school level for the past 13 years. His interests include team teaching, co-constructing inquiry-driven curriculum with students, and pursuing teacher research. His recent research agenda includes studying how student reading and thinking can be supported through the use of art, drama, and technology.

Jeff is currently an assistant professor at the University of Maine, where he teaches courses in middle- and secondary-level literacy. In Maine, he coordinates the fledgling Adolescent Literacy Project and summer institutes in literacy and technology. He is also the recent recipient of the NCTE Promising Researcher Award (1995) for his work "Reading Is Seeing," regarding the use of visual artwork to help reluctant readers. He enjoys speaking, presenting, working with students and schools. You may visit his home page at http://130.11.68.40/Wilhelm.html